INVOLUNTARY LABOUR
SINCE THE ABOLITION OF SLAVERY

INVOLUNTARY LABOUR SINCE THE ABOLITION OF SLAVERY

A SURVEY OF COMPULSORY LABOUR THROUGHOUT THE WORLD

BY

W. KLOOSTERBOER

FOREWORD BY J. J. FAHRENFORT
Professor emeritus of Ethnology
at the University of the City of Amsterdam

GREENWOOD PRESS, PUBLISHERS
WESTPORT, CONNECTICUT

Library of Congress Cataloging in Publication Data

Kloosterboer, Willemina.
Involuntary labour since the abolition of slavery.

Translation of Onvrije arbeid na de afschaffing van de slavernij.
Originally presented as the author's thesis, Amsterdam.
Reprint of the ed. published by E. J. Brill, Leiden.
Bibliography: p.
1. Forced labor--Case studies. I. Title.
[HD4871.K613 1976] 331.1'173 76-9771
ISBN 0-8371-8887-3

Originally published in 1960 by E. J. Brill, Leiden

Reprinted with the permission of N. V. Boekhandel and Drukkerij voorheen E.J. Brill

Reprinted in 1976 by Greenwood Press, a division of Williamhouse-Regency Inc.

Library of Congress Catalog Card Number 76-9771

ISBN 0-8371-8887-3

Printed in the United States of America

CONTENTS

FOREWORD BY J. J. FAHRENFORT VII

INTRODUCTION 1

CHAPTER ONE
The British West Indies and Mauritius 3

CHAPTER TWO
South Africa 17

CHAPTER THREE
The Netherlands West Indies 32

CHAPTER FOUR
The Netherlands East Indies 41

CHPATER FIVE
The United States of America 57

CHAPTER SIX
The Portuguese colonies in Africa with particular reference to West Africa 67

CHAPTER SEVEN
Latin America 79

CHAPTER EIGHT
Madagascar 107

CHAPTER NINE
Belgian Congo 119

CHAPTER TEN
Kenya 141

CHAPTER ELEVEN
Haiti 154

CHAPTER TWELVE
Liberia 161

CHAPTER THIRTEEN
Soviet Russia 174

CHAPTER FOURTEEN
Conclusions 191

Literature on compulsory labour in general 216

FOREWORD BY J. J. FAHRENFORT

Professor emeritus of Ethnology at the University of the City of Amsterdam

The study of unlettered peoples which we call Ethnology, Ethnography, Social Anthropology, and Cultural Anthropology has recently concentrated more on the present circumstances and changes in the social organization of such peoples than on what might be called antiquarian ethnology. Scholars have come to recognize that it is not only of interest to study social development before the appearance of powerful Western influences, but also to examine the responses of the "primitive" cultures to the continually closer contact with the West.

Nonetheless, the detection of sociological laws inherent in the social structures of the past is also important, the more so where these laws appear to be equally valid for more advanced societies. In "Slavery as an Industrial System", H. J. Nieboer has given what in my opinion is a classic example of what can be achieved in the field of sociology by combining the functional with the comparative method. It is, however, not clear why he has limited himself to a definition of slavery according to which a slave is the property of his master. The concept of property is not exact: it conveys a whole range of gradations from an absolute to an extremely weak right of disposal. Nieboer did not in fact require this conceptual limitation for his thesis because his argument is equally applicable to compulsory labour in which the operator is not the owner of the labourers in his service.

This point is developed clearly by Dr. Kloosterboer, against various backgrounds. Even after slavery was declared unlawful over the entire world, those whose interests were involved found many ways to create compulsory labour when free labour was impossible or difficult to obtain. The fact that conditions are rapidly changing, particularly with the emancipation of many former colonies, does not mean that all compulsory labour has already disappeared. But even when it has done so, the delineation of a piece of social history, especially of one in which the pattern is so consistent, will retain its importance for every student of the social sciences in the broadest sense of the term.

Amsterdam, December 1959

INTRODUCTION

The Dutch author H. J. Nieboer, in his thesis *Slavery as an Industrial System* (1900), indicated that the occurrence or non-occurrence of slavery in a society is dependent on the economic state of that society. Slavery as a rule will not exist if the circumstances—which he seeks particularly in the land situation—are such that there is an offer of voluntary labour. On the other hand, if this voluntary labour is not available, then, in most instances, slavery will occur.

The abolition of negro slavery in the course of the 19th century would appear in the light of this theory to have been premature. Generally speaking, the circumstances in the colonies at the time were not such that an offer of sufficient voluntary labour could be anticipated. But then it was in fact so that the impetus for abolition came from groups not directly involved in slavery. The slave-holders themselves were violently opposed to abolition, and, being overruled, it was not long before they substituted new forms of compulsory labour.

It is indeed not clear why precisely slavery should exist if there is not sufficient voluntary labour. As labour systems, serfage, debt-slavery, and even contract labour under penal sanction fulfil exactly the same function [1]. The form compulsory labour takes will in the first place depend on the spirit of the times. Public opinion in the West would never have approved of the re-institution of slavery as such after abolition, no matter how acute the labour shortage. In these circumstances, however, other forms of compulsory labour were resorted to—often leaving the victims not much better off than before.

In the following chapters we will examine when and how compulsory labour has been imposed in different countries since the abolition of slavery. First, however, we must determine the boundary between voluntary and compulsory labour. In a certain sense almost all labour can be classed as compulsory; by far the majority of people do after all work out of necessity to support themselves and not

---

[1] J. J. Fahrenfort drew attention to this in his article Over vrije en onvrije arbeid (On Voluntary and Compulsory Labour) in the Dutch journal Mensch en Maatschappij, 1943, p. 31.

because they are particularly keen to. But this is not the sort of compulsion we are concerned with here. In our society everyone may at least decide for himself whether he would rather work for his bread or not work and starve. No direct external compulsion is exerted.

We will term that labour compulsory from which the labourer cannot withdraw if he so wishes without being liable to punishment, and/or for which he has been accepted without his willing consent to it. The motive for the imposition of this labour must moreover be to gain profit—or have profit gained.

There are a few forms of labour which cannot be considered as compulsory even though they satisfy the first mentioned requirements; e.g., penal servitude as customarily imposed from corrective considerations. Neither does the fact that sailors are liable to punishment for breach of contract mean that their labour is compulsory in the sense meant here, since this compulsion is for quite another and obvious reason. In the same way, the labour called upon by governing bodies in cases of necessity falls outside the scope of this investigation. Another matter is the labour on public works as imposed by the authorities. If it here concerns works also of importance to the labourers themselves, and if the duration of the labour is not excessively long, then, in our terms of reference, the labour performed cannot be considered as compulsory. Indeed a parallel can be drawn in these cases with taxation as imposed on our society. However, if the works laboured on are of little or no benefit to the people as such, and if very heavy labour of long duration is demanded—as has often been the case—then once again the economic motive becomes dominant, and in our terms of reference the labour must be classed as compulsory.

The occurrence of compulsory labour will be investigated in a wide range of countries as regards both circumstances and—in the many cases where it is a matter of colonial territory—the nationality of the ruling class. A complete record has not been attempted, but most of the important cases have been represented.

CHAPTER ONE

THE BRITISH WEST INDIES AND MAURITIUS

England confirmed the abolition of slavery in 1834 and became the first country to do so. The colonies most affected by this measure were British Guiana, the West Indian islands belonging to Britain, and Mauritius in the Indian Ocean. After all there were large estates here, for the most part sugar plantations, and the labour force was made up of Negro slaves. We will examine in which way the labour requirements were met after abolition.

In the West Indies—with the exception of Antigua—complete freedom was not immediately granted to all slaves in 1834 [1]. Only children under the age of six were freed. For the remaining Negroes an apprenticeship system was introduced, which in effect meant that the former slaves were now compelled to work for their former holders without payment for a further number of years; in most cases six years but in a few instances four. The holders, however, no longer had complete rights over their former slaves. A few directives were given. For example, a maximum number of working hours was determined; 45 hours a week for 'apprentices' in agriculture —and these were in the majority. It was hoped that they would offer to work for wages in their spare time; and to encourage this it was decreed that 'apprentices' could buy their freedom from further services at a fixed price.

Under this system the former slaves could not as yet consider themselves particularly well off. As is to be expected the planters were not always of good will, and the Government in London had to be continually taking action to bring about improvements in the colonial legislation, especially against the legislative body in Jamaica, where almost half the Negroes of the British West Indies lived. Cruelties frequently occurred both on the plantations and in the prisons where they amounted to atrocities; so much so that various members of the Anti Slavery Society—disbanned after abolition became a reality—felt obliged to take up action again.

---

[1] The following is taken from British Slave Emancipation, 1833-1849, by William Law Mathieson, 1932.

However, the apprenticeship system was only intended as a first step to complete freedom, and we will leave it at that. In fact it came to an end in 1838, which was for most 'apprentices' two years earlier than at first intended, whilst on one of the islands, Antigua, the planters had preferred to declare complete freedom for all the Negroes right from scratch in 1834.

A dire shortage of plantation labourers arose as soon as the apprenticeship system came to an end. The Negroes did not feel much inclined to work, and especially not on the plantations since to their minds slave-driving was an inherent factor in such labour. In the beginning all wished to be free and the result was chaos. Although this state of affairs sorted itself out to some extent later it still remained extremely difficult for the planters to find labourers. Where there was little density of population and much uncultivated land, as in British Guiana, Jamaica and Trinidad, the more energetic Negroes were in a position to buy their own plots of ground with the money they had been able to save in their time as 'apprentices'. Many, desiring a change, decided on other forms of labour, becoming shopkeepers, small merchants, fishermen and even carriers; and frequently those parents who stayed on at the plantations would send their children to the towns. And all this mainly because of the association between plantation labour and slavery. Even from those who stayed on at the plantations, or returned there after some time, not much work was to be expected since they could, with the produce of the small holdings which had been theirs of old, either support their families entirely or manage, if the plots were too small, by adding the wages of a few days' labour a week. Only a very small number indeed felt the urge to work so as to have more than just the minimum requirements in the way of food and clothing, but even these Negroes were not prepared to work as many hours a day as had been customary before.

Under these difficult circumstances the planters attempted in various ways to get a better hold on their labourers. The settlers in Antigua were first faced with this problem, having, as already stated, not felt much for the introduction of an apprenticeship system in 1834. Within a few months of abolition a law called the Contract Act was passed on this island and enforced in anticipation of approval from London. By this act Negro labour was drasticly regulated.

As soon as a contract was concluded between planter and labourer the following stipulations applied:

1. If the labourer was absent from work for half a day or less (!) without good cause he forfeited his wage for the whole day.
2. If he was absent for two consecutive days, or for two days in fourteen, he was liable to a week's imprisonment with hard labour.
3. For negligence of various kinds during work he could be convicted to up to three months hard labour.

The employer on the other hand was only liable for breach of contract to a maximum fine of £5. What is more, even a verbal contract made in the presence of two witnesses was considered valid.

Although it is true that the Government of the mother country did not accept the regulation in this form, it did pass it with a few modifications; and in its final form the act contained a remarkable clause stating that the occupation of a tenement entailed on a Negro the same obligations as the conclusion of a verbal labour contract. It is clear that this, on an island where there was as good as no uncultivated land left, amounted to forced labour for the greater part of the Negro population.

For many years this law was in force in Antigua, and through it the labour situation there became much more favourable for the planters than on the other islands. For when the labour problem arose elsewhere a few years later the home country was no longer prepared to sanction similar measures.

Even without the Contract Act, however, ways and means were found of imposing plantation labour on part of the Negroes. Many of the Negro families, who for generations had had the use of shacks and small holdings on the plantations, were now made to pay for the privilege of this occupation in labour and not in money, as would have been reasonable in a system of voluntary labour. As a rule only the head of the family was obliged to work, but then he had to do so almost continuously. On Barbados, for example, it was customary to demand nine hours a day five days a week. In some instances all members of the family had to assist. On the densely populated islands the planters speculated with this measure realizing how little opportunity the Negro had of moving away, but mainly—and this applied everywhere—banking on the Negro's attachment to his shack and small holding.

More than half the Negroes of the British West Indies lived in Jamaica, and here it was that abolition was most stubbornly opposed by the planters. After its realization they were not content to make the Negro work for his use of a small holding, but so regulated the matter that the wage worked out at less than the rent of the tenement. In this way the people were more or less faced with a form of debt slavery.

Moreover, in 1840 a law was passed in Jamaica against "vagrancy". A "vagrant" according to this law was any man who migrated from his home leaving his wife and children unprovided for. In the absence of a police officer, it was decreed that anyone could arrest such a person. Thus another attempt at hindering the migration of Negroes from the plantations.

In Mauritius, however, the settlers went much further in their endeavours to keep the Negroes at work after abolition became a reality on February 1st, 1835, six months later than in the West Indies. Even in the same year an ordinance was passed whereby the greater majority of the population were faced with a situation hardly to be considered as any better than slavery. The main clauses of the ordinance read as follows [1]:

All persons under the age of sixty years, capable of labour (that is, women as well as men) and unable to prove that they follow a business or possess sufficient means of subsistence, shall be bound to take up a trade, or find employment, or hire themselves as field labourers, within a period to be fixed by the police. In the event of failure to perform this duty, the offender is to be delivered to the police to be employed on the public works. And if after three months any such person shall not have found employment, he may be sentenced to be placed on a plantation or in a factory, to be there employed for a period not exceeding three years. No regulations were included to cover such matters as wage, working hours, &c. And one's troubles were not necessarily over after three years of forced labour since a following clause decreed that anyone who had not found other work after completion of this term could again be put to work in the same way. It was made difficult, if not impossible, for the labourer to find new work by a further clause holding anyone guilty of enticing a labourer away from the plantation of his holder liable to pay damages and a fine. A comprehensive registration of all labourers, coupled with a decree making it compulsory for every labourer to carry on his person an identification card issued by the

[1] Report of the Royal Commissioners appointed to enquire into the treatment of immigrants in Mauritius, 1875, p. 29, &c.

police (and to be renewed with every change of employer), made it even more difficult for them, particularly seeing that these regulations were most rigorously and unsympathetically enforced. In fact someone even temporarily unemployed could find himself convicted to forced labour despite his not having committed any crime, and his chances of ever getting away from the plantation to which the police sent him were very slender indeed.

One can imagine that this state of affairs did not improve the way in which the planter (till shortly before, slave-holder) treated his labourers. Furthermore, a labourer who attacked his master or his master's representative was, in terms of the ordinance, liable to a maximum of 12 months' imprisonment, with or without hard labour. And if three or more labourers should collaborate in an attempt to leave the plantation or improve the conditions of labour, they would be liable to six months hard labour. In addition one later had to work two days longer for every day spent in jail.

Finally it was even made possible in the ordinance to put children over eight to work as apprentices up to their 21st year. And, because it could apparently not be taken for granted that the ordinance as it stood would be sufficient to bring the free population to work, another clause was introduced by which contraventions of any kind by unemployed persons could be all the more heavily penalized. A farther going system of labour compulsion is hardly imaginable.

When the ordinance was sent to the Minister of Colonial Affairs for approval he was singularly dismayed, and, to the indignation of the Governor, the Council and planters of Mauritius, he promptly turned it down. In the meantime the ordinance had already been in force for almost a year and we shall moreover see that many of the clauses found their way into the legislation in the course of the following years, although they then mainly pertained to another section of the population.

Every attempt to get the former slaves to work seemed doomed to failure. In British Guiana and most of the islands in the West Indies—including the larger ones, Jamaica and Trinidad—the Negroes could easily manage without having to labour on the plantations since there was still a lot of free land available. There was a rapid increase in the number of independent Negro farmers in these territories [1]. On the whole they showed little initiative, cultivating only what was

---

[1] See for example Mathieson, op. cit., p. 69, 71.

strictly needed, and for the rest living in idleness [1]. This was possible in such a climate; and they were at any rate a lost cause as plantation labourers.

Also in Mauritius many of the freed slaves were able to get along without working for the whites. Some acquired land of their own [2], while the majority were fishermen by day and thieves at night [3]. In all these territories the labour shortage remained acute despite every measure to overcome it.

It was only on the more densely populated, smaller islands in the West Indies (Antigua, St. Kitts and Barbados), and where there was hardly any uncultivated land left, that the greater majority of the Negroes returned of their own accord to their old plantations—due to lack of other possibilities [4].

In those territories where the labour shortage remained acute the planters were quick to seek a solution in another direction entirely. Both in the West Indies and Mauritius they started drawing labour from elsewhere. The first attempt in the West Indies, with Portuguese from Madeira and Negroes from the West Coast of Africa, proved unsuccessful. Results were satisfactory only when the planters started importing Indians, and—in the West Indies—small numbers of Chinese. Indeed in the end the labour problem was in fact solved in this way.

Indians started arriving in large numbers in Mauritius soon after abolition. In the West Indies a stop was put to the immigration after an initial start in 1838, but by 1844 a regular stream of Indian coolies started arriving here too. Chinese emigration was mainly to British Guiana, and the greater proportion arrived between 1853 and 1874. In all about 450,000 Indians emigrated to Mauritius, 200,000 to British Guiana and 150,000 to Trinidad (far fewer to the other West Indian islands). About 16,000 Chinese arrived in British Guiana. The immigration of British Indians continued for many years. On Mauritius it ended in 1911, when there were a sufficient number of labourers on the island. In 1917, at the proposal of the Government of India, the British Government prohibited all immigration of contract labourers.

This Indian and Chinese immigration followed the pattern of the

---

[1] Mathieson, op. cit., p. 136-138.
[2] Id., p. 232.
[3] Id., p. 232, 236.
[4] See Mathieson, op. cit., Chap. 1: Developed Colonies.

indentured-labour system by which the emigrants signed a contract in India or China committing themselves to work, usually for a full 5 year period, in the country to which they were sent. They received free passage and the contractors were required to provide regular work at reasonable wages as well as housing and medical attention. In the West Indies the immigrants also had the right on a free passage, or (later) partly free passage, back to the country of origin after working a number of years, mostly ten.

Most characteristic of this Indian and Chinese labour, however, was the penal sanction: Contrary to what we know in Western law, there were criminal laws to cover breach of contract. Desertion and absence from work, and even negligence of various kinds, was punishable, often with imprisonment. This gave to this labour an involuntary aspect. After all there was no way of terminating one's service when one wished, no matter how unhappy the circumstances. And the involuntary nature of this contract labour was considerably enhanced by the way in which the labourers were recruited and put to work, and the way in which the coolies were sometimes kept on even after the contract period had expired.

Let us examine this in more detail [1].

Often the recruiting was done in such a manner that there was hardly any question of a free choice on the part of the labourers. This became particularly known of China [2]. The poverty-stricken Chinese were tempted with loans, after receipt of which they were immediately in the power of the recruiting agents because of the Chinese laws pertaining to debt slavery. Naturally they were also tempted with false promises of a glorious future in the foreign countries. Many of the agents were notoriously unsavoury characters. What is more they were mostly paid in proportion to the number of coolies delivered, and consequently they did not carry out their man hunts very scrupulously. The system was known as the "buying and selling of pigs". The Chinese were intimidated into gambling away their future, or they were made drunk and carried off, or just simply carried off by

[1] Unless stated to the contrary the following information concerning Mauritius and British Guiana has been taken from the Report of the Royal Commissioners appointed to enquire into the treatment of immigrants in Mauritius 1875; and from the Report of the Commissioners appointed to enquire into the treatment of immigrants in British Guiana, 1871.

[2] See for example Persia Crawford Campbell, Chinese Coolie Emigration to countries within the British Empire, 1923.

force. Sometimes torture was used to make them declare that they were emigrating of their own free will. Once won over, they were locked up in barracks till such time as they could be transported by ship. Little consideration was shown en route; far too many were packed into small vessels not meant for passenger transport at all. Many died. With increasing government control the conditions improved somewhat later but were never made adequate enough. When an English ship again left with labourers for the West Indies in 1873 after the shipment of coolies had ceased for some years, the horrors on board were so bad that public opinion in China as well as in England—where the old Anti Slavery Society again became active—demanded a çessation of all emigration under the contract system. In 1874 the activities of the British West Indian Emigration Agency came to an end, and a few years later the organisation was altogether disbanned.

The recruiting of coolies from British East India was done on similar lines [1]. In the early stages the people were generally enticed away under false promises regarding the labour conditions that awaited them. The work would be light, living cheap, and the voyage to Mauritius would take only ten days, whereas it in fact took two months. That a coolie could be punished for labour wastage was generally not known at all by the emigrants. Here too the re-rcuiting officers were paid in proportion to the number of coolies they delivered, with, of course, disastrous consequences. Women would be separated from their husbands and families, and those who wished to go to a specific colony because they had friends or family there would be brought by deceit to the depot of another colony. Here too transport conditions were shocking, and here too steps were eventually taken to bring about improvements in recruiting and shipment, but many of the evils were difficult to root out and for many years complaints continued to be heard against the deception of the agents, whereby emigrants did not know what it was they were putting their signatures to.

The coolies had also very little freedom on arrival in the colonies. In Mauritius they were originally delivered to planters by merchants who made the traffic in coolies their profession. This was later prohibited but the coolies were not any better off through it. When

[1] See for example: Report of the Royal Commissioners appointed to enquire into the treatment of immigrants in Mauritius, 1875.

recruiting became largely an official matter, the authorities would bring into the colony as many coolies as *they* deemed necessary, or as many as the often sadly depleted treasury would allow. As a result competition among the planters was extremely fierce and the wildest scenes would follow as soon as a shipment of coolies arrived. The police had to stand by to prevent acts of agression against coolies by planters who thought they had a right to them. Go-betweens had a wide field of action and everything was made far worse by corrupt officials in the Immigration Office. Once again we find steps being taken to improve things, but for a long time these proved ineffectual, and for many years it was quite a common occurrence for members of one family to find themselves allocated to different employers.

Once at work, the question of penal sanction becomes of particular importance in studying the position of the coolies. In Mauritius unlawful absence, i.e. absence from work without the permission of the employer and without good cause, was punishable; as was desertion, definable as unlawful absence made worse by the circumstance that the labourer was not found at home for three consecutive days. For desertion one could be convicted, under an ordinance of 1867, to three months imprisonment. For unlawful absence the punishment meted out could take the form of *either* a) loss of wages and food rations corresponding to the duration of absence, with payment of such restitution to the employer that the labourer loses a total of two days wages for one day's absence—the so-called double-cut—*or* b) the contract period to be lengthened by the number of days absent, *or* c) a maximum of 14 days' imprisonment.

The double cut was an extremely severe sentence, made more so by the fact that this sentence could be imposed by the planters themselves, and the onus as to whether there had been a good cause for absence or not lay with the planter. Furthermore, for many years it was possible to demand the double cut in labour and not in money.

The manner in which the penal regulations were executed by both magistrates and employers was frequently even harsher than had been intended by the legislation. It would often be forgotten that the three mentioned penalties for unlawful absenteeism were alternatives, and it repeatedly occurred that a labourer found himself faced with a further period at the end of his service even though the double cut had already been applied, and in some instances despite the fact that he had even been imprisoned for those same wasted labour days. The reasonable regulation decreeing that unlawful absence was not punishable if payment of wages was more than two months overdue (often indeed applicable) was ignored time and again. Some magistrates would impose a prison sentence applying to desertion in cases of unlawful absence, thus three months instead of 14 days. However, this form of laxity was as common in reverse; for since desertion could only be punished with imprisonment, it was often to the benefit of the planter to describe an obvious case of desertion as unlawful absenteeism; thus, the double cut or prolongation of service rather than gaoling was imposed. Both magistrates and planters showed considerable latitude in their views as to what was and was not to be unlawful absenteeism. Thus, for example, a labourer making his way to the protector or magistrate to complain of ill-treatment might find himself charged with unlawful absenteeism because of his not being at work. And the double cut was also demanded for days spent in gaol. Some planters even went so far as to declare a labourer unlawfully absent, and impose the double cut, simply because he had not completed his allotted tasks for the day. And as regards the deserters, they might quite easily find themselves classed as vagrants; thus liable to a much longer term of imprisonment. All in all the coolies were pretty much at the mercy of the arbiters.

In British Guiana the regulations covering penal sanction were as follows: A contract labourer was liable to a fine or two months hard labour for a) absenteeism without good cause, b) refusing or neglecting to carry out orders, c) drunkenness in working hours, d) using threatening and abusive language toward his superiors, etc. This regulation went coupled with another decreeing that the labourer could, as well as the above, also forfeit his wage for work done badly or not completed. And it was not necessary to bring such cases before the magistrates since the supervisors on the plantations were entitled to impose this forfeiture themselves—meaning in effect that the labourers were entirely dependent on their bosses.

For desertion—here defined as absence from work for seven consecutive days—a contract labourer was liable to a penalty twice that pertaining to unlawful absenteeism, *or* to a prolongation of service by a period twice as long as the period of desertion. Yet another regulation to combat desertion was passed, making it possible for the planters and their supervisors as well as the police to arrest and return any labourer found two miles or further from his place of work without a pass. Needless to say this regulation caused the contract labourers undue hardship seeing that freedom of movement was made almost entirely impossible, and, worse still, it was made very difficult indeed to take complaints to the authorities appointed for this purpose.

All kinds of unlawful practices served to make the situation even more unbearable for the coolies. In both British Guiana and Mauritius it was usual to make deductions from an already meagre wage for any form of petty offence, such as negligence, cheekiness, and so on. Although the planters were supposed to settle such matters in the magistrates court they found it far simpler to solve them in their own way, thus enhancing uncertainty and increasing the dependence of their labourers. Another common practice was to demand more labour than the many hours already allowed by law.

In other respects too the coolies were often shockingly treated, especially in Mauritius. Labourers refusing to work for some reason or other were forcibly dragged from their huts by quarter-guards, and mishandling was sometimes so rough as to be fatal. Although periodic inspection of the plantations was prescribed by law practically nothing ever came of it, the few officials assigned to this task having not enough time to do their work at all efficiently, and being in any case entirely in the hands of the planters.

Neither were the coolies able to make their complaints known. In the first instance it was very difficult for them to go to the authorities concerned since the planters prevented them from leaving the plantations, and if they did go they were quite liable to find themselves charged with unlawful absenteeism, and faced with all the consequences thereof. However, the worst of it was that judgement was so very partisan. More often than not the verdict would be very hard on the contract labourer and very much in favour of the planter. Outrages committed by the planters were punished lightly and often condoned whereas labourers, if charged, would receive sentences far in excess of the penalties laid down by law for these offences. If a planter or one of his supervisors arrested an Indian as a deserter and it later appeared that his accusation was unjust the chances of his being punished were very small even though the law prescribed this. However, if an Indian laid a charge against his master and showed himself unable to adequately substantiate his charge, he might easily find himself convicted for making "frivolous and malicious complaints", even though the marks of ill-treatment might still be visible on his body.

The contract labourers therefore did not receive, or at least received in very small measure, the protection they so urgently needed in view of their weak position in relation to the planters, their being on foreign soil, and their being bound to work for an employer for a number of years. This placed them at the mercy of the planters, and in such circumstances there can have been no question of freedom.

However, they had only signed for a specific period. Let us therefore examine the coolie's position on completing his contract period. First in British Guiana. Here there existed for him the possibility of being shipped back to his own country after a period of ten years, i.e. five years after completion of his first contract period. If, however, he were to remain in British Guiana he would find very little opportunity to support himself other than as a plantation labourer. There was no regulation making it possible for him to acquire land of his own, and, although trading and hand-crafts were open to all, the opportunities here were very limited. It was possible however to become a free plantation labourer.

In fact by about 1870 there were from 8,000 to 9,000 free Indians in British Guiana as opposed to from 17,000 to 18,000 who had signed up for a second period of five years on completion of their first term of service [1]. But only the cleverest, who had succeeded in saving some money, were able to become free. The majority had no option but to sign up again for a further period. The colonists devised ways and means of exercising pressure to achieve this end, in the first place by granting a not unreasonable sum of money on renewal of a contract, but also by violent insistence. This insistence came not only from the planters but from the immigration agents as well—so much so that their other duties suffered because of it. And it would even appear that the very severe laws were not in the first place designed to be enforced but that waiving of legal consequences might be given in exchange for a renewed contract.

However, the coolie's position in Mauritius was even more unfavourable. Here too pressure was applied on the coolies to make them sign again, and here too much use was made of the law as an instrument of pressure. As in Guiana, a coolie would be promised freedom of legal consequences if he signed up for a further period.

---

[1] Report of the Commissioners appointed to enquire into the treatment of immigrants in British Guiana, 1871, § 513.

That was one method, another was to bring the coolie who refused to sign before the magistrate for every petty offence in the hope that he would in this way eventually yield. But the worst of all was that even those who had freed themselves of contract labour despite all this pressure were not yet left in peace. As early as 1844 a regulation was passed defining a „vagrant" as someone able but unwilling to work, becoming thereby a menace to society and because of it liable to a maximum of 28 days imprisonment; which term was later extended to 6 to 9 months on repetition. In 1867, however, a new and much more stringent regulation came into force which in reality entailed compulsory labour for all Indians [1].

Every old immigrant no longer working under contract had in future to be in possession of a valid pass only issued by the police if it could be shown by the applicant that he was in regular employ. An immigrant whose contract had expired and who did not wish to sign up again had to be in possession of such a pass within 8 days (in special circumstances 15 days), which is to say that he had in that time to ensure himself of new employment. If this period was transgressed he was liable to a fine of £ 2 or 7 days imprisonment. Somebody found without a pass was taken to the immigration depot where he had to prove that he was executing work of one sort or another. Should he not succeed in satisfying the authorities on this point he would be looked upon as a "vagrant" and treated as such. The police had the power to with the approval of the authorities concerned enter immigrants' dwellings to examine all passes. On top of all this it was decreed that immigrants were not allowed to move out of their districts, except in special circumstances, the reason being that such a measure would simplify control. Somebody found outside his own district could be arrested and brought to the immigration depot where his case would be examined. All in all, a remarkably stringent regulation!

And it was applied as severely as possible. In fact the immigrants were hunted down in the same way as had been customary in the days of slavery. An Indian walking in the streets stood a great chance of being held up by a policeman, and—as was often the case—if the policeman could not read the pass, which was written out in English, he would simply take him along to the police station. The magistrates

[1] Report of the Royal Commissioners appointed to enquire into the treatment of immigrants in Mauritius, 1875. Chapters 10 & 11. Also § 2013, 2015, 2019, 2042.

cooperated with the police in applying the law as strictly as possible, and it was not a rare occurrence for an immigrant to be convicted as a vagrant even though actively employed. In addition, it should be borne in mind that after 1852 the immigrants had no rights whatever on a free or even partly free passage back to their own country. They were thus entirely at the mercy of the colonists and the lives they led during and after the contract period did not differ all that much from slavery.

The system of contract labour, no matter how reasonable in theory, can thus be seen as having led to most unfavourable results in practice. The many serious abuses connected with the recruiting, with the treatment in the colonies, and with the practices after the completion of the contract periods made of the system a real plague for many years, and with penal sanction gave it a marked aspect of compulsory labour.

LITERATURE

Campbell, Persia Crawford, Chinese Coolie Emigration to Countries Within the British Empire, London, 1923.

Clementi, Cecil, The Chinese in British Guiana, 1915.

Davy, John, The West Indies before and since slave emancipation . . ., London etc., 1854.

Duchesne-Fournet, Jean, La main-d'oeuvre dans les Guyanes, Paris, 1905.

Immigration ordinances of Trinidad and British Guiana, London 1904, Cd. 1989.

McNeill, James, and Chimman Lal, Report to the Government of India on the Conditions of Indian Immigrants in four British Colonies and Surinam, London, 1915, 2 vols.

Mathieson, William Law, British Slave Emancipation, 1838-1849, London etc., 1932.

Nath, Dwarka, A history of Indians in British Guiana, London etc., [1950].

Report of the Commissioners appointed to enquire into the treatment of immigrants in British Guiana, London, 1871, C 393.

Report of the Committee on Emigration from India to the Crown Colonies and Protectorates, London, 1910, Cd. 5192-5194.

Report of the Royal Commissioners appointed to enquire into the treatment of immigrants in Mauritius, London, 1875, C 1115.

CHAPTER TWO

SOUTH AFRICA

In another British colony of the time, the Cape Colony, abolition of the slave-trade in 1807 might almost be said to have produced greater turmoil than slave emancipation did in 1834. For here the natives of the territory, primarily Hottentots, were not used as slaves, whereas there had been a regular traffic of slaves for some 150 years from Madagascar and Mozambique, and from British and Netherlands India [1]. Cutting off this source of supply left the farmers with labour problems, and it was at this point that they looked to the natives as a possible labour force.

These, as has been said, were mainly Hottentots. With the advent of the Dutch they were by degrees robbed of their land, and by about 1800 there was no land available for them any longer to lead their former nomadic existence. They either roamed the country aimlessly, feeding off wild vegetation, or lived on the land of the Europeans. Some of this last group were put to work by the Boers, but, since they showed little inclination to work and since there were sufficient slaves about, many among them did little to no work.

By 1807, when the slave-trade came to an end, the colonists felt little obliged to tolerate all this, and in 1809 regulations were passed with a view to altering the situation [2]. Every Hottentot had in future to have a "place of fixed abode". Migration was not permissible without a pass issued by the specified authorities. Anybody found roaming about without this pass would be picked up as a "vagrant" and allocated to a farmer as a labourer; and it was the duty of every European to demand to see the pass of any suspect "vagrant".

By these measures the Hottentots were in reality forced to enter the employ of the Europeans. After all, the "place of fixed abode" could hardly be on land of their own since they no longer had any, and neither was roaming from place to place possible any longer.

---

[1] Sheila T. van der Horst, Native Labour in South Africa, 1942, p. 7/8.

[2] Select Constitutional Documents Illustrating South African History, 1795-1910 . . . . edited . . . . by G. W. Eybers, 1918, p. 17/18. See further for measures relating to the Hottentots: W. M. McMillan, The Cape Colour Question, 1927. And: J. S. Marais, The Cape Coloured People, 1652-1937, 1939.

They were therefore forced to live on European-owned land. However, the Europeans now only allowed this if a labour contract was entered upon.

Matters were made far worse for the Hottentots by the inconsiderate way in which the authorities enforced the pass laws. A Hottentot not wanting to remain in the employ of a farmer on completion of his contract could from the office concerned receive a pass permitting him to go out and look for work. Often, however, this pass was valid for far too short a period—sometimes only a few days, and then again one day, or 12 hours—and if he did not succeed in finding work in that time he had to return to the office of issue or stand liable to arrest for "vagrancy";—in both cases being put to work by the higher authorities.

And often the farmers too showed very little consideration for their labourers. It was a common occurrence for a labourer to be kept on by his employer at the end of a contract period, whether he liked it or not. Food and clothing, damages to property, medical attention, and even time lost through illness would all be accounted to him and by far outweighed his meagre wages. Consequently, being in debt to the farmer, there was nothing for it but to serve a further contract period.

Another far-reaching regulation was promulgated in 1812. The authorities were empowered through this regulation to allot Hottentot children between the ages of 8 and 18 who had been provided for by a farmer up to their eighth year to that farmer as apprentices, or, if the farmer did not appear suitable, to another. Although the apprentices had to work for their masters, the masters were not obliged to educate them. The farmers by this law were not only given the rights on the labour of young people but also indirectly on the labour of their parents since these were more or less forced to work on the farms where the children were being kept if they wished to retain any contact with them.

It is obvious that under these circumstances the wages to the Hottentot labourers must have been very low indeed. It is true that there were regulations designed to protect their interests, but who was to know? Hardly the Hottentots, and officials of every grade were entirely in hands of the colonists.

Some of the Hottentots found shelter on the mission stations established for that purpose during this period. In some respects they could consider themselves privileged. For one thing they could not be allocated to a farmer if found outside their place of abode without a pass, and for another, their children were not affected by the regulations covering the apprenticeship system. The mission stations, however, were in most cases not sufficient in extent or quality of ground to ensure a livelihood for the people living there. Therefore most of the natives accommodated on the stations had no other choice but to work on neighbouring farms. Yet there were always a number who preferred poverty on the mission stations to labouring for the Boers. Naturally in the eyes of the Boers such idleness was wrong, and therefore a very high tax was imposed on the Hottentots of these settlements. To pay this tax it became necessary for them to work on the farms for longer or shorter periods. What is more, for a certain period of the year they were required to do compulsory labour for the public authorities. So we see that in one way or another practically all the Hottentots were forced to work for the Europeans.

However, the humanitarian movement responsible for the abolition of slave-trade in 1807 remained active in England, and in 1828 the position of the Hottentots was completely reversed by a new ordinance. The pass system, for one, was abrogated, and the apprenticeship system reformed. This really meant a cessation of compulsory labour, for roaming about was now allowed again and farmers no longer had rights over children merely because they had provided for them in their early childhood. And with the emancipation of slaves in 1833 the humanitarian movement achieved its greatest victory.

But these reformations only infuriated the majority of Europeans at the Cape. Many Hottentots indeed left their service in 1828, and "vagrancy" increased considerably. The colonists began pressing for a new law against "vagrancy", a movement which gained ground after abolition, so much so that in 1834 the Legislative Council of the Cape Colony proposed a law which was to force the coloured population (Hottentots and freed slaves) to work. Instantly great herds of Hottentots, who had for a few years at least enjoyed comparative freedom—comparative in the sense that there was still no land available for them—crowded onto the mission stations. However, in England the Government, with whom the final decision rested, remained adamant, and the proposed law was defeated.

The introduction of one reform after the other and the refusal of the British Government to revert to the old principles can be said to have been the main provocations causing a group of indignant colonists to embark on the Great Trek of 1836/37. Many hundreds of Boers moved north and settled outside the colony where, as Piet Retief, their leader, declared in a manifesto, they would "know how to maintain the right relationship between servant and master" [1]. Wherever these Boers went in those territories later to be known as the Orange Free State, Transvaal and Natal they took possession of the land of the Bantu natives. This eventually led to a system of "labour tenancy" which meant in effect that natives could have the use of a small holding on the Boer farms in exchange for labour. This system only developed by degrees, however, and in the first years the farmers experienced difficulties in procuring sufficient labour, especially in the busy seasons; notwithstanding their small labour requirements. Cattle farmers, for example, seldom needed more than one or two herders, a few farm-hands and some domestic help. Yet to meet these needs the republican settlers resorted to direct labour compulsion; hardly surprising considering their mentality on leaving the Cape.

In the first form of compulsory labour resorted to, natives were called up by the authorities and distributed among the Boers. They then had to labour for anything up to 14 consecutive days. This labour went under the name of taxation even though it was used to further private ends. However, the worst of it was that the farmers frequently demanded more labour from the natives than officially allowed. The natives were not so familiar with the regulations, and in any case defenceless.

The second form of compulsory labour was still more abused. This labour was procured by means of an apprenticeship system. In the promulgated regulations it was decreed that natives could be allocated to work as apprentices for farmers up to their 25th year. The great demand for these apprentices, especially as domestic help, led to large scale kidnapping of native children. Quite a few persons made it their job to buy up children from natives who had stolen them, and they would carry off wagon loads of these children at a time![2]

Such outrages were rampant. The leaders of the republics were not able to see that the laws were properly observed. There was no police force, and the interests of the officials were closely allied to those of the farmers.

[1] Eybers, op. cit., p. 144.
[2] Van der Horst, op. cit., p. 57.

In the British administrated Cape Colony the settlers, many of them of Dutch stock, observed the regulations of 1828 and 1833 (abrogation of compulsory labour for the Hottentots, and slave emancipation), and consequently there was a more liberal attitude toward the native population. Yet here too measures were adopted with a view to exerting pressure on the natives to make them work, especially in the forties and fifties when the economic growth of the colony brought with it an increasing demand for labour [1].

The Bantus had penetrated the Cape Colony by this time and soon became the main native group. The northward migration of colonists and the southward spread of various Bantu tribes resulted in one Kaffir War after the other, and both groups were brought into closer contact with each other than ever before. The Europeans at the Cape at first conscientiously endeavoured to keep the formidable Bantu races at a distance for fear of possible trouble, but after losing the compulsory labour of the Hottentots in 1828 they began to look to the Bantu as a possible labour force and therefore allowed them to settle on their farms [2]. Also, by about this time the Hottentot race became extinct through intermarriage with the freed slaves and—to a lesser extent—the Europeans. This intermarriage brought into existence a "coloured" group which joined the Bantus in forming a labour reservoir.

The first measure to ensure a labour supply was taken in 1841 with the proclamation of an ordinance governing employer—employee relations. This ordinance was drawn up in such a way as to bind the servant more closely to his master and included penal sanction for such matters as desertion, negligence at work, and insubordination. And in 1856, when the settlers were granted a share in the administration of the colony, these regulations were made more rigid—although it should be mentioned that more regulations protecting native interests were also passed.

However, the natives were mainly brought to work by indirect measures. For example, native settlements in white areas were encouraged in anticipation of a favourable effect on the labour situation. The policy to make ownership of land in the reserves individual and not communal was also adopted with this end in mind. Another method was to impose taxes. And yet another way was

[1] Van der Horst, op. cit., p. 26.
[2] W. M. McMillan, Bantu, Boer and Briton, 1929, p. 67.

to encourage natives to wear European clothes and buy European goods. Trade restrictions were raised. But the results probably went further than was intended, for the natives were immediately surrounded by innumerable traders, who sold on credit to such an extent that many natives were soon hopelessly in debt [1]. All the same, many natives were won over to work for the Europeans in this way.

To facilitate the labour movement, magistrates took it upon themselves to act as mediators, and any Boer needing labourers had simply to apply to them. Besides all this there was also the increasing shortage of arable land which eventually compelled the natives in the Cape to work for the Europeans.

In Natal, annexed by Britain soon after the Great Trek, the need of a labour force was greater than elsewhere in South Africa since sugar-cane cultivation was the primary industry here. Taxation and other measures for procuring such a labour force all proved ineffectual, and it was for this reason that coolies from British India were brought to the colony.

However, generally speaking there was not such a great need of a labour force in South Africa at this time, and that need was certainly neglígeable to the needs which arose with the commencement of diamond mining in 1870 and gold mining in 1886. Now suddenly labourers were needed in vast quantities, not only for the mining industry but also for all the other industries which sprang up as a result of it. Railways had to be built, harbours improved, and agriculture became of increasing importance with the growth of the towns. Thus in a matter of years the labour requirements rocketted—to remain high (except perhaps during depressions).

True there was also a greater offer of labour at this time, and many factors were at work to increase this offer. The native land problem grew more acute after 1870—eventually becoming almost impossible. The reserves were far too small to sustain a growing native population, and the farming methods employed too primitive. The authorities were not very active in introducing better methods, and in 1932 a government commission came to the conclusion that the situation was getting steadily worse. Due to erosion and other causes the impoverished soil could provide for less and less people. Most of the natives in the reserves were in debt, and because of the general

[1] Van der Horst, op. cit., p. 19.

poverty—mainly due to over-population—their health was deteriorating [1]. On the other hand the needs of the natives were growing because of their intensified contact with white civilisation. Thus many natives were now offering their services to the Europeans of their own accord. But this increasing offer of labour was in itself not enough, and therefore various steps were taken to stimulate the migration of natives from the reserves to the European employers.

To begin with, various taxes were imposed on the natives. Although there were other reasons for this, the main one remained unalterable. To pay taxes one has to earn, and to earn one has to work. Even today these taxes are apparently still deemed essential to ensure a steady flow of labourers to the industries, so they are still imposed—even though quite unfair.

Under the taxing system all native men of 18 and over have to pay a uniform tax, which is high in proportion to their average earnings. Moreover, all natives possessing a small holding in the reserves have to pay another uniform tax as well. Whether the native is earning or not makes absolutely no difference since the taxes are there and have to be paid. Members of other races, however, only pay taxes over and above a specified minimum income. In some rural areas this has led to the paradoxical situation in which the white farmers do not pay taxes because they do not have a sufficiently high income, whereas their servants do pay, and a relatively high tax at that. And in the towns poor whites, coloureds, Asiatics and natives might live together under the same conditions and all equally poor, but only the natives would pay direct tax [2]. And the main tax a native has to pay often amounts to more than his monthly wage. Moreover, tax collecting is as a rule most inconsiderately carried out. Natives have been known to be arrested while attending a church service, because their tax payments were overdue. On one occasion even a funeral service was held up and all the participants arrested for the same reason [3]. This is all much more serious when one realizes that also the indirect taxes are in themselves already a heavy burden on the natives [4].

There was at one time a tax which made it even more imperative

---

[1] Report of Native Economic Commission 1930-1932, pp. 10, 173, 182, 183.

[2] Report of Native Economic Commission 1930-1932, p. 225.

[3] Western Civilization and the Natives of South Africa, Edited by I. Schapera, 1934, p. 286.

[4] Report of Native Economic Commission 1930-1932, p. 227.

for the natives to work. Namely between 1894 and 1905 when in some districts natives who possessed no land of their own and who had not worked for a specific time for Europeans had to pay a certain amount to the revenue office. As the Prime Minister of England put it when proposing this law, such a tax would "help the natives to overcome their idleness, it would teach them the value of work and would give them an opportunity to do something in return for the wise rule of the Europeans" [1].

The policy of making ownership of land in the reserves more individual was another measure with the same end in view, and it was applied more strictly after 1894. Naturally there were other reasons for this policy, but there is no doubt that it was mainly prompted by the thought that in this way more natives would have to leave the reserves for the industries.

And finally, having seen that the limited extent of the reserves has a definite effect on the labour situation, it is difficult not to believe that this overcrowding has for a part been the result of a determinate labour policy.

These measures to draw more natives from the reserves were mainly to benefit the industries, and if one examines the situation in the European rural areas one finds measures of similar intent in operation. For example, it was decreed that farmers having more natives living on their farms than absolutely essential to the running of the farms were to pay a fixed premium for every superfluous native. This regulation had the desired effect since many natives were indeed put off the farms [2], and—again taking into consideration the overcrowded state of the reserves—they had no alternative but to migrate to the towns. To achieve the same ends in other instances, laws were passed limiting the number of native families living on a European farm to five.

In 1879 an even more direct step was taken to promote native labour when a law to combat "vagrancy" was introduced in the Cape Colony [3]. This law is still operative today [4] and decrees that anybody without "legal and sufficient means" is culpable, while persons offering shelter to such "idle and disorderly" people are equally liable to prosecution.

---

[1] Taken from Van der Horst, op. cit., p. 149.
[2] Van der Horst, op. cit., p. 148.
[3] Van der Horst, op. cit., p. 123.
[4] Lord Hailey, An African Survey, 2nd ed. 1945, p. 666. Report of the Ad hoc committee on forced labour, 1953, p. 77, 409 etc.

All these mainly indirect measures indeed served to bring the natives into the employ of Europeans, and in larger numbers than anywhere else in Africa. Yet they were not enough if a really sufficient and regular supply of industrial labour was to be ensured; and it was for this reason that the large undertakings deemed it necessary to do their own recruiting. Carefully planned and well organised recruiting took place on a large scale, but here too dubious practices occurred which suggest that the native employees were not always free in their choice.

On the diamond fields it began right from the word go in 1870. The employers offered guns to the natives who had worked for them. The native chiefs, feeling insecure in view of the European rule, were so keen on this that they exerted all their influence on their subjects to send them to the industry [1]. Direct bribing of the chiefs also took place [2]. Such practices repeated themselves later when the gold mining industry got under way. Labourers frequently complained that their chiefs had "sold" them to the recruiting agents [3], and the European administrators also on more than one occasion lent the agents a helping hand in their task [4]. Like the chiefs, these officials as a rule were able to exercise much influence on the natives, whereby an advice was often as good as a command. On the whole those most guilty of abuses were the recruiting agents operating independently, and the most common deception was to give a completely false picture of conditions in the mines. When the recruiting system was later to a large extent organised the situation improved in this respect. The administration also endeavoured to bring about improvements in the recruiting system, both independently in the various provinces before Union, and again after Union through the Native Labour Regulation Act of 1911, which, among others, imposed a code of behavior on recruiting agents. The agents, however, continued for many years to grant loans to natives so as to get them in their power, and when an amendment to the act eventually limited the amount that could be loaned considerably, this still did not prevent a trader-agent from giving extensive credit to a

---

[1] Van der Horst, op. cit., p. 69-71.
[2] Id., p. 71.
[3] Id., p. 133.
[4] For example see I. Schapera, Migrant Labour and Tribal Life, 1947, p. 149, 151.

native so as to later be able to force him to go to work on the mines to pay off his debt [1].

Many mine labourers are drawn from outside the Union, mainly from Portuguese East Africa. In the beginning false representations, etc. also played a role here, though this was not strictly necessary seeing that many natives were only too glad to conclude a contract, thereby escaping the labour obligations pertaining to all able males in the Portuguese colonies [2]. However, this will be discussed in a later chapter.

Neither are the natives really free once they are working on the mines. In the early stages of diamond exploitation the freedom of movement of the labourers was restricted to prevent desertion. A pass was required to leave the diamond field, and this pass could only be acquired on presentation of a document signed by the employer declaring that the contract period was over. Any native labourer found outside the area without a pass was of course committing an offence. The natives could therefore not move from their place of work for the duration of their contracts without risking prosecution. And a similar, though stricter, rule was later applied to the gold mining industry. The Native Labour Regulation Act of 1911 redrafted the regulations covering employer-employee relations, but penal sanction on breach of contract and the pass system were retained and have been up to recent times [3].

It is widely known that the labour conditions in the South African urban areas, though much improved in comparison to the early days of mining, are still unfavourable in many respects. The contract period for recruit labourers on the mines is about 11 months ("volunteers" are more free in their choice). During their period of service most labourers live in mine compounds, which they may not leave without authority. Most of these compounds are no more than a miserable arrangement of barrack-type dwellings, and they are supervised by native boss-boys, notorious in the extreme for their uncouth and violent ways; not that the labour supervisors on the mines proper are any better behaved.

There is an official eight hour working day; to this should really be added the time taken in travelling to and fro between the mines

[1] Leonard Barnes, Native Labour on the Transvaal Gold-mines, The Contemporary Review, Vol. 145, 1934, p. 66.

[2] Raymond Leslie Buell, The Native Problem in Africa, 1928, Vol. 1, p. 31.

[3] Report of the Ad hoc Committee on Forced Labour, 1953, p. 74-77.

and the compounds, which can be quite some distance apart. Most labourers work on a basis of daily tasks. If the daily task is not completed, the day's wage is forfeited and another day is also added to the contract period.

And then there is the question of wages. It is all too well known that these are kept extremely low intentionally. In 1897 the native wages were made uniform throughout the mines and amounted to about two-thirds of the average wage earned before that time. Furthermore, between 1897 and 1930 this nominal wage remained more or less static, meaning in effect a marked depreciation in the actual wage value. The lowest paid European workers receive eight times as much in wages as the natives even though performing work no more demanding than that reserved for natives.

But, no matter how low the native wages in the industries, they are still considerably higher that the traditional wages paid to native farm labourers. This, together with the other dubious attractions of the towns, resulted in too large an exodus of labourers from the country, which, in time, led to what could be considered as a satisfactory provision of labour for the industries and an acute shortage of labour on the farms.

Various steps have been taken in the course of the 20th century to remedy this situation. The Natives' Land Act of 1913 might be said to be the most sweeping measure, since by this act natives were definitely forbidden to either buy or hire land from Europeans outside the specified territories intended for them. One of the main motives for this act was to introduce segregation with respect to Bantu and European landed property; but an equally important motive was to bring the many natives with small holdings on European farms—whether by crop-sharing or cash arrangement—into a different relationship with the landowners. The native was now to become either a labourer or labour tenant, in which case he would retain the right of occupation of his small holding in exchange for labour during a certain number of days per year. Because of this law many natives were indeed compelled to enter into a labour relationship with their landlords, and mostly on terms stipulated by the latter. After all, the reserves were—and are—over-populated, and natives with their own small holding are usually too attached to their cattle and piece of cultivated land to easily forsake these for a life as industrial labourers.

In 1932 a new law pertaining to the Transvaal and Natal, the

Native Service Contract Act, was passed, certain regulations of which were designed to bind the natives still more closely to their landlords. For example, it was decreed illegal to employ a native living on European-owned land outside the reserves unless he could show a declaration from the landowner stating that his services were not required for the duration of the contemplated period of employment. Nor were the authorities allowed to issue passes authorising the natives to look for work in the towns without the consent of the landowner-employer. Also, it was strictly forbidden to employ native youths under the age of 18 without the consent of the landowner. On the other hand, the headman of a *kraal* on European-owned land could now legally conclude a labour contract with the landowner on behalf of youths under 18, without the consent of these youths being necessary. And the penalties for breach of contract were made stricter—flogging could now even be administered to youths under the age of 18. It would certainly appear evident from these regulations that it was increasingly difficult to keep the native youths on the farms.

These measures to prevent farm labourers from migrating seem strict enough as they stand, yet many farmers would have liked to have taken matters much further [1]. According to them the pass laws should have been so strict as to make it practically impossible for the natives to leave the farms at all. Refusal to accept offered work—on the usual terms—should have been made punishable by laws as should roaming about for more than three weeks at a time. And any native unable to prove that he had worked for a European for at least nine months out of twelve should be likewise punishable. What is more, the authorities should have been given power to allocate native labourers to such farmers as required them. Since labourers were being drawn to the industries because of better conditions it was concluded as only natural that housing in the towns should be made less attractive, and that wage discrepancies should be evened out by declaring farm labourers tax-free, and imposing a higher tax on industrial labourers to meet the difference. Fortunately the Government was not prepared to sanction such extravagances.

Let us examine the conditions of farm labour more closely [2].

---

[1] Farm Labour in the Orange Free State, 1939, p. 40-42.

[2] See particularly: Report of Native Economic Commission 1930-1932, pp. 49-58, 185-204. And: Farm Labour in the Orange Free State, 1939.

A labour tenant must be prepared to work for his landowner-employer for six months of the year in Natal and three months of the year in the other provinces. In quite a few cases, however, a longer period of labour is asked for and received—even to the extent of nine months. Furthermore, in many cases the landowners call upon their tenants to work when they need them so that the tenant cannot work off his tenancy in one time but must instead be prepared perhaps to make two days available in the week, or even have no fixed arrangement at all and be entirely at the landowners beck and call. Such a system is of course most unfavourable for the natives since they cannot really at any time work for someone else to supplement their meagre incomes.

In the case of both labourers and labour tenants it is customary for the whole family to assist; the women mostly doing domestic work, and the men and youths working in the fields. Since 1932 it has even been so that if one of the members of the family fails to meet his obligations toward the landowner, the landowner has the right to put the whole family off the land; and this can be seen as another regulation to prevent desertion.

As is generally the case with farm labour, working hours are long and irregular. The rewards are particularly meagre. Only a small percentage of the wages is paid in money (also in the case of labourers), the rest to be made up with food, and the right of the use of a small plot of land. However, the food is usually insufficient and the plot of land far too small to keep a family on. Because of the small income in money, the tenants are hereby placed in a very vulnerable position. At times of drought or crop failure they are faced with extreme poverty and often would not be able to keep their head above water were it not for the farmers' loans. They are also frequently forced to borrow from the farmer-landowners when extra expenses crop up or when taxes have to be paid. In fact very few farm labourers or labour tenants are not involved in debt, and some farmers make it a point to encourage a certain amount of borrowing so as to make it impossible for a native to leave unless he finds an employer willing enough to take over his debts for him. The amount of money owing to a former employer is stated on the pass which is necessary when looking for work, thus if the debt is large the chances of finding new employment are very slender. Since these passes are issued by the former employers, the natives are very dependent on them, and the whole system cannot be otherwise than open to abuse.

Finally, farm labourers, and sometimes even labour tenants are punishable for breach of contract in accordance with the Master and Servants Acts which are strongly biased in favour of the European farmers. As a consequence of all this, both farm labourers and labour tenants cannot be said to be in a free position.

But it is particularly the strongly prejudiced attitude of the law courts and police which make it most difficult for the natives, and this applies to both country and town. The police can be often extremely tactless and dishonest in their dealings with natives, and in a dispute between a European and a native, the former will almost always be favoured. Serious outrages by Europeans are connived at, while petty offences committed by natives meet with severe sentences [1]. This all naturally places the native in a very vulnerable and dependent position.

Although we have not been able to show that any direct pressure is exerted to make a section of the population work in the Union of South Africa—either for private persons or even (since a long time) on public works—it can certainly not be said that the natives work quite voluntarily and without compulsion of one sort or another. The Union is the only country in Africa where by far the majority of the natives are dependent on paid labour. This, as we have seen, is mainly because of over-population and a shortage of available land, and in these circumstances indirect measures are for the most part sufficient to ensure a steady supply of native labour for the industries and mines. However these indirect measures are rigorously enforced, particularly with regard to the heavy tax pressure; and the recruiting system instituted by the industries does the rest. One can only speak of a real labour shortage with respect to the rural areas—and mainly because the farmers steadfastly refuse to pay higher wages and provide better working conditions; and here extreme measures have been taken both officially and unofficially on the part of the Boers to bind the natives more closely to them. Furthermore, pass laws and penal sanction pertain to all native labourers whether in the country or in the towns, and must restrict their freedom to a large extent. Where it has been deemed desirable, therefore, the European settlers in South Africa have also shown themselves prepared to adopt labour compulsion, if in most cases indirectly.

---

[1] See for example: Western Civilization and the Natives of South Africa, Edited by I. Schapera, 1934, p. 291-294.

LITERATURE

Barnes, Leonard, Native Labour on the Transvaal Gold Mines, In: The Contemporary Review, Vol. 145, 1934, p. 64-71.
Buell, Raymond Leslie, The Native Problem in Africa, New York, 1928, Vol. 1, p. 1-159: South Africa.
Farm Labour in the Orange Free State, Report of an investigation undertaken under the auspices of the South African Institute of Race Relations, Johannesburg, 1939.
Lord Hailey, An African Survey, A study of problems arising in Africa South of the Sahara, 2nd ed. London, etc., 1945.
Haines, E. S., The Economic Status of the Cape Province Farm Native, In: The South African Journal of Economics, Vol. 3, 1935, p. 57-79.
Handbook on Race Relations in South Africa, Edited by Ellen Hellmann, London etc., 1949.
Horst, Sheila T. van der, Native Labour in South Africa, London, 1942.
Leubuscher, Charlotte, Der südafrikanische Eingeborene als Industriearbeiter und als Stadtbewohner, Jena, 1931.
Marais, J. S., The Cape Coloured People 1652-1937, London, 1939.
McMillan, William Miller, Bantu, Boer and Briton, The making of the South African native problem, London, 1929.
— The Cape Colour Question, A historical survey, London, 1927.
— Complex South Africa, An economic foot-note to history, London, 1930.
Lord Olivier, The Anatomy of African Misery, London, 1927.
Phillips, Ray E., The Bantu in the City, A study of cultural adjustment on the Witwatersrand, New York etc., 1938.
Read, C. L., The Union Native and the Witwatersrand Gold Mines, In: The South African Journal of Economics, Vol. 1, 1933, p. 397-404.
Report of the Ad hoc Committee on Forced Labour, Geneva, 1953, (United Nations — International Labour Office).
Report of Native Economic Commission 1930-1932, 1932, (Union of South Africa).
Robertson, H. M., 150 years of Economic Contact between Black and White, A preliminary survey, In: The South African Journal of Economics, Vol. 2, 1934, p. 403-425; Vol. 3, 1935, p. 3-25.
Schapera, I., Migrant Labour and Tribal Life, A study of conditions in the Bechuanaland Protectorate, London etc., 1947.
Select constitutional documents illustrating South African history 1795-1910, Selected and edited with an introduction by G. W. Eybers, London, 1918.
Tinley, J. M., The Native Labor Problem of South Africa, Chapel Hill, N.C., etc., 1942.
Western Civilization and the Natives of South Africa, Studies in culture contact, Edited by I. Schapera, London, 1934.

CHAPTER THREE

THE NETHERLANDS WEST INDIES

Having examined the situation in the British West Indies (Chap. I) we need not spend much time on the Netherlands West Indian colonies, in which slavery came to an end in 1863, seeing that the situation in the latter in general terms very much resembled that in the former after emancipation there in 1834. The colonists in both instances were confronted with more or less the same difficulties, and took to more or less the same measures in solving them.

We must draw a distinction here between Surinam on the one hand and the islands on the other. On the islands there were not so many liberated slaves—11,654 in all, as compared to 33, 621 in Surinam [1]—nor was there such a great demand for labour—since staple products were not grown in great quantity; the principal means of livelihood being trade. Moreover, the situation on the islands was such that the inhabitants were after a time not able to provide for their own needs without working for the whites [2]. Thus most of those liberated remained at their former work or, if they went away, soon returned to it. The abolition of slavery can therefore be seen to have created no unusually complicated difficulties here.

Not so in Surinam. Here the large estates, especially the sugar plantations, were of primary importance to the country, and made heavy demands on the labour potential. Moreover, there was a great deal of uncultivated land available on which the Negroes could relatively easily provide for their own requirements. As is to be expected, the abolition of slavery created a serious labour problem here—which led to the re-institution of a system of compulsory labour; in this case, a system of contract labour subject to penal sanction.

The need for new labour did not follow directly upon abolition in 1863, seeing that the slaves here got as little immediate freedom in 1863 as the slaves in the British West Indies had in 1834. The liberated slaves were placed under government supervision for the first ten

---

[1] Encyclopaedie van Nederlandsch West-Indië, 1914-1917, p. 642.

[2] C. A. van Sypesteyn, Afschaffing der slavernij in de Nederlandsche West-Indische koloniën, In: Het Bijblad van de Economist, 1866, p. 66.

years [1], and during this period all persons between the ages of 15 and 60 were obliged to sign labour contracts. Anyone not signing a contract within three months of the date of abolition was to be put to labour by the administration on the government plantations or on public works. Anyone not fulfilling the terms of his contract would be liable to a fine or imprisonment with forced labour on the public works of from 8 days to 3 months. In addition, idleness and „vagrancy" were made penal offences in the same year, 1863.

But these were all intended as temporary measures to tide over the period of transition. There was little hope, after what had been learnt from experience in British and French Guiana, that the freed slaves would in this way grow accustomed to a life as wage earners. Nor did that happen. The Negroes hated the plantation labour which they had had to do for so long as slaves, and they sought every opportunity to move away as soon as they could either to the towns or elsewhere to start a little "place" of their own where they would be free to raise what they needed for themselves in their own good time. In short, the former slaves were lost to the large estates after 1873—and the colonists had therefore to look further afield for their labour supply.

Chinese labourers and Portuguese from Madeira had been brought into Surinam in as early as 1853, when it first became clear that emancipation was on the way. There was a further influx of West Indian people, especially from thickly-populated Barbados, soon after abolition. But the greatest immigration took place after 1870 when the Dutch signed a treaty with England, whereby British Indians were allowed to be recruited for Surinam, and later (after 1890) the labour supply was further increased with the regular arrival of Javanese. Altogether 34,848 British Indians entered Surinam between the years 1873 and 1916, and 30,905 Javanese between 1890 and 1929 [2]).

All these immigrants came as contract labourers [3], i.e., they had signed a contract for a certain period—here always 5 years—to work on the plantation to which they would be assigned—and

---

[1] See for this period of State supervision especially: C. A. van Sypesteyn, op. cit., in: Het Bijblad van de Economist, 1866, p. 1-85.

[2] Ernst Snellen, De aanvoer van arbeiders voor den landbouw in Suriname, 1933, p. 78.

[3] In the years 1930 and 1931 about 1,500 free immigrants from Java were admitted.

in return the employers were obliged to provide housing, medical attention, etc., as well as pay the wages determined by the Government. Penal sanction was the first element of non-freedom involved in this labour. Because they had gone to great expense to import their labourers, the planters felt they had the right to ensure that they really worked for their full period of 5 years; and the only way to ensure this amply was to make breach of contract a penal offence. The penalties involved were:

a) In 1873: a maximum fine of 25 guilders and/or imprisonment with forced labour to a maximum of 14 days.
b) After 1916: for refusal to work etc., a maximum fine of 25 guilders or a maximum of 6 weeks' imprisonment; for desertion, a maximum fine of 50 guilders or a maximum of 2 months' imprisonment.

However, this aspect of non-freedom was considerably enhanced by the fact that the labourers in most cases did not know what was awaiting them, or were even sent to Surinam against their will.

The manner of recruitment of these labourers was often as bad as that of the coolies for British Guiana [1], as decribed in Chapter One. In Java, the recruiting agents were also paid on a commission basis, and they were for the most part ruthlessly unscrupulous. They were only concerned with rounding up as many people as possible, and naturally not with *how* this was to be done. It was customary to portrait the life awaiting the victims in Surinam in glowing terms, and all forms of deceipt and trickery were resorted to. The recruiters were hated intensely in Java. Those taking the oath on assuming membership of one branch of the Sarekat Islam had to swear that they "would not steal, would not recruit, and would not lie" [2]. The corruptability of many of the native chiefs completed the system—so that there was absolutely no question of voluntariness on the part of the coolies. As soon as they had signed a contract they were locked up, sometimes for months, in depots—and anyone caught after escaping from one of these was liable to a fine and imprisonment [3]).

---

[1] See for instance J. W. Meijer Ranneft, Misstanden bij de werving op Java, In: Tijdschrift voor het Binnenlandsch Bestuur, dl. 46, 1914, afl. 1, p. 1-17; afl. 2, p. 54-72. Also: Gouvernementswerving, In: Koloniaal Tijdschrift, jg. 3, 1914, p. 920-923.

[2] J. W. Meijer Ranneft, op. cit., In: Tijdschrift voor het Binnenlandsch Bestuur, dl. 46, 1914, afl. 2, p. 62.

[3] J. van Vollenhoven, Rapport over de werving, emigratie, en immigratie van arbeiders en de kolonisatie in Oost-Indië en Suriname, 1913, p. 24.

Finally, there followed the voyage to the West. Although later improved, conditions were frightful, and until well into the 20th century Javanese recruitees were treated with complete unconcern for some of the most rudimentary principles of human rights [1].

Also, when once in the new country there were circumstances which accentuated the fact that they were not free. In the period immediately following on abolition the European planters proved themselves unable to immediately change their attitude toward their inferiors with the result that there was not much change in the practices on the plantations [2]. Even in 1915 complaints were still being heard of unprovoked savagery and brutal treatment on the part of overseers, especially against Indonesian labourers [3]. Often the labourers, especially the Indonesians [4], were given very little opportunity to present their grievances. To be sure, the diverse rulings for the protection of the labourers and for inspection of the plantations were not bad in theory [5]; but the *agent-general* was far too busy with other things to find the time to make adequate inspection tours. And the District Officers, whose duty it was to see all the plantations in their district once a month, were also responsible for following up penal offences committed by the immigrants—and these certainly did not as a rule discern any sign of the protector in the officers [6]. Actually, even in 1909 there was no one in the colony—and therefore also not in the immigration department—who knew the language of the Javanese labourers [7], which fact was not exactly conducive to good understanding or justice. Moreover, the wages were much lower than they had been led to expect in Java [8], and were indeed exceedingly low according to official reports [9]. Few fetched even the minimum wage stipulated by the authorities (up to 1920, 60 cents (about 1/4 d) a day for men). This was possible be-

[1] G. J. Kruijer, Suriname en zijn Buurlanden, 1953, p. 80.

[2] Id., p. 73.

[3] J. Ismael, De immigratie van Indonesiërs in Suriname, 1949, p. 60.

[4] The British Indian coolies were under the protection of the British consul in Paramaribo, so in a more favourable position.

[5] James McNeill and Chimman Lal, Report to the Government of India on the Conditions of Indian Immigrants in Four British Colonies and Surinam, 1915, pp. 151, 169.

[6] De Economische en financieele toestand der kolonie Suriname, 1911, p. 189/190.

[7] Kruijer, op. cit., p. 80.

[8] De Economische en Financieele Toestand etc., 1911, p. 178.

[9] Id., p. 180 ff. McNeill and Chimman Lal, op. cit., pp. 153, 155, 166.

cause they were paid by piece work, and the tarifs for this were far too low. In fact, the average day's pay of Javanese labourers was no higher than 35 cents—about 9d. [1]. Although this was equivalent to normal wages in Java, it should be remembered that the cost of living was much higher in Surinam. There was insistence on higher wages in the Dutch Parliament in 1916, because then the labourers would be able to feed themselves better and therefore be stronger! [2]. Needless to say, only the pick of the labourers were in a position to save any money [3]. Most of the Javanese returned home poorer than when they had left it [4]—despite the fact that women did contract labour alongside their husbands. Is it surprising then that many of the Javanese told a missionary working among them (in 1909) that they thought they had been cheated [5]. If in addition to all this, we take into account that sometimes (although probably not often) the people had to wait some time at the end of their contract period for a ship to take them back to their own countries—causing them to incur debts through which they could be compelled again to sign a new contract [6]—then we can only conclude that contract labour in Surinam constituted compulsory labour in many respects; some legal (penal sanction), but perhaps many more illegal—though none the less real. The British Consul in Paramaribo in 1911 warned against emigrating to Surinam because of, among other things, "veiled slavery" [7].

Compulsory labour under penal sanction was brought to an end in the early thirties. No more British Indian coolies arrived in the country after 1917, as a result of the ban by the British Indian Government on emigration for contract labour—and here after more and more Javanese were brought in. But eventually the situation changed. Many more immigrants were beginning to stay in Surinam on the expiration of their contract periods. Some signed new contracts, but most—after serving one or two contract periods—settled as small farmers, either in special areas set aside for them by the Government, or on land made available to them by the planters. In the latter case the arrangement made was that the former contract labourer

[1] Ismael, op. cit., p. 59.
[2] J. M. Plante Fébure, West-Indië in het Parlement, 1897-1917, 1918, p. 7.
[3] McNeill and Chamman Lal, op. cit., p. 155.
[4] Plante Fébure, op. cit., p. 68.
[5] Kruijer, op. cit., p. 80.
[6] Plante Fébure, op. cit., p. 67.
[7] Id., p. 64.

would continue to work one or two days in the week on the plantation in exchange for the use of a small plot. But even when it was not arranged in this way, eventually there were sufficient people settled on the plantations—and in the special reserves usually near the plantations—to form a labour reservoir from which labour could be drawn. In 1931, there were—as a result of these developments—3,569 free labourers employed on the plantations, as opposed to 2,598 contract labourers [1]. Moreover, in this period—before the world crisis of 1929 and the following years but to an even greater degree after that—the economic situation changed for the worse, which reduced the demand for labour. Thus the time was ripe for a repeal of contract labour under penal sanction. The Government supplied the impetus which brought this about. Because of the difficult economic situation, the planters asked Government permission to lower the wages of the contract labour already in service. This was agreed to, on condition that among other things, the penal sanction was relinquished. This was accepted without much opposition. Also because of the slump, new contract labourers were not brought in, and so this system of compulsory labour came to an end after having lasted for almost sixty years.

However, we must turn our attention to another form of compulsory labour which was prevalent in Surinam for some time; namely, debt bondage, with particular reference to the *balata* industry. The first concession for the exploitation of this product was given in 1889, and the industry rapidly developed till about 1910-1914, when it was responsible for 40% of the Surinam export trade, and employed from 8 to 9 thousand people [2]. After this, there was a considerable fall in production, although it still remained a principal source of export revenue until recently. The conditions of labour in this industry are of a very unusual nature. Balata is obtained from the bast or inner bark of the bully tree which grows in the jungles of Surinam. To get to it involves travelling for two or three weeks, in small boats on rivers with cataracts, and on foot over hills and through swamps. The labourers—almost exclusively Negroes—had to spend the balata season (from January to August) in the jungle, living in primitive huts in very unhealthy zones. Needless to say there was always—and particularly in the top production years—a

[1] The recruiting of labour in colonies and in other territories with analogous labour conditions, 1935, p. 98.

[2] Kruijer, op. cit., p. 204.

continual shortage of labour; which led to an undesirable situation. The various concessionaries competed fiercely with each other to get labourers, and the main tactics were to offer very high advance payments. The illiterate Negroes were naturally very keen on these and were willing to accept all manner of contracts, without even knowing their contents. Only when it was already too late did they discover how bound down they were, since the contracts were very much in favour of the employers. For example, they stipulated [1] that the labourer was obliged to do all the work assigned him, that he might not leave the concession or shed without a pass signed by the overseer even in cases of illness, and that if he was not present at the time set for departure he was to pay a fine as well as repay any damages caused by the delay. The worst stipulations were those concerning the system of advance payments [2]. If at the end of a contract term a labourer had not repaid his advance, his contract would be automatically extended to cover a new contract period. In many cases, this stipulation was made all the more difficult to bear by the proviso that the advance could only be repaid with *balata* deliveries (thus, not in cash). When we consider that the advances in the years of greatest production would be anything up to £ 120, and that food and implements had to be purchased from the employer at very high prices, it is clear that labourers were bound to their employers, notwithstanding the reasonable pay. As a matter of fact labourers were only able to pay off their advances in one year if circumstances were particularly favourable. Most, however, went from one contract into another without ever being able to clear their debt. And their labour was also subject to penal sanctions, the contractees being subject to the strict provisions of the „Herziene strafverordening van 1874" (Revised Penal Ordinance of 1874). For desertion a maximum fine of 50 guilders and/or imprisonment with or without forced labour to a maximum of three months could be imposed [3]. All in all, it is hardly surprising that there were complaints of serious abuses in the *balata* industry [4].

This did not, however, last very long. A new "Balata Ordinance"

---

[1] See for instance the specimen contract in „De Balataindustrie in Suriname", supplement by Fred. Oudschans Dentz, 1911, p. XXII-XXVI.

[2] C. A. J. Struycken de Roysancour and J. W. Gonggrijp, Het Balata-vraagstuk in Suriname, 1912, p. 49-52. De Balata-industrie in Suriname, 1909, p. 79, 80.

[3] Struycken de Roysancour en Gonggrijp, op. cit., p. 57/58.

[4] Plante Fébure, op. cit., p. 6.

was passed in 1914, setting a rather low limit to the amount that could be advanced, and soon thereafter the worst of the abuses disappeared. Nevertheless, one suspects that this was due more likely to the fact that the boom period of the balata industry was over, and far fewer workers were required. While the number of people employed in 1912 and 1913 was still in the region of 7,000, by 1917 the number had fallen to about 2,700 [1]).

We must therefore conclude that in Surinam too it was the great demand for a labour force—both in the balata industry and on the plantations—which led to a system of compulsory labour; and that these systems were abrogated only when they had become largely unnecessary in view of the changing circumstances.

LITERATURE

De balata-industrie in Suriname, 1909.

—— Supplement by Fred. Oudschans Dentz, Paramaribo, 1911.

Burger, J. W., Vergelijkend overzicht van de immigratie en blijvende vestiging van Javanen en Britsch-Indiërs in Suriname. In: De Economist, jg. 77, 1928, p. 422-447.

Duchesne-Fournet, Jean, La main-d'oeuvre dans les Guyanes, Paris, 1905.

De economische en financieele toestand der kolonie Suriname, Rapport der commissie benoemd bij besluit ... van 11 Maart 1911 ..., 's-Gravenhage, 1911.

Ezerman, R. A., Een en ander omtrent de koeliewerving. In: De Indische Gids, jg. 34, 1912, p. 1261-1294.

Getrouw, C. F. G., De stemming van de bevolking vóór, tijdens en na de emancipatie van de slaven in Suriname. In: De West-Indische Gids, jg. 34, 1953, p. 3-12.

A glimpse of the existing conditions in the balata industry in Dutch Guiana. In: The India Rubber World, August 1, 1913.

Gouvernements-werving. In: Koloniaal tijdschrift, jg. 3, 1914, p. 920-923.

Gülcher, J. M., Immigratie en kolonisatie in Suriname. In: Verslag van het Indisch Genootschap, 1892, p. 96-116.

Huizinga, D. S., De Surinaamsche loonsverhooging van 1920. In: De West-Indische Gids, 1927/28, p. 111-130.

Ismael, Joseph, De immigratie van Indonesiërs in Suriname, Leiden, 1949.

Kalff, S., Javanese emigrants in Suriname. In: Inter-Ocean, vol. 9, 1928, p. 544-548.

Kom, A. de, Wij slaven van Suriname, Amsterdam, 1934.

Kruijer, G. J., Suriname en zijn buurlanden. Lichtplekken in het oerwoud van Guyana, 2e herz. druk, Meppel, 1953, (Terra-Bibliotheek).

Lier, Rudolf Asueer Jacob van, Samenleving in een grensgebied. Een sociaal-historische studie van de maatschappij in Suriname, 's-Gravenhage, 1949.

[1] Rapport der studie-commissie naar aanleiding van haar bezoek aan Suriname (Suriname Studie-Syndicaat), 1919, p. 141.

McNeill, James, and Chimman Lal, Report to the Government of India on the conditions of Indian immigrants in four British Colonies and Surinam, London, 1915, 2 vols. (Cd. 7744/7745).

Meijer Ranneft, J. W., De misstanden bij de werving op Java. In: Tijdschrift voor het Binnenlandsch Bestuur, dl. 46, 1914, afl. 1, p. 1-17; afl. 2, p. 54-72.

Plante Fébure, J. M., West-Indië in het Parlement 1897-1917, Bijdrage tot Nederlands koloniaal-politieke geschiedenis, 's-Gravenhage, 1918.

Plasschaert, E. K., Der Forstbetrieb in Surinam, München, 1910, p. 154-163: Balata.

Rapport der studie-commissie naar aanleiding van haar bezoek aan Suriname, Rotterdam, 1919. (Suriname Studie-Syndicaat).

Snellen, Ernst, De aanvoer van arbeiders voor den landbouw in Suriname, 1933.

Staal, G. J., Ontwrongen bezwaren. In: De West-Indische Gids, 1926/27, p. 235-248.

Struycken de Roysancour, C. A. J., en J. W. Gonggrijp, Het balata-vraagstuk in Suriname, 1912.

Sypesteyn, C. A. van, Afschaffing der slavernij in de Nederlandsche West-Indische koloniën, Uit officiële bronnen samengesteld. In: Het Bijblad van De Economist, 1866, p. 1-85.

Vollenhoven, J. van, Rapport over de werving, emigratie en immigratie van arbeiders en de kolonisatie in Oost-Indië en Suriname, 's-Gravenhage, 1913.

CHAPTER FOUR

THE NETHERLANDS EAST INDIES

Slavery was abolished in the Netherlands East Indies in 1863. However, in this archipelago of the East, slavery had never been widespread, and certainly of not such significance as another system of forced labour which was abrogated at about the same time, namely the culture system instituted in 1830. Under this system the Javanese were required to set aside one fifth of their cultivable land for the cultivation of crops assigned to them by the administration, and non-farming Javanese were required to work in the agricultural industries for a fifth part of the year (66 days). The culture system had entailed a heavy burden on the greater part of the Javanese population, and had met in Europe itself with considerable opposition, both on ethical and economic grounds. Those opposing it on ethical grounds were initially more against the many abuses which arose in practice than against the idea as such. But the system in itself could no longer be said to have a real place in the society of those days. The liberal movement advocating freedom for the individual entrepreneur had made its influence felt in the Netherlands, and people were no longer able to tolerate a system of State cultivation not allowing for free participation of the individual. As a result of this opposition steps were taken in 1854 toward the gradual replacement of compulsory cultivation by a system of voluntary agreements between private individuals on the one hand and the native population on the other.

The less important State cultures such as pepper, cloves, nutmeg and tobacco were the first to go, and the really big switch over came in 1870 when the administration commenced to gradually yield its assumed rights on the cultivation of the principal product, sugar. Thereafter coffee was the only product of any real importance to the State, but it was not long before these interests were also abandoned.

For the natives of the East Indies, the abrogation of compulsory cultivation was naturally a big step forward toward freedom from involuntary labour. But it did not get them all the way there since there still remained other compulsory services to be performed for the various governing bodies: the so-called *pantjendiensten* for the inland chiefs, the *herendiensten* on public works for the Dutch Government, and the *desadiensten* on works of public utility in the *desas* (hamlets or larger villages); and the combined total of these obligations in terms of compulsory labour must not be underestimated [1]. For example, in the *herendiensten* alone a native could be demanded to work for a maximum of first 52 and later 42 days in every year, and, by a regulation of 1864, twelve hours work was stipulated. The *pantjendiensten* for the native chiefs were an equal hardship on the population since it was in these services that most abuses occurred.

However, endeavours were soon made to put an end to these forms of personal service since they were not concordant with liberal ideas. The *pantjendiensten* were the first to go—in 1882, and the *heren* and *desa* services were increasingly handicapped by restrictive regulations. Not that this brought any immediate relief, however, for the economic development of Java (especially after the principle of private initiative made a decided *entree* in about 1870) led to a demand for better road communications etc.; and thus compulsory labour, became at first even more widespread despite it being objectively restricted [2]. When regulations were imposed drasticly curtailing the *herendiensten*, it was customary for the authorities to now classify those operations which formerly came under this heading as *desadiensten* [3]. And it was some time before these services were completely abrogated: the *herendiensten* in the thirties in Java and Madura and in 1941 in the Outer Islands.

Although a heavy burden in practice, theoretically these services could be considered as a form of taxation in a country where the monetary system had not as yet fully evolved, and were therefore not necessarily objectionable in principle. Quite a different matter, however, is the labour which the Indonesians had to perform for their European masters on the privately-owned estates.

The administration in ceding these estates in the 18th and early

---

[1] See: T. F. Tjoeng, Arbeidstoestanden en arbeidsbescherming in Indonesië, 1947, Chapter II.

Bruno Lasker, Human Bondage in Southeast Asia, p. 174-181.

F. Fokkens, Eindrésumé van het ... 1888 ... bevolen onderzoek naar de verplichte diensten der inlandsche bevolking op Java en Madoera, 1902-'03, 3 volumes.

C. J. Hasselman, Eindverslag over het onderzoek naar den druk der dessa diensten op Java en Madoera, 1905.

[2] J. S. Furnivall, Netherlands India, 1939, p. 185.

[3] Hasselman, op. cit., p. 66/67.

19th century also handed over the traditional manorial rights over the native tenants, including the right to demand labour from the men. The tenants here were often in an unenviable position compared to the inhabitants of the rest of Java [1]; so much so that Lasker claims it is perhaps not without significance that the first scene of anti-European riots occurred on private lands [2]. These rights, once acquired, were so respected by the Netherlands Government that it was loath to intervene directly in matters relating to the labour of Javanese tenants on the estates; and when the Netherlands ratified the Forced Labour Convention of 1930 they expressly exempted from its application the "services performed for landowners in certain parts of Western Java" [3]; thus at the outbreak of World War II this form of compulsory labour was still legal. The Government did, however, try to alter the situation indirectly in the 20th century by following a policy of buying back the private estates; and an end was made to the compulsory labour on those estates which were not bought back during the Japanese occupation. When the Dutch returned in 1946 they abided by the new situation, and from henceforth personal services could only be demanded with the special permission of the administration.

More important than the foregoing, however, is the question of how the private planters—whose number was small at the time of the culture system, but who after 1870 became more and more evident—recruited their labour. Let us commence by examining the situation in Java. Here the earliest method was to conclude contracts with the *desa* chiefs. In practice, this amounted to bribing the chiefs who then rounded up and sent the required number of labourers. These had no option but to comply whether they wished to or not since to revolt against the authority of the chiefs was to court disaster [4]. Thus there can be no question of their labour having been voluntary. Opposition on the part of the liberals in the Dutch Parliament led to a ban on the concluding of contracts with the chiefs in 1863; and from henceforth all agreements were to be drawn up with the labourers individually.

This caused great consternation among the planters, quite unjust-

---

[1] Bruno Lasker, Human Bondage in Southeast Asia, 1950, p. 84.
J. S. Furnivall, Colonial Policy and Practice, 1948, p. 341.
[2] Lasker, op. cit., p. 178.
[3] Lasker, op. cit., p. 365, note 6.
[4] P. Endt, Wanderarbeiterverhältnisse in den farbigen Kolonien, 1919, p. 34.

ifiably so since there were a sufficient number of Javanese so dependent on wage labour as to make labour compulsion in any form unnecessary. Many became landless because of the increasing density of population and because of the European's ability to acquire the best native land for himself despite the regulations designed to prevent this. In 1870 and shortly afterwards it was decreed in the Agrarian Law and the regulations based on it that Europeans could acquire on long leasehold any land *not* under cultivation, and could rent (but not buy) cultivated land on short term leases. However, it was not difficult to get the natives to hire their land even if this should prove to be right against their own interests by simply tempting them with attractive advance payments. Thus there existed a large group of natives who no longer had any land of their own, and who were therefore compelled to work for the Europeans from time to time. Generally speaking, employers were not up against a shortage of labourers as such, but up against the difficulties of irregular labour [1]. Most Indonesians simply worked when and for as long as it was absolutely essential for them to do so to meet their immediate requirements.

Attempts were made to guarantee more regular labour, and the Government was continuously urged to pass laws making breach of contract a punishable offence. In Java a regulation had been in operation from as early as 1851, whereby servants deserting their work could be prosecuted, but it was never clarified whether this regulation could also be made to apply to employees other than domestic servants. Besides the problem of employer-employee relations only became really urgent after 1870. In 1872 we find a law passed which proscribes a fine of from 16 to 25 guilders or 7 to 12 days forced labour on the public works for any "servant or workman" deserting his service or not wishing to work without good cause. But as a result of strong opposition in the Dutch Parliament this regulation was repealed seven years later, though a concession was made through another ordinance in the *Wetboek van Strafrecht voor Inlanders* (Penal Code for Natives) which decreed that anyone taking advantage of his employer by deliberately accepting an advance payment only to break his contract prematurely would be liable to prosecution. However, such a concession had little significance seeing that in most cases deliberate fraud was difficult to prove.

---

[1] Philip Levert, Inheemsche arbeid in de Java-suikerindustrie, 1934, p. 139.

Pressure on the Government to reintroduce penal sanction continued right into the 20th century, although there was at the same time one group of employers who did not support this movement for fear that penal sanction would mean more expensive labour since it was bound to go coupled with regulations for improved labour conditions [1]. The Government, however, adamantly adhered to its belief that penal sanction would be superfluous in over-populated Java; yet, as a point of interest, they found it necessary to declare that the ordinances pertaining to the desertion of seamen were applicable to those labourers working on the harbour works at Tandjong Priok and in the Madura strait in 1880/1882 [2].

Because of the attitude of the Government, other methods of assuring regular labour were resorted to by the entrepreneurs, and one such method was to set out the terms of contract so stringently as to involve the labourers in what amounted to human bondage [3]. Wage deductions would be made for orders not properly carried out, and no wages would be paid at all for work already performed if the labourer left before his contract expired. And, for temporary absence without cause, if the labourer had received an advance payment he forfeited the right to anything he might have earned toward it. Another frequent clause contained the terms under which labourers were to stand in trust for each other, all the members of a certain group being held responsible for the individual debts of any among them. Such a group could comprise a specific team of labourers, all the members of a family, the inhabitants of a specific village working in an undertaking, or just simply all the labourers in service of an undertaking. The terms of contract for transport drivers were particularly severe. The drivers used their own wagons and draught animals, and under one or two very shrewd clauses they lost these if they were judged to be in default. Generally, it was stipulated that wages for overtime would be paid at the start of the next season, since it was hoped that the labourers could then be induced to sign up again. As Paets tot Gansoyen said, "all the juridical skill in (Dutch) India was employed in phrasing the contracts as rigorously as possible" [4]; and the matter as such is not made any less contemptible by

---

[1] Endt, op. cit., p. 80. Levert, op. cit., p. 144.
[2] Levert, op. cit., p. 143/144.
[3] Levert, op. cit., p. 148-152. Endt, op. cit., p. 65/66.
[4] Cited in Levert, op.cit., p. 151.

the fact that the clauses were not put into practice so much as used as a means of intimidation.

Besides the contract system, there was yet another method of binding the labourers to their work in Java, viz., by the creation of a debt relationship. Because of the widespread poverty, potential labourers could be easily tempted with advance payments or loans, which, if once accepted, immediately put them under an obligation to work for the creditor at least until such time as the debt had been fully paid off. This was in accordance with an old Javanese tradition, whereby the recipient of a payment, the so-called *pandjer*, felt morally obliged to labour on certain projects agreed upon. The extent to which the advance system was used by Europeans rather depended on the prevailing labour situation, the amounts advanced increasing in direct proportion to the scarcity of labour. Furthermore, they also endeavoured to artificially increase the needs of the population by giving them a taste for luxuries of one sort or another [1].

In more recent times, the virtual enslavement of contract workers through debt occurred more often under Asian than under European management. Examples of such enslavement are to be found in P. de Kat Angelino's Batik Report of 1930/31. In the batik industry the women workers were practically never able to become debt-free. Deductions were made from their already meagre salaries toward settlement so that they would be forced to borrow anew as soon as there was any question of the slightest extra expense. Such wretchedness was enough to deprive the majority of them of any joy in life [2].

Some women would run away, notwithstanding their debts, and at the time of Angelino's writing this was happening more frequently, indicating a general undermining of the forces of tradition [3]. In such cases employers would wend their way to the village chiefs or police who were only too prepared in view of a forthcoming reward to persuade the women to return to their work and remain there until their debts were settled [4]. As a rule, no physical force had to be resorted to since the mere sight of a police officer in there homes was enough in itself to convince the women that they would do better to return to their work .[5] Any intervention on the part of the chiefs

---

[1] Lasker, op. cit., p. 129.
[2] Part Two, p. 25.
[3] Part One, p. 55.
[4] Part Two, p. 28 etc.
[5] Part Two, p. 31.

was of course quite illegal, but more often than not the illiterate Javanese were in no position to distinguish between services to which they could be legally conscripted by the authorities (viz., *desadiensten*) and labour for private persons, over which the *desa* chiefs had no authority whatever. Often they would be given the impression that the administration had something to do with it all, by the simple expedient of having the contracts concluded in the presence of a village authority [1].

If necessary, the Europeans would also avail themselves of the willing cooperation of the authorities—Javanese and European— in recruiting and keeping labourers [2]. In most cases all a *desa* chief had to do was make an announcement to the effect that such and such an undertaking was in need of labourers and the natives would be left wondering whether this was really an announcement and not a calling up notice for some *desa* service; and anyway these potentates had such power over their subjects that a hint was often as good as a command. The chiefs also acted as witnesses at the concluding of contracts. In this way the impression was given here too that the authorities were concerned with the employment—which made desertion more difficult. If a labourer should still happen to run away before having fulfilled his obligations under the contract, the chiefs were called in again, and a little pressure from this source went a long way. European authorities have also been known to cooperate, quite illegally, by punishing those labourers who consistently failed in their obligations, and punishing in such a way as to really make them think twice before committing a "breach of contract" again [3].

Thus we see that employers found ways and means of getting along even without the Government granting the penal sanction some of them so ardently desired. Fortunately these practices, including the deeply-ingrained advance system, became of less significance in the course of time; primarily because of a) the increasing offer of labour in Java, and b) the continual efforts of the Netherlands Indian Government to suppress such systems by a policy of restriction.

All that remains for us is to examine whether the Javanese people were better placed during the liberalistic period—in which an end was made to slavery and compulsory labour under the culture system — than before it. And this was certainly not the case. After all, the

[1] Part Two, p. 33/34.
[2] Levert, op. cit., p. 93, 167-170.
[3] Levert, op. cit., p. 93.

liberals can hardly be said to have pursued a policy in which the welfare of the natives took first place, their primary aim having always been freedom for private enterprise. Just as the Conservatives, they saw the colonies as vast industries producing profits for the mother country [1]. As Multatuli expressed it, "the one party wanted to gain as much as possible from (Dutch) India, and the other party wanted to gain from (Dutch) India as much as possible" [2]. While Europeans and Asians made tremendous headway in terms of wealth during the liberalistic period, the Indonesians themselves became poorer and poorer [3] as a result of a) the growing scarcity of land in a country with a rapidly increasing population, b) the tendency of the Europeans to take up more and more of this scarce land for their own use, and c) the decrease in wages, particularly after the economic crisis of 1883-1885 [4]. Labour conditions grew progressively worse as more and more State-run industries were made over to private persons [5], and Endt declares [6], that the labourers on the majority of the private undertakings were badly treated. This is further illustrated by the fact that some employers were against the introduction of penal sanction since this was certain to come coupled with regulations demanding humane treatment—which would naturally cost more. It was only with the advent of the so-called ethical politics about 1900 that attempts were made to bring about improvements in the working and living conditions of the Javanese. But then, people were beginning to recognize that a prosperous Java might even be to the advantage of the mother country as well as to the people themselves; and it is not entirely without significance that the Netherlands cotton industry in its ever increasing expansion was at about that time seeking a wider market for its products in these far distant islands of the East Indies [7].

We can therefore only conclude that the situation of the native after the abolition of slavery and official compulsory labour was not improved. There was indeed more labour freedom in Java under liberal politics, but then there was no question of a labour shortage

[1] Furnivall, Netherlands India, p. 174/175.
[2] L. van Keymeulen, Multatuli. In: Revue des deux mondes, t. 110, 1892, p. 805.
[3] Furnivall, Netherlands India, p. 214.
[4] Id., p. 214.
[5] Lasker, op. cit., p. 176.
[6] Endt, op. cit., p. 49/50, 60.
[7] Furnivall, Netherlands India, p. 227.

there and the restriction of freedom which reappeared was primarily directed at making labour more reliable.

Problems of quite a different nature arose in the Outer Provinces. This region was very lightly populated and the people were not suited to regular work. When the exploitation of these areas got under way, the labour problem was clearly the greatest difficulty it faced. In 1863 the first tobacco planter arrived in Sumatra[1], and the spread of tobacco cultivation and shortly afterward the rapidly rising rubber culture created a great demand for labour. But there was no question of getting free labour, and slave labour was equally impossible because slavery had been abolished in the Netherlands Indies. The solution was then found in the importation of first Chinese and then principally Javanese labour under the system of contract labour with penal sanction.

Even the very first colonists in Sumatra recruited Chinese workers from Penang and Singapore through the agency of professional recruiting officers there. Such recruitment was as notorious as it was ruthless. For example, people would be invited to attend a shadow show, and on arrival would be taken captive and forcibly removed to Deli [2]. And then in the Provinces, employers complained of complete lack of labour assurity. All they had to safeguard their interests was the same ordinance of 1872 as pertained to Java, proscribing certain sentences for breach of contract. This regulation, they claimed, was altogether insufficient for the far more difficult situation in the Outer Provinces. Petitions were drawn up, and the Government was convinced of the necessity of introducing a special ordinance relating to the Provinces; this being the very same Government that had repealed penal sanction in Java a few months previously [3]. At any rate, the Coolie Ordinance of 1880 was passed, and although at first only applicable to the Sumatra East Coast districts it was later amended slightly and made applicable to the other islands as well. Further amendments were made from time to time, and this ordinance has been in operation till recent times.

Most characteristic of the Coolie Ordinance is the section dealing with the sentences which can be imposed on a labourer found guilty of not fulfilling his obligations [4]. For desertion or determined refusal

---

1 Karl Josef Pelzer, Die Arbeiterwanderungen in Südostasien, 1935, p. 89.
2 Endt, op. cit., p. 80.
3 See page 44.
4 For the contents of the Ordinance, see for example: H. J. Bool, De arbeidswetgeving in de residentie Oostkust van Sumatra, 1904.

to work the penalty was to be a fine of 50 guilders or forced labour on the public works for a maximum of one month (three months on relapse), while a decree was later added enpowering the police, or an employer or his staff on behalf of the police, to return to his work any coolie found to have run away. For refractory conduct, abuse or threats against employers or their staff, extreme idleness, and the like, a coolie could be brought before a magistrate and sentenced to pay a small fine or do a maximum of 12 days forced labour. Finally, no coolie could leave his place of work without written permission, and it was emphatically decreed to be his obligation to work regularly and to carry out the orders of his superiors.

On the other hand, there were also directives pertaining to the treatment of labourers, who had naturally to be generally well treated, and to receive decent housing and medical attention. A ten hour day was stipulated, and no contract could be for longer than three years, although to this period could be added the time a coolie spent absent due to leave, illness of more than one month, desertion, or a prison sentence which had had to be served. Moreover, coolies had the right on a free passage back to their own country if they did not wish to sign up again when their contract expired. The penalty for infringements on the part of employers was a maximum fine of 100 guilders.

The stated aim of the Coolie Ordinance was to give the employers some labour assurity in consideration of the high costs involved in bringing coolies to the islands. But what this amounted to in reality was that the labourers were completely at the mercy of their employers, and this gave rise to some shocking cases of abuse [1], particularly in the beginning.

The first cases of malpractice were to be found in the recruitment, initially organised by professional agents who were by no means the pride of their nation. Since they were paid on a commission basis, it was hardly to be expected of them that they would stick to the maxims of fairplay. False representations and outright deception were more likely to be the methods adopted, that is if they had not already employed the use of opium and gambling to incur their victims in debt bondage [2].

Nor was the situation on the plantations admirable. For not a few

---

[1] Furnivall, Netherlands India, p. 353.
[2] Endt, op. cit., p. 207.

of those responsible for running them, the power which they had over the labourers bound by penal sanction had a corrupting influence, and abuses, by Europeans as well as Asiatic overseers, were all too common[1]. The regulations contained in the Coolie ordinance to protect the labourers were very frequently ignored[2]. The work was often too heavy, and work was demanded on official days of rest[3] (two per month). All manner of discriminations were indulged in by employers; *inter alia* uncontrolled deductions on the already meagre wages[4], illegal compoundment[5], and "forgetting" to mark up the books when labourers worked extra days to catch up on wasted time[6]. As Lasker puts it[7], it was "labour without protection, capital without conscience". One only has to read the advertisements of the time, reprinted in the booklet, *De Millioenen uit Deli* (The Millions from Deli) by J. van den Brand, to realize the mentality of the settlers toward the labour question; here "bright, young and healthy workers" are offered at so much a head between advertisements for draught animals and riding horses.

There was also much trouble as a result of the capture and return, by or on behalf of the planter, of deserting coolies—first illegally and later legally. Much harshness was brought to bear here, and innocent people were often victimized[8]. Then there was the matter of debt bondage, whereby coolies who were in debt to their masters could be compelled to stay on after the completion of their contract periods[9], and it was customary to make concerted efforts to ensure that labourers became involved in debt toward the end of their terms of service, usual methods being to encourage gambling and prostitution on the plantations, something which would otherwise never have been tolerated[10]. Daily shadow shows by travelling artists were arranged and foremen moved about among the labourers freely distributing loans. No wonder then that many labourers found that their debts far outweighed their earnings when it came to the day of

[1] See for example the writings of J. van den Brand.
[2] Endt, op. cit., p. 128.
[3] Id., op. cit., p. 146.
[4] Id., p. 133. M. van Blankenstein, De Poenale sanctie in de practijk, 1929, p. 61-67.
[5] Endt, op. cit., p. 95.
[6] Id., p. 133.
[7] Lasker, op. cit., p. 221.
[8] Van Blankenstein, op. cit., p. 22/23.
[9] Endt, op. cit., p. 94, 103, 145.
[10] Van den Brand, De millioenen uit Deli, p. 63-65.

reckoning, and in such circumstances there was nothing for it but to sign up again for a further contract period.

Since the officials were known to work in close collusion with the planters, the coolies could in no way count on their support. This was mainly due to the fact that the planters and their staff offered the only social contact in the outlying districts. Often too, officials would be won over with bribes, if in a disguised form. For example, it was customary for an official to put up his house and furniture for auction before being transferred to another district, and the prices fetched from the planters all rather depended on whether he had won their favour during his term of office or not [1]. Needless to say, the coolies were not given much opportunity to defend themselves in court. Employers or their staff would take labourers to the charge office, issue a list of complaints against them, and expect summary on the spot sentences without closer investigation [2]; and then it was not unusual for officials to curry favour by imposing heavier sentences than allowed by law [3]. On the other hand, offences by Europeans, if they ever got into court, were repeatedly condoned or simply hushed up [4]. In Van den Brand's opinion, not even one per cent of the culpable offences committed by Europeans during the time he spent in the Outer Provinces were followed up [5]. Indeed it was difficult to do anything even under circumstances in which the officials tried to carry out their duties since, although a coolie had the right in accordance with the Coolie Ordinance to leave the plantation for the purpose of taking any complaints to the controller, it was easy for the foremen to prevent him from doing so; and if he still insisted they could always resort to the expedient of hushing it up betimes [6]. The atrocious conditions led to many cases of assault against the foremen, and much desertion [7].

Just as in Java, improvements began to be introduced at about the turn of the century when the Social Democrats first began to have some say in Dutch politics, contesting the power of capital, which till then had in reality been governing the Government [8];

---

[1] Van den Brand, op. cit., p. 16 etc. Van Blankenstein, op. cit., p. 10 etc.
[2] Van den Brand, op. cit., p. 22, 56, 57.
[3] Id., p. 21.
[4] Id., p. 15, 22 etc.
[5] Id., p. 24.
[6] Id., p. 54/55.
[7] Endt, op. cit., p. 166-169. Van Blankenstein, op. cit., p. 15, 22.
[8] Furnivall, Netherlands India, p. 225, 350. Id., Colonial Policy and Practice, p. 231.

and it was the Social Democratic influence which in the end brought about a complete reversal in colonial affairs. The primary aim of the Government was no longer to promote labour *supply* but to ensure labour *protection* [1], and the most important step in this direction was the institution of a labour inspection in the Outer Provinces in 1904/1908. From this time on employer-employee relations were to be better regulated, and attempts were made to curb the malpractices inherent in recruitment, which proved to be the most difficult problem.

Naturally, the situation could not be changed overnight. The planters had long been inclined to simply ignore any regulations that displeased them [2], and in the early stages of the new movement inspectors did not have sufficient powers to intervene effectively [3]. The situation remained particularly bad in cases of new exploitations [4] and as regards recruitment; here rather awful cases of ill-treatment are known to have occurred even in recent times,[5] although it should in all fairness be stated that the gradual replacement of professional agents by agents sent out solely on behalf of individual planters proved a definite step forward toward better control, so much so that conditions could be described as generally fairly reasonable by the end of World War I [6]. Soon the planters too began to realize that undernourished and dissatisfied labourers are not the best of workers, and might even prove to be a liability [7]. The general improvement in labour conditions during the first decades of the century is further reflected by the decreasing death-rate from the high peak of about 1900 [8].

Finally also atempts were made to abolish penal sanction. As a matter of fact, circumstances had changed a lot in the course of time. It was found that many coolies were staying on in the new land after their contract periods expired, and they or their descendants were forming a reservoir of labourers willing to work voluntarily there where the conditions of labour were favourable. Moreover, after a time it was even found possible to bring in free labourers from Java.

---

1 Furnivall, Netherlands India, p. 354.
2 Endt, op. cit., p. 162.
3 Id., p. 158.
4 Id., p. 149.
5 Van Blankenstein, op. cit., p. 20, 42 etc.
6 Lasker, op. cit., p. 222, 223, 224.
7 Id., p. 222.
8 See the figures in Van Blankenstein, op. cit., p. 31/32.

By 1929 almost one-fourth of the coolies in the Outer Provinces were free labourers [1], and it seemed that this percentage could easily be improved upon; thus a specific, rapidly rising, increase in the percentage of free labourers was proscribed by decree in 1931.

At first the planters opposed this reformation [2] but two factors quickly caused them to change their minds: a) the amendment to the United States tariff law, whereby it was prohibited to import goods into the United States which had been manufactured under penal sanction; and b) the economic depression resulting in an over-abundance of labour on the plantations. The American ban affected the tobacco industry in Sumatra, and the planters soon realized that it would be wiser in the long run to work exclusively with free labour and support the abolition of penal sanction. Thus it was that the percentage of free labourers rose more rapidly than proscribed—from under 25% in 1929 to 93% in 1934 [3]—making it possible to completely abolish penal sanction in 1941. And it would furthermore appear that this switch over did not present undue difficulties [4].

In conclusion, we see therefore that in the Netherlands East Indies too slavery (and the culture system)—after having been made impossible—were replaced by other forms of compulsory labour whenever this seemed at all desirable. In Java compulsory labour was not resorted to on a large scale since there was no shortage of labour there—only the lack of continuity in labour giving rise to difficulties. In the Outer Provinces, free labour was an impossibility in the early stages of exploitation and compulsory labour was promptly introduced, to disappear again as soon as it became unnecessary from an economic point of view. Intervention by a foreign power—not from unselfish motives—only served to hasten the process of abrogation.

LITERATURE

Blankenstein, M. van, De poenale sanctie in de practijk, Rotterdam, 1929.
Blommestein, A. F. van, De nieuwe Koelie-Ordonnantie voor de Oostkust van Sumatra, (Ind. Stbl. 1915 no. 421), Amsterdam, 1916.

---

[1] J. H. Boeke, Indische Economie, 2nd ed., Vol. 1, 1947, p. 173.
[2] Id., p. 172.
[3] Id., p. 173.
[4] Id., p. 173.

Boeke, J. H., Indische economie, 2de herz. druk, Dl. 1, Haarlem, 1947.
Boeijinga, K. J., Arbeidswetgeving in Nederlandsch-Indië, Leiden, 1926.
Bool, H. J., De arbeidswetgeving in de Residentie Oostkust van Sumatra, Utrecht, 1904.
Brand, J. van den, De millioenen uit Deli, Amsterdam etc., 1902.
—— Nog eens: De millioenen uit Deli, Amsterdam etc., 1903.
—— De practijk der Koelie-Ordonnantie, Amsterdam etc., 1904.
—— Slavenordonnantie en Koelie-ordonnantie, Amsterdam etc., 1903.
Delden, C. H. van, Bijdrage tot de arbeidswetgeving in Nederlandsch Oost-Indië, 's-Gravenhage, 1895.
Endt, P., Wanderarbeiterverhältnisse in den farbigen Kolonien (mit besonderer Berücksichtigung von der Ostküste von Sumatra, Niederl.-Indien), Amsterdam, 1919.
Fokkens, F., Eindresumé van het ... 1888 ... bevolen onderzoek naar de verplichte diensten der inlandsche bevolking op Java en Madoera, Batavia etc., 1902-'03, 3 vols.
Furnivall, J. S., Colonial Policy and Practice. A comparative study of Burma and Netherlands India. Cambridge, 1948.
—— Netherlands India, A study of plural economy, Cambridge, 1939.
Guyot, Georges, Le problème de la main-d'oeuvre dans les colonies d'exploitation: la côte est de Sumatra, Paris etc., 1910.
Hasselman, C. J., Eindverslag over het onderzoek naar den druk der dessadiensten op Java en Madoera, Batavia, 1905.
Heyting, H. G., De koelie-wetgeving voor de Buitengewesten van Nederlandsch-Indië, 's-Gravenhage, 1925.
Kalma, J., De poenale sanctie. Kan zij afgeschaft worden? Buitenzorg 1928.
de Kat Angelino, P., Batikrapport, Weltevreden, 1930-'31, 3 vols. (Publicaties van het Kantoor van Arbeid, No 6-8).
Kool, J. W., Art. 328a Wetboek van Strafregt voor inlanders (Ind. Staatsblad 1879, no. 203), Alkmaar, 1884.
Kooreman, P. J., De Koelie-Ordonnantie tot regeling van de rechtsverhouding tusschen werkgevers en werklieden in de Residentie Oostkust van Sumatra, Amsterdam, 1903.
—— Nog eens: De Koelie-Ordonnantie tot regeling van de rechtsverhouding tusschen werkgevers en werklieden in de Residentie Oostkust van Sumatra, Amsterdam, 1903.
Kupers, E., Het vraagstuk van de poenale sanctie op de Internationale Arbeidsconferentie te Genève, 1930.
Lasker, Bruno, Human Bondage in Southeast Asia, Chapel Hill, N.C., 1950.
Levert, Philip, Inheemsche arbeid in de Java-suikerindustrie, Wageningen, 1934.
Middendorp, W., Twee achterlijke arbeidssystemen voor inboorlingen in Nederlandsch Oost-Indië (heerendienst en poenale sanctie), Haarlem, 1929.
Mulier, W. J. H., Arbeidstoestanden op de Oostkust van Sumatra, Medan, 1903.
De nieuwe Koelie-Ordonnantie voor de Residentie Oostkust van Sumatra, (By J. S. C. Kasteleyn), 1916. (Internationale Vereeniging voor de Rubbercultuur in Nederlandsch-Indië).
Notes on the labour conditions and recruiting of labour for estates, mines and other industries in Netherlands East India, Semarang etc., 1914. (Netherlands East-Indian San-Francisco Committee, Department of Agriculture, Industry and Commerce, no. 18).

Pelzer, Karl Josef, Die Arbeiterwanderungen in Südostasien. Eine wirtschafts- und bevölkerungsgeographische Untersuchung, Hamburg, 1935.
Tjoeng, Tin-Fong, Arbeidstoestanden en arbeidsbescherming in Indonesië, Gouda, 1947.
Verslagen van den Dienst der Arbeidsinspectie en Koeliewerving in Nederlandsch-Indië.

CHAPTER FIVE

THE UNITED STATES OF AMERICA

In the Southern states last to accept abolition, slavery came to an end in 1865. The emancipation of so many thousands of Negro slaves at first caused a chaotic situation. As elsewhere, here too the Negroes were quite adverse to labour immediately after liberation, and a great many left the plantations where they had been slaves. And since, as the Governor of Mississippi declared [1], "to work was the law of God", a number of laws were created in the South, the so-called Black Codes, with a view to keeping the Negroes on the plantations [2].

The contents of the Black Codes varied from state to state. Generally, however, they included regulations against "vagrancy", i.e., idleness could be punishable; thus many Negroes were compelled to conclude labour contracts. And to prevent those who had signed a labour contract from forsaking their work before the end of the contract period (usually a year), it was decreed that such labourers were to be arrested and brought back to their employers, while in many instances they were to lose the right to their wages for the period preceding the breach of contract.

The governments of Louisiana, South Carolina and Mississippi adopted the most radical measures. Here virtually all coloured people were forced to enter the employ of Europeans; the term "vagrancy" was employed in the widest possible sense, and the sentences covering it were in fact tantamount to forced labour.

Thus it was decreed in Mississippi in 1865 that all Negroes and mulattos apparently without regular employment after a certain date would be considered "vagrants" and, as such, liable to a maximum fine of $ 50 plus imprisonment not exceeding 6 days. If unable to pay the fine—and such was the position of practically all emancipated slaves—the "vagrant" was to be allocated to work for anyone

---

[1] Taken from Vernon Lane Wharton's book, The Negro in Mississippi 1865-1890, 1947, p. 83.

[2] The following has been mainly taken from: H. A. Wyndham, The Atlantic and Emancipation, 1937, Part III: The United States. Also: Vernon Lane Wharton, The Negro in Mississippi 1865-1890, 1947.

prepared to pay it as well as the costs of the case for him; on the understanding, that is, that in those instances where a Negro had deserted the service of an employer that employer would be given first option.

Although it is true that some of these regulations applied also to Europeans, they were at any rate not those regulations sanctioning forced labour, and the others were very seldom applied. Another regulation applying only to the non-white section of the population decreed that anyone unable to pay a tax imposed on all Negroes would be viewed as a "vagrant"—and could thus be hired out to an employer. Furthermore, any Negro unable to pay a fine could similarly be hired out, no matter what the fine happened to be for.

The Negroes were for all practical purposes entirely in hands of the local authorities since only very few were able to pay the sum of from $ 25 to $ 150 needed to appeal to a higher court after conviction by the local Bench.

Referring to breach of contract, it was decreed in Mississippi that every "civil officer" was by duty bound to arrest and return to his employer any Negro labourer found to have deserted, and that all other persons were *allowed* to do this. A substantial reward was forthcoming for the return of labourers who had deserted—this reward to be later deducted from the labourer's wages—while anyone providing food or protection in any form to such deserters would be liable to a heavy fine, even imprisonment; the same sentences also applying to anyone found guilty of encouraging a labourer to commit a breach of contract.

An apprenticeship system was devised for minors, whereby those minors whose parents were not able or not willing to support them were to be allocated as apprentices to employers, preferably their former holders; and the approval of the parents was not required in this matter.

Also far-reaching were those regulations which made it very difficult for the coloured people to hire land. In fact, such regulations were passed in various states. In South Carolina, the same goal—to retain the former slaves as plantation labourers—was striven after by rigorously limiting the Negroes' possibilities of choosing work other than plantation or domestic labour. And these regulations were not intended as temporary measures, but as permanent fixtures.

Such measures, however, met with violent opposition in the North, and they became invalid with the passing of the Civil Rights Act and the 14th Amendment to the Constitution in 1866. This was not to mean an immediate change in the situation. In some states the Black Codes remained in force and even in those states where they were repealed there was not much change in practice at first: Since public opinion supported it the whites continued to treat the Negroes almost as before. However, the worst of these abuses ceased in the course of time [1].

Eventually even all forms of labour compulsion became unnecessary seeing that even without it the vast majority of Negroes were more or less obliged to work for Europeans. Only a very small number of emancipated slaves was able to obtain land of their own, although at the time more than half the land in the United States was "public land", i.e., 1,048 million acres out of a total of 1,920 million acres in 1860 [2], and of this public domain 46 million acres were in the Southern states Florida, Alabama, Mississippi, Louisiana and Arkansas [3]. But nobody would ever have dreamt of giving this "public land" away for nothing; all the same, it was fairly cheap, but the Negroes did not have the money to buy. Even the cultivated plantation land depreciated considerably in price as a result of the economic collapse in the South after the Civil War; yet from the census of 1880 it would appear that only a very small number of Negroes were land owners [4]. This was also partly due to the reluctance of the Europeans to sell land to Negroes—though the importance of this factor has frequently been exaggerated [5]. All in all we see therefore that—taking into consideration the limited possibilities outside agriculture—the majority of Negroes had no option but to work on the land of Europeans. And because of the unsatisfactory experiences with wage labour, this work for the most part very soon assumed the form of "share-cropping", a system of labour which made the worst of the earlier forms of labour compulsion all the more unnecessary and meaningless.

Nevertheless, labour compulsion was later reverted to again in the United States, be it on a much smaller scale; e.g., at times of

---

[1] See for example Vernon Lane Wharton, op. cit., p. 92/3.

[2] Ernest L. Bogart and Donald L. Kemmerer, Economic History of the American People, 2nd Ed., repr., 1948, p. 438.

[3] E. Merton Coulter, The South during Reconstruction 1865-1877, 1947, p. 108.

[4] C. Vann Woodward, Origins of the New South 1877-1913, 1951, p. 205.

[5] Merton Coulter, The South during Reconstruction 1865-1877, 1947, p. 111.

seasonal pressure, and when circumstances were such that it was very difficult to find labourers in other ways. This labour compulsion mostly took the form of a binding debt relationship between employers and employees. Thus it occurred for example that labourers would be recruited from cities and towns far from the location of work, and be given money in advance by agents to cover travelling and other expenses. Invariably the agents would give a much finer description of the conditions of labour than the reality warranted, but any labourer deserting before his debt was paid could be arrested and brought back to his work;—for he had been guilty of accepting money on "false pretenses", a misdemeanour made punishable in the South by law. In such cases a new agreement would usually be drawn up, whereby the labourer promised to work for his debt in exchange for clemency. Once intimidated in this way, it was a simple matter to make sure that his debt did not decrease too rapidly. Naturally such a system was open to malpractices and led to some very rough handling of the Negroes. Frequently the labour would be performed under the supervision of armed guards, and at night labourers would be locked up to prevent escape.

Such practices occurred in many fields of activity; not only on the plantations, but also in the mines, in industry etc. And not only the Negroes suffered, but also Europeans, and then mostly those who had only just immigrated. Also, such forms of involuntary labour not only occurred in the South but also in the North; namely, in the remoter districts where it was difficult to procure an adequate labour force.

At the turn of this century the lumber companies in Maine, New England, experienced difficulties in meeting their labour requirements. Agents were then sent out, mainly to Boston, to recruit labourers with tempting portrayals of the situation. They might say, for example, that the location of work was near a town, where the labourers would frequently be able to go for recreation. But after signing up and receiving an advance payment, the people would be brought to the outposts of the civilized world, and then would have to walk another 60 or 70 miles because there were no transport roads; and would have to live in the middle of the forests in most unpleasant conditions, without any chance of recreation. When the labourers deserted their work in large numbers, the lumber companies succeeded in getting a law passed in Maine similar to those as existed in the Southern states against not settling loans by work. Although the regulations were less severe here, the authorities, as elsewhere, were on the side of the entrepreneurs, and interpreted the regulations in their favour so that the labourers were altogether powerless and bound to their work entirely. No matter how they had been deceived, they still had to work till their debt was paid off, or else face a prison sentence [1].

For many years Mexicans had been entering the United States illegally, either fleeing of their own accord from the estates to which they were bound in their own country [2] or recruited by people who made it their job to procure cheap labour in this way for the industries, mines, railways, and particularly the farms in the States [3]. Neither was *their* labour altogether voluntary. Having come to do seasonal work, they were often compelled to stay on permanently by some means or other, usually a debt relationship [4]. Moreover, they were always used for the most unpleasant work [5], and the living conditions they had to contend with were most atrocious [6].

The Negroes in the South, however, were still being treated even more atrociously. In the season in which many labourers were needed, the planters simply rounded up Negroes and put them to work on their plantations, claiming that they were in debt to them; and there they had to work from 12 to 16 hours a day, as a rule without wages, till the busy season was over. They would then be let free—till the next busy season [7].

Besides this, yet another method was used to get people to work against their will, and this method was also applied almost exclusively to Negroes. It was customary in the South to punish infringements with a fine, to be replaced by a period of forced labour if the fine could not be paid. However, in many cases such convicted persons would be distributed to undertakings as labourers, and soon after the

---

[1] Peonage, The Complete Report of the Immigration Commission on this Subject, 1911. (Abstracts of reports of the Immigration Commission, Vol. 2), p. 447-449.

[2] Carey McWilliams, North from Mexico. The Spanish-speaking People of the United States, 1949, p. 105.

[3] Id., p. 178/9.

[4] Id., e.g., p. 150, 181.

[5] Id., p. 178, 215.

[6] Id., e.g., p. 183, 190, 215. See further regarding the labour of Mexicans in the United States: Paul S. Taylor, Mexican Labour in the United States, 1928/1932, 2 vols.

[7] Mary Church Terrell, Peonage in the United States. In: The 19th century and after, Vol. 62, 1907, p. 312.

Civil War it became the practice to hire them out. Later the system changed somewhat, in so far that employers now paid the fine and received the convicts in their service [1]. These then had to work in their employ till they had earned the fine plus the expenses incurred for their transport etc. Needless to say the wages were extremely low in these instances, and it took the convict some time to settle his debt, especially when one considers that the employer sometimes had to pay a certain amount to the authorities concerned to be able to take over convicts, thus adding to the expenses which had to be paid off. It would even happen that the convicts were hired out to the highest bidder, and in this way a price could be attained far surpassing the normal fine charged. On the other hand, it wasn't very difficult to involve the convict labourers in more and more debts. Should they try to escape, they would be arrested anew and be convicted for breach of contract. Thus it could take many years for a convict put to work in this way to regain his freedom.

The prosecution also cooperated exemplarily with the planters and other employers. Substantial fines would be charged for the smallest of infringements. Walking on the grass where this was not allowed and other petty misdemeanours could involve a Negro in debt slavery difficult to escape; and the authorities would be especially thorough in clamping down on such infringements when a busy season was approaching, in which the labour problem would be bound to arise. The authorities involved would more often than not be related in some way or other to the big planters, and their salaries were paid out from the fines. Even today all the lesser authorities in more than half the Southern states receive their salary from fines [2].

Employers procuring their labour force in the way described above could do practically anything they liked with that labour force, and the conditions in the convict camps were notoriously shocking. The labourers had to work extremely hard for from 14 to even 20 hours a day for a meagre, or, in some cases for absolutely no wage. The food was often very bad and housing was particularly atrocious. Men and women would be crowded together in barracks far too small and in every way inadequate. Heating was unknown or at the best of times insufficient, making for a frightful winter, and lack of ventilation would often prove to be the greatest plague

[1] See: Peonage. The Complete Report of the Immigration Commission on this Subject, 1911. Mary Church Terrell, op. cit.

[2] Arnold Rose, The Negro in America, 1948, p. 179.

in summer. Needless to say the barracks were well locked at night, and in some cases the convicts had to sleep chained to each other. Also, in many camps they would be locked up over the weekends, from Saturday evening to Monday morning. Treatment was on the whole rough, fatalities due to assault being a frequent occurrence. Because of their relations in higher circles, employers would be mostly acquitted in such cases. That the death rate was high is hardly surprising under the circumstances; and according to some observers the convicts were at least as badly off as the former slaves [1].

Another form of debt slavery evolved from the "share-crop" system [2]. Under the "share-crop" system he who cultivates the land does not pay the owner hire in money but hands over a share of his crop to him—usually a half. We have seen that very few Negroes succeeded in acquiring land of their own after abolition; by far the majority had to be content with working on the European-owned plantations. In the beginning the relationship with the landowner varied from paying hire for a small holding to wage labouring, but it was not long before the "share-crop" system became predominant, and today still this system plays an important role in the economy of the South. Although their number decreased considerably after about 1935, 25.3% of the Negroes working in agriculture in 1940 were share-croppers [3].

Since the share-croppers usually have no money of their own, all the necessary farm implements, and frequently also food and clothing, are provided by the landowner, mostly at a very high rate of interest—37% per year average in 1934! [4] At the end of each season the value of the implements etc. plus interest is subtracted from the proceeds of the share of the crop owing to the cropper. It can easily happen in times of drought, or when there are crop failures for other reasons, that a Negro's debt becomes greater than his share in the crop; in which case the landowner in some states is entitled by various laws not only to expropriate the cropper's possessions

---

[1] See Terrell, op. cit., p. 309.

[2] The following has been primarily taken from:
Edward Byron Reuter, The American Race Problem, 1927, p. 235 etc.
Arnold Rose, The Negro in America, 1948, p. 87 etc.
Vernon Lane Wharton, op. cit., p. 71/2.
Allison Davis, Burleigh B. Gardner and Mary R. Gardner, under the direction of W. Lloyd Warner, Deep South, 1941, Chapters 17 and 18.

[3] Arnold Rose, op. cit. p. 85.

[4] Arnold Rose, op. cit., p. 89.

toward settling the debt, but also to compel him to work on the plantation as a labourer until the debt has been fully paid. In most cases the Negro must immediately borrow more money so as to be able to provide for his family and commence the labour of the new season; thus if circumstances are against him he can find himself more and more deeply involved in debt. There are in fact planters who encourage this by offering tempting articles to the labourers and croppers so that they might become so deeply involved in debt as to never be able to leave the plantations at all. Many planters have their own shops on the plantations, in which case the croppers are not provided food, clothing and small luxuries directly from the landowner, but are told to purchase these from the shop. Credit is, of course, given, and prices are usually exorbitant, which leads once again to the Negro becoming involved in debt.

On the whole, the share-croppers lead a pitiable existence [1]. Many are so poverty-stricken, that starvation is often a widespread occurrence at certain times of the year (even nowadays). They are entirely dependent in their labour. Seeing that it is in the interest of the plantation owner that the crop should be as high as possible, all work on the plantation is carried out under his supervision, and the share-croppers have no independence at all, sometimes even having to work in "labour gangs". The customary way of getting the most out of the Negroes is to threaten them with physical violence, and actual ill-treatment is not uncommon.

However, one should bear in mind that no matter how bad the situation may have been for the victims of the various forms of debt slavery, involuntary and compulsory labour has never been prevalent on a really large scale in the United States since slave emancipation. It was neither necessary, as we have already seen, from an economic point of view since the Negroes had no option but to work for the Europeans. More often than not, debt slavery was indulged in as a way of getting really *cheap* labour, though another important factor was that the planters had grown accustomed to dependent Negro labour in the days of slavery. Thus it was that they had no scruples about compelling the Negroes in one way or another to do specific work for them when a large labour force was required, such as during the busy season for example. Furthermore, some-

[1] Allison Davis, Burleigh B. Gardner and Mary R. Gardner, under the direction of W. Lloyd Warner, Deep South, 1941, Chapters 17 and 18.

times debt slavery was resorted to as the only way of procuring sufficient labour in the remoter districts, and in such instances also white people were subject to this form of labour compulsion. Public opinion in the North has always sided very strongly against any form of compulsory or involuntary labour; so much so that forced labour, except as a form of punishment, was prohibited in as early as 1865 and 1866 by the 13th and 14th amendment to the constitution; and a special law was introduced to combat debt slavery in 1875. In the beginning the effect of this was not felt very strongly in the South. In many states there were laws sanctioning debt slavery, although restrictive regulations were later introduced, prohibiting the hiring out of convicts to private individuals for example. The system only lost its legal sanction in 1910 when the Supreme Court, in a decision on a particular case, declared unconstitutional those State laws unter which debt slavery was tolerated. In 1911 the "Immigration Commission"—from the report of which more has been quoted—came to the conclusion that there was no longer much debt slavery to be found in the South, and that the remnants of it were being vigorously combated on the whole, as opposed to the North where the few cases of it had not been followed up as they should have been. During World War One, debt slavery among Negroes increased again in the South—as a consequence of the fact that many wished to migrate to the North because of the higher wages paid there. But this increase was only temporary. In his book which appeared in 1946, "Negro Labor, a National Problem", R.C. Weaver speaks of "instances of peonage (that) occasionally remind us that forced labor still exists in our Southland" [1].

Although serious immediately alter abolition, and giving proof of extreme discrimination against the Negro race, compulsory labour in the United States can be said to be a thing of the past.

LITERATURE

Bogart, Ernest L., and Donald L. Kemmerer, Economic History of the American People, 2nd ed., New York etc., 1947.

Coulter, E. Merton, The South During Reconstruction 1865-1877, Baton Rouge etc., 1947, (A History of the South, vol. 8).

Davis, Allison, Burleigh B. Gardner and Mary R. Gardner, under the direction of W. Lloyd Warner, Deep South, Chicago, 1941.

Kendrick, Benjamin B., Agrarian Discontent in the South 1880-1900. In: Annual Report of the American Historical Association for the year 1920.

[1] Page 4.

McWilliams, Carey, North from Mexico. The Spanish-speaking People of the United States, Philadelphia etc., 1949.

Peonage. The Complete Report of the Immigration Commission on this Subject, 1911, (Abstracts of reports of the Immigration Commission, Vol. 2 — Reports of the Immigration Commission — Senate documents. Nr 747).

Reuter, Edward Byron, The American Race Problem, New York, 1927.

Rose, Arnold, The Negro in America, London, 1948, (A condensation of "An American Dilemma", by Gunnar Myrdal).

Taylor, Paul S., Mexican Labor in the United States, Berkeley, Cal., 1928/1932. 2 Vols. (Univ. of California publications in economics, vols. 6, 7).

Terrell, Mary Church, Peonage in the United States. In: The Nineteenth Century and After, vol. 62, 1907.

Weaver, R. C., Negro Labor, a national problem, New York etc., 1946.

Wharton, Vernon Lane, The Negro in Mississippi 1865-1890, Chapel Hill, 1947. (Studies in History and Political Science).

Woodward, C. Vann, Origins of the New South 1877-1913, Baton Rouge etc., 1951.

Wyndham, H. A., The Atlantic and Emancipation, Oxford etc. 1937, (A report in the Study group series of the Royal Institute of International Affairs).

CHAPTER SIX

THE PORTUGUESE COLONIES IN AFRICA WITH PARTICULAR REFERENCE TO WEST AFRICA

In 1836 Portugal prohibited the traffic of slaves to and from its colonies, and the decision to abolish slavery altogether was taken in 1858—all Portuguese slaves were to be emancipated within 20 years. In actual fact, abolition was effected nine years earlier than planned, namely in 1869. Portugal later again gave evidence of its anti-slavery views by being among those countries to participate in the Congo Act of 1885 and the Brussels Anti-Slavery Conference of 1890.

In the Portuguese colonies, however, matters took quite a different course right from the start. By 1869 all Portuguese slaves had indeed become "libertos", but they were free in name only since they were still compelled to work without wages. This continued till 1875 when it was decreed that an end was to be put to the "libertos" system within one year; in that time all former slaves were to acquire their freedom, but—would have to hire out their services for two more years, preferably to their former holders. And this decree applied to all persons above the age of seven! Moreover, the law of 1875 already contained clauses against "vagrancy". Africans convicted of this offence were to be put to work in service of the State. However, this was all to be changed in 1878; according to the law there was to be no longer any question of compulsory labour after then, and all natives would become really and truly free.

The colonists in Portuguese Africa were extremely indignant about the abolition of slavery, and indeed they were faced with a difficult problem; for how were they now suddenly to find labourers without using compulsion? It was in these circumstances that the law governing labour relations in the colonies appeared in 1878.

At first sight, the regulations seemed innocent enough: employer-employee relations would in future be governed by labour contracts, and there would be official control on the concluding of these contracts. The natives had, in the consideration of the legislators, not yet attained such a level of civilisation as to be able to maintain their privileges as free citizens. However, it was immediately decreed that the officials presiding over the conclusion of contracts would receive a fee for every contract signed in their presence; and—"vagrancy" was again to be met with severe punishment. Naturally this was leaving the door wide open to new forms of compulsory labour—and much use was made of it. It was now declared that every African was by nature a vagrant and had thus to be compelled to work. This led to the idea of obligatory labour applying to all; as formulated in a regulation of 1902: on each and every able native rests—apart from cases of force majeure—the moral and legal obligation to support himself by work. In so far as they were well-intentioned, the regulations of 1878 were not strictly adhered to in the colonies where the overriding factor was the necessity to acquire cheap native labour in sufficient quantity; thus regulations in any sense favourable to the natives were simply ignored. Planters and officials—whose interests were after all closely allied—tried in every way to get the Africans to work; often relying on the cooperation of native chiefs who were easily bribed. Thus the former slaves found slavery replaced by compulsory labour, which was not at all to their advantage, according to many observers, and which became progressively worse as it continued for several decades.

On the plantations in the interior of Angola, the former slaves were kept on as contract labourers. The conditions of labour, however, remained exactly the same in every respect, and their children grew up without even knowing that a reformation was supposed to have taken place.

Moreover, an officially sanctioned yet veritable trade in Africans was now being conducted in Angola. Large numbers of natives were rounded up in the interior by enticement or force and driven down to the coast where they were crowded together into depots—large courtyards with high impenetrable walls, and often the very places used in the days of slavery. From here they were sold, under guise of contract labour of course, to anyone requiring labourers.

Many of the natives traded in this way were destined for the islands of St. Thomas and Principe off the West coast of Africa. Here the cocoa industry flourished spectacularly at the turn of the century; providing one-fifth of the world production in 1905. The small local population appears to have been quite unsuited for this type of labour, but not so the Angola natives, and from 1900 to 1910 there was an average import of about 4,000 natives per year.

The circumstances of this traffic, and the consequent treatment, received especial publicity in the first decade of this century through the works of three Englishmen who had spent some time in Portuguese West Africa studying the labour system [1].

There were three categories of recruiting agents; those who worked independently at their own risk, those in the employ of rich entrepreneurs, and those in the employ of the State. In all three cases, however, they worked on a commission basis, and all adopted the most shameless tactics in recruiting natives. The most prevalent methods used were a) to grant loans to the natives which most were unable to repay, thereby falling into the agent's power, b) to bribe chiefs and c) simply to "kidnap" natives on a large scale.

Once recruited, the natives were brought together to form caravans, and then the endless trip to the coast began, sometimes from as far afield as the hinterland districts bordering on the Belgian Congo. Up to 1902 the caravans were frequently made up of as many as 1000 people. Many collapsed under way from hunger and thirst, and from the gruelling march; if there was any chance of them reaching the coast alive, they were driven further; if not, they were either killed or left to die; and human skeletons could be seen in profusion along the routes taken. Agents considered themselves lucky if they got six out of ten natives to the coast alive, and as many as two-thirds of the people on a caravan trip have been known to die.

For those who survived the journey there followed the formality of concluding a contract, under official control of course. In reality they were sold to the planters, and once on the plantations they were entirely at the mercy of the planters and had to work extremely hard for very little. Escape was almost impossible but some tried it and the authorities co-operated in tracking them down and returning them to the plantations. However, the worst of it was that the natives were not let free at the end of their contract periods, mostly five years; all the more proof that the contract system was nothing more than a guise. One contract was followed by another, and all under official control, so that practically all the labourers remained to their dying day on the plantations to which they had been recruited, being quite powerless to do anything about it. The children born on the plantations were automatically trained as labourers. From an early age they were given small duties to perform, and at

[1] Henry W. Nevinson, A Modern Slavery, 1906.
William A. Cadbury, Labour in Portuguese West Africa, 2nd. ed., 1910 (In which is included a report by Joseph Burtt).

fourteen they became officially contract labourers with no prospects of escape. Under such a system the natives were faced with a situation tantamount to slavery and quite as bad; but then, contract labour on the Portuguese islands has always been known to have been one of the blackest chapters in the history of native labour in Africa [1].

At about the same time, the rubber industry became of increasing importance in Angola. The export of rubber started in as early as 1867 but increased enormously as a result of the acute world shortage in the early years of this century. And naturally, once again it was the Africans who had to do the work [2]. Under the compulsion of their chiefs, who were richly rewarded by the Europeans, great numbers of natives—men, women, and children—journeyed every year in long caravans to the uninhabited, unhealthy and almost inaccessible rubber districts along the Eastern border of Angola. Very often they had to travel hundreds of miles, and the whole trip there and back took many months. Extracting the rubber was hard work in itself since deep notches had to be cut; and then finally, there was the long return journey, everyone carrying as much rubber as he could. Not all those who had gone out returned to their villages; many died en route, not able to take the terrible journey, the arduous work, and, in some cases, the starvation suffered if too little food had been taken with. Back in the inhabited world again, the natives traded their rubber with the Europeans for textiles, simple ornaments and alcohol —and they had to give a lion's share of these to their chiefs, who thus profited as well as the colonists. The State did not concern itself directly with the workings of this trade, but all were highly pleased to observe the effects of it on the export earnings.

In about 1910 there was a sudden drop in the world price for rubber, resulting in an economic crisis in Angola, and it was at the same time that Portugal became a republic. Thus, new ideas, also as regards the colonies, in the mother country at any rate, and at the same time less immediate demand for labour, so that the moment seemed especially favourable for a change in policy. However, the colonial mentality dies hard, and in 1911 yet another law was introduced, making it even easier than before to impose compulsory labour on the Africans.

---

[1] Lord Hailey, An African Survey, 2nd ed., 1945, p. 651. According to the Report of the Ad hoc Committee on Forced Labour (1953, p. 63/4) contract labour on St. Thomas is still tantamount to compulsory labour, or practically so

[2] Grande enciclopédia portuguesa e brasileira, Art. Angola p. 648.

In the years that followed, however, other regulations were passed to counteract this. Most of these covered the contract system, and were to protect native rights: officials were no longer to receive a fee for every contract concluded in their presence, the methods of recruiting were to be strictly controlled, corporal punishment was to be prohibited, and there was even to be a body of inspection to see that the regulations were enforced. In short, it was proclaimed that the Africans in the Portuguese colonies were to be well-treated from henceforth.

This looked all very nice on paper but nothing ever came of it in practice. Angola soon got over its economic crisis, and the rapid development there led to greater demands for labour. This development was mainly in the field of agriculture, as is illustrated by the following figures: the export of the principal crop, maize, was 29 tons in 1911, 2,107 tons in 1913, 4,052 tons in 1914, and 37,059 tons in 1922; coffee exports rose from 4,458 tons in 1914 to 11,721 tons in 1934 (i.e., an increase of 200% in 20 years); and the export figures for the third product of importance, sugar, were even more impressive—1,717,524 kgs in 1910 to 21,095,141 kgs in 1933 [1]. Moreover, there was a marked advance in the construction of roads, railways and bridges after the establishment of the Republican administration. One of the ways of encouraging road construction was to present district authorities who had been responsible for the construction of more than 100 kms of roadway with a free motor car! Thus the colony went through a period of general expansion in every respect [2].

In Mozambique the activities of the colonists also proved very productive. This is illustrated by the export figures for the two main products, sugar and sisal: sugar exports were an average of 31, 235 tons per annum in the years 1911-1915, 46,152 tons in the years 1921-1925, and 67,321 tons from 1926-1930; for sisal the figures were 362 tons averaged between 1911 and 1915, 1,593 tons between 1916 and 1920, and 7,417 tons between 1926 and 1930 [3].

Returning to Angola, it is evident that measures to promote the provision of labour were bound to appear there since the natives were far from willing to accept wage labour of their own accord.

---

[1] Enciclopédia portuguesa e brasileira, Art. Angola, p. 656 and 672.

[2] Enciclopédia portuguesa e brasileira, Art. Angola, p. 654 and 657.

[3] Moçambique, 1931. (Publ. en l'occasion de l'Exposition Coloniale Internationale): L'agriculture, par C. A. de Melo Vieira, p. 18.

Besides, the new administration did not ever intend to give the natives complete freedom. In as early as 1913 the official line of action for all authorities included such measures as preventing idleness among the natives by getting them to work, either as paid labourers or on their own initiative [1]. And in the following year, 1914, a sweeping regulation pertaining to native labour was introduced, whereby it was emphatically established as a first principle that every able native was morally and legally obliged to support himself by work [2]. As we have seen this was not an entirely new viewpoint; the interdiction on vagrancy immediately after abolition amounted to the same thing, and the idea as such had been explicitly expressed in a regulation of 1902; but now for the first time this principle was worked out in detail and became the basis of the whole labour system.

One was considered to have fulfilled one's obligations to work if one possessed either sufficient capital to be independent, or drew an adequate income from agriculture, trading, a craft or free profession [3], or had been a wage earner for a certain number of months in the previous year—the number of months to be determined separately in each colony. In Mozambique a period of three months was stipulated, in St. Thomas, six months, and in Portuguese Guinea, eight months [4]. He who had no means of his own, or had not spent the required number of months working as a wage earner, would be placed at the disposal of the authorities who would find work for him varying in duration from three months to a year. The public services and all private individuals could apply to the authorities concerned for labourers. The public services, however, were to be given preference if there were not a sufficient number of labourers available to meet demands. The cooperation of native chiefs was to be sought as far as possible, both in rounding up natives not fulfilling their obligations to work and in compelling them to work.

---

[1] Enciclopédia portuguesa e brasileira, Art. Angola, p. 652.

[2] For full particulars of this regulation, see: Forced Labour, report and draft questionnaire (International Labour Conference, 12th session, Geneva, 1929), p. 117 etc.; 184 etc.; 206 etc.

[3] In practice it was of course not considered enough if one was able to support one's own family, for in that case the colonists would not have been able to get any labourers.

[4] The period stipulated in Angola is not stated in the abovementioned publication.

Moreover, the chiefs were to be paid for their cooperation, the amounts to be stipulated by local ordinances.

Anybody refusing to work after having been taken into custody by the authorities, or anybody deserting or attempting to escape while being taken to his location of work, would be convicted for vagrancy and would be liable to from eight to three hundred days imprisonment with forced labour. People thus convicted would in the first place be put to work in the public services, and would only be allocated to private individuals if they could not be absorbed by the services. The convicts were provided with food and clothing, but received no wages in the public services, and those working for private individuals were to receive half the customary wages for native labour. Anybody still refusing to work or attempting to escape after having been convicted to forced labour was to be sent to a detention camp, or banished from the colony.

Women and invalids, persons over sixty and under fourteen, native chiefs, and natives of a few other categories would be considered exempt from any obligation to work. The exception to this general rule was to be found in St. Thomas where it was decreed that the obligation to work also applied to women between the ages of fourteen and fifty.

It was repeatedly and emphatically declared by the authorities that labour in the colonies was voluntary [1]. Only those who refused to realise their obligation to work of their own accord would be compelled to do so. Needless to say, it was argued that these were educationary measures designed to civilize the natives, and as such they were enforced [2].

The 1914 regulations also contained clauses protecting the rights of working Africans, at any rate those working voluntarily in the public services. A minimum wage was stipulated—but then not one minute of the working day was to be wasted, for such waste "for no matter what reason" would lead to a wage deduction. The working day was officially fixed at nine hours, and there was to be one day of rest in the week. Medical attention was also promised. At the same time, it was decreed that anyone not adhering to the conditions of his contract and absenting himself from work for more than fifteen consecutive days would be liable to the same conviction as applied to

---

[1] See for example: Forced Labour, 1929, p. 114, note 4.
[2] Id., p. 116.

"vagrants" (i.e., from eight to three hundred days forced labour). It was moreover stated that any native deserting after having been recruited had to repay any advance payments made by the recruiting agents; if he failed to do so he would be convicted to forced labour until the debt was fully settled.

On a later occasion it was again stated, almost redundantly, that it was the duty of every governing authority to do his utmost to promote the recruitment of natives. They had to make it clear to the natives that it was their moral duty to cooperate in the opening up of the colony since this was in their own interests [1]. Employers experiencing difficulties in finding labourers were to ask for the assistance of the governing body, and this was again emphatically expressed in 1921 [2].

The results of these regulations based on the principle of obligatory labour were shocking to the extreme in all the colonies—and this has even been admitted to a certain extent by the Portuguese Government [3]. The trade in natives, for that is what it really amounted to, continued in Angola, and in some respects even grew worse than already described. The governing body set about recruiting natives by bribing the chiefs, or by threatening them with imprisonment if they did not cooperate satisfactorily; and the recruited Africans were made to work for the State or for the local authorities, or otherwise made available to planters in Angola itself and in St. Thomas—still called "the land of no return" [4]. The labour demanded of them by the Europeans took so much of their time that the natives were no longer able to cultivate their own land properly. The legally stipulated period of obligatory labour was long enough in itself, yet the planters found ways and means of keeping them on still longer. They were of the opinion that the period of service would be over far too quickly if they counted in every working day, thus every pretext not to count in a day was taken advantage of, even though the native labourer might very well have worked on that day. In this way they tried to make a period of three months last

---

[1] Forced Labour, 1929, p. 210/211.

[2] Id., p. 211.

[3] Id., p. 13, note 1. See for this period also: Modern Slavery in Africa. In: The Nation, vol. 121, 1925, p. 195-196. (Extracts from the notes of Prof. Edward Alsworth Ross, who published a report in 1925 after visiting Portuguese Africa). I have not been able to obtain a copy of the report itself. See also John H. Harris, Slavery or "Sacred Trust?", 1926, p. 45-52.

[4] Harris, op. cit., p. 49.

say four months; and it was a simple matter for a planter to offer to pay a native's tax for him if he wished to keep him on the plantation, for by so doing the native could be compelled to remain until he was able to pay back the loan. This might take some time since the natives received practically no wages at all for their work. By law, the employers had to hand over the native wages to the authorities, who were solely responsible for paying the labourers; but the amount always dwindled en route in some way or other so that little remained for the labourer, and on going to the office concerned to receive his wages he might quite easily be told to return again in a few months time. If he still had courage to do so, he might find himself flung out of the office, still minus wages—and that would be that. Often the labourers did not dare to go to the offices to receive their wages for fear, apparently justified, that they would immediately be noted down for a longer period of service. Naturally, all native labour was covered by contracts, but more often than not the natives would apply their finger prints to these without even knowing the terms of the contract; and if they hesitated in signing violence would be resorted to. Generally speaking, the Africans found they were in a worse position after the proclamation of the republic than before, many having to work longer hours to receive less in return. From both Mozambique and Angola, large numbers tried to escape to neighbouring territories [1].

Besides the compulsory labour discussed above, which was partly in service of the administration and partly in service of private individuals, Africans were also required to labour on works of general importance as a sort of taxation paid in natura [2]. There were many protective regulations governing this form of compulsory labour; from time to time compulsory labour of this kind for private individuals was prohibited, and in 1926 it was decreed that on public works it would only be permitted in cases of special emergency. However, such protective regulations were not always taken into account. Roads were constructed—far more than necessary according to Prof. Ross—with called up labourers who received no payment, nor, in many cases, food [3]. Frequently these labourers were for the most part women [4]. Thus this labour can be seen as a further heavy burden added to the other compulsory labour.

---

[1] Modern Slavery in Africa, p. 196. Harris, op. cit., p. 50/51.
[2] Forced Labour, 1929, p. 120 etc.; 185 etc.
[3] Id., p. 127. Modern Slavery in Africa, p. 196.
[4] Forced labour, 1929, p. 128, note 1. Modern Slavery in Africa, p. 196.

The labour system, of which a brief account has been given above, came to an end in 1928. Probably it was partly under the influence of foreign criticism of the conditions of labour in the Portuguese colonies that the principle of obligatory labour was abandoned now. But it was maintained in the new law that followed that every able native was at least morally obliged to assure himself of a livelihood through labour and thereby to work "in the general interest of mankind" [1]. From henceforth officials would no longer be allowed to recruit labourers for private individuals [2], but at the same time it was stated as general policy that all government officials, and particularly those who by virtue of their office came into daily contact with the native population, were obliged to assist the recruiting agents in their work as much as they could [3]. This was stated even more explicitly in regulations that followed [4]: while it was forbidden to accompany agents on their recruiting tours or allow them a police escort, they could assist them by indicating the localities likely to give satisfactory results. Moreover, they were to advise the chiefs and the subjects to go to work, at the same time making it quite clear that this was not compulsory. False rumours likely to impede the agents in the performance of their duties were to be combatted with all legal means at their disposal. Finally, the agents were to be given all the moral and material support that might be of service to travellers in the interior, as long as this did not in any way arouse suspicion that there was official pressure on recruitment.

The laws which today govern the colonial policy of Portugal are the "Acto Colonial" of 1930 and the "Carta Orgânica do Império Português" of 1933. These laws also contain clauses forbidding all direct assistance by officials in recruitment, although the right of the colonial administration to encourage labour from an educational point of view is preserved [5].

Despite these reformations in the legislation, compulsory labour still occurs on a fairly large scale in Portuguese Africa, at least until recently, which is made abundantly clear in Basil Davidson's "The

---

[1] The recruiting of labour in colonies and in other territories with analogous labour conditions, 1935, (International Labour Conference), p. 99. See also for contemporary situation: Report of the Ad hoc Committee on Forced Labour, 1953, p. 59 etc.

[2] The recruiting of labour etc., p. 131.

[3] Id., p. 140.

[4] Id., p. 141.

[5] Hailey, op. cit., p. 650.

African Awakening", published in 1955 and based on personal observations of about that time as well as on a report made by a member of the Portuguese National Assembly concerning the situation in the Portuguese colonies in 1946. Essentially, the system would seem to have changed very little since the early days of colonial development [1], although it is now not quite as drastically and ruthlessly enforced. Employers requiring labourers notify the Governor-General, who then allocates a certain number, advising the local administrator to conscript these through the local chiefs and headmen. For the sake of public opinion abroad, contracts are signed, but usually only between the officials concerned and the native chiefs; nevertheless, the natives thus put to work are called "contratados". It is hardly necessary to add that the officials regularly receive token money from employers. In 1954, 379,000 natives were conscripted in this way by the administration [2], while about 400,000 offered their services "voluntarily"—though even here one wonders when one considers the methods adopted by the recruiting agents of various large undertakings whether their "offer" to work was really made of their own free will [3]. The fear of compulsory labour is so widespread that many hundreds of natives still continue to escape across the borders every year, especially in Angola where the acute depopulation can be ascribed mainly to this factor [4].

From the preceding it is quite clear that slavery in Portuguese Africa has been largely replaced by compulsory labour.

LITERATURE

Apontamentos para a história da abolição da escravidão nas colónias portuguezas, Lisboa, 1880.

Bourne, H. R. Fox, Slave traffic in Portuguese Africa. An account of slave-raiding and slave-trading in Angola and of slavery in the islands of San Thome and Principe, London, c. 1909.

Burtt, Joseph, Slavery in Anno Domini 1913. In: The contemporary review, vol. 104, July-Dec. 1913, p. 216-222.

Cadbury, William A., Labour in Portuguese West Africa, 2nd ed., London etc., 1910.

Correspondence respecting contract labour in Portuguese West Africa, London, 1912, Cd. 6322.

---

[1] See chapters 18 to 21, and in particular p. 202 etc.
[2] Davidson, p. 202.
[3] Davidson, p. 221.
[4] Davidson, p. 192, 204.

Further correspondence respecting contract labour in Portuguese West Africa, London, 1913, Cd. 6607.
—— London, 1914, Cd. 7279.
—— London, 1915, Cd. 7960.
Further correspondence respecting contract labour in Portuguese South-West Africa, London, 1917, Cd. 8479.
Davidson, Basil, The African Awakening, London, 1955, Chapter 18-21.
Forced labour. Report and draft questionnaire, Geneva, 1929. (International Labour Conference, 12th session, 1929). pp. 114-133, 184-187, 206-223.
Grande enciclopédia portuguesa e brasileira, Lisboa etc., Vol. 2, c. 1940, Art. "Angola".
Lord Hailey, An African Survey, a study of problems arising in Africa south of the Sahara, 2nd ed., London etc., 1945.
Harris, John H., Slavery or "Sacred Trust"?, London, 1926, p. 45-52.
—— Portuguese slavery: Britain's dilemma, London, 1913.
Moçambique, Paris, 1931. (Publ. en occasion de l'Exposition Coloniale Internationale).
Modern Slavery in Africa. In: The Nation, vol. 121, 1925, p. 195-196. (Extracts from the notes of Edward Alsworth Ross).
Nevinson, Henry W., A Modern Slavery, London etc., 1906.
—— More changes, more chances, London, 1925.
The recruiting of labour in colonies and in other territories with analogous labour conditions, Geneva, 1935. (International Labour Conference).
Report of the Ad hoc Committee on Forced Labour, Geneva, 1953. (United Nations-International Labour Office).
Swan, C. A., The slavery of to-day; or, the present position of the open sore of Africa, London, 1909.
Thornhill, J. B., Adventures in Africa under the British, Belgian and Portuguese flags, London, 1915, Chapter 11: Portuguese slavery in Angola.

CHAPTER SEVEN

LATIN AMERICA

In most of the Latin American countries Negro slavery was definitely abolished shortly after 1850. In Venezuela and Ecuador abolition came in 1854, in Columbia in 1851; Brazil followed suit considerably later: abolition became a reality there in 1888. Nevertheless, most Latin American slaves were freed rather early if we take the United States—where slavery was abolished in 1863—as criterion. But by 1900 forced labour had again made its appearance in those countries which had freed their slaves, and it came in a form which was harder to bear for most of the victims than the former slavery had ever been. Those on whom this compulsory labour was imposed were for the most part Indians or mestizos. There were relatively few Negroes in most of the Spanish-American countries. This brings us on to an examination of how the Indians were used for labour by the whites after the conquest of the Americas. We will see how soon after a ban on slavery other forms of compulsory labour followed similar to those which later appeared in many countries after the abolition of negro slavery.

Real slavery was not very widespread among the Indians of Spanish America [1]. Right from the start, the only Indians who could be held as slaves were those who had been taken prisoner during the wars of conquest (which were considered just), and those who were already slaves held by their own people, provided they were bought by purchase or were received as a tribute. However, it was not long before enslavement was entirely forbidden [2]: the first step being taken in 1530, and the decisive ruling being given in 1542 [3].

But the Spanish could not live in the Americas without the labour of the natives, since for them to do manual labour themselves in the tropics—where colonization began—was practically an impossibility. Moreover, the early colonists were not from the working classes, and it was certainly not their intention on coming to the

---

[1] Lesley Byrd Simpson, The Encomienda in New Spain, 1929, p. 24.

[2] Silvio Zavala, New Viewpoints on the Spanish Colonization of America, 1943, Chap. 5.

[3] Id., Chap. 6.

newly discovered territories to work as labourers. Thus they were dependent on native labour for their subsistence, and this need was greatly enhanced when gold was discovered. The Indians, however, were not in the least interested in working for the whites. Hardly surprising then that they were compelled to do so. Slavery was indeed strictly limited and later banned, but there were other methods conceivable.

The encomienda system was the labour system that marked colonial life in the first 50 years of colonisation [1]. The intent of this system, which was partly based on the feudal system as practised at that time in Castile [2], was to combine the recruitment of the necessary labour with the cultural mission, considered as one of the most important elements of colonization. An encomienda was the allocation of a number of Indians—usually from 30 to 300—to a Spanish colonist or even to an ecclesiastical functionary; the term allocation being used in the sense that the Indians had to work for the encomendero—he to whom they were allocated—and/or deliver produce to him, in exchange for which the encomendero had to provide for their spiritual and material welfare. To the former belonged instruction in the Christian religion and the application of the basic elements of European culture; to the latter, the provision of food, clothing, housing etc.

The encomenderos had no absolute power over the Indians allotted to them. These remained the direct subjects of the Crown which exercised its rights on administration and justice through the royal functionaries and, in respect to local administration, through the old Indian chiefs.

Obtaining an encomienda did not, in the beginning at any rate, mean that one also automatically became owner of the land on which the allotted Indians lived [3]. This land remained the property of the Indians themselves or the Indian communities, or, in certain circumstances, became the property of the Crown. Land allotment by the Crown was independent of the allocation of Indians.

The term of an allotment was varied. Initially, the encomendero had the right to his encomienda for a relatively short period of

---

[1] See on this especially: Leslie Byrd Simpson, op. cit. Also: Silvio Zavala, op. cit., Chapters 7 and 8.

[2] See: Robert S. Chamberlain, Castilian backgrounds of the repartimiento-encomienda, 1939.

[3] Silvio Zavala, op. cit., p. 80 ff.

two or three years only, but later it was declared that an allotment of Indians held for the lifetime of the encomendero and his heirs, or even one or two generations longer. After the death of the last of these heirs, the Indians were again placed at the disposal of the Crown, which retained the right to allot them to another colonist or let them go free. However, it was not unusual for the period of encomiendas to be repeatedly lengthened for a further generation.

Payment for Indian labour was antithetical to this system, the obligation to work or supply produce being the most fundamental element in it. The Crown did several times rule that a certain wage should be paid to the encomienda Indians, but generally speaking wage-earning was almost non-existent in practice.

What was the position of the Indians under the encomienda system? Except for a few favoured groups, to wit, the tribes which had not offered resistance to the conquest, and generally also the chiefs and sometimes other native nobility, all Indians who were not slaves were given in encomienda, so that the members of every ordinary family were subjected to compulsory labour of one sort or another. As a rule obligatory labour applied to persons between the ages of 18 or 14 and 50. However, children under the age of 14 could be ordered to do work suitable to them, such as weeding. For women, the rules varied. Sometimes it was forbidden to make them work, and sometimes it was only forbidden to let them do the heavier types of work, such as in the mines. But the encomenderos either ignored these provisions or met them inadequately, as would appear from the fact that such regulations had to be continually repeated—not to mention the probably exaggerated descriptions of Las Casas [1] and others.

The Indian situation during the first period of colonization—restricted to the islands in the Caribbean Sea—differed somewhat from later times when the principal colonial area was in the country today known as Mexico. On the islands, labour for the whites took a great deal of the Indians' time—unbearably much when we consider that these people were not accustomed to regular labour. This is indicated by the legal provisions for the protection of the natives. In 1512 it was decreed that the Indians were to work for periods of 5 consecutive months on the mines interspersed with

---

[1] Frequently cited by Simpson, op. cit., and by Konrad Erb, Behandlung der Indier in Theorie und Praxis . . ., 1906.

40 day rest periods in which they were to care for their land. A year later this regulation was replaced by another decreeing that they were to work 9 months a year for the Spaniards, and were to be compelled to work on their own lands or for the Spaniards for wages in the remaining three months. The intention was, as was added, to prevent their spending their time in indolence and to teach them to live as Christians. We may assume that the periods stipulated in the ordinance were the minimum of what the encomenderos tde manded of their Indians. Rest days and daily free time during he- period of labour were meted out most grudgingly. In 1513 it was determined that the Indians had a right to one free day per month, which they would be allowed to spend at home. But the rider was quite illusionary, since the majority of Indians worked great distances from their homes.

In Mexico, the whole question of Indian labour was approached from another angle; partly because of the different circumstances there, but also in order to avoid the catastrophic effects which the labour in the service of the encomenderos had had on the Indians of the Caribbean islands. In Mexico it was not so much a matter of demanding personal services as of imposing the Indians to deliver produce (not only agricultural but also textiles and ceramic products). It is clear that also the latter demands, in contrast to our system of taxation, constituted compulsory labour for the Indians. Normally, they grew only sufficient to meet their own requirements, but now, to be in position to render tributes to the whites, they had to do work which they would not otherwise have done; whereas our taxes are generally only a reduction on that part of our incomes which is for personal use. Nevertheless, it must be conceded that the replacement of personal services by tribute was a definite mitigation of the compulsory labour, since in the final analysis, less control is imposed on those who are affected. However, in practice this principle of minimised personal service was not adhered to in Mexico. The time came when it was declared that the tribute was not to be paid in kind but in money exclusively and, if this was impossible, the Indians could be called upon to "earn" the equivalent by labouring in the mines. As the Indians had no money, what this really amounted to, of course, was personal services.

Actually, an attempt was made to prevent the colonists from demanding too heavy a service. Cortes, the conquerer and first Governor of the territory, specified that not more than 20 consecutive days of labour could be demanded, during which the Indians should not be made to work longer than from sunrise to one hour before sunset, with one rest hour at midday; and that, after having worked such a period of 20 days, an Indian might not be called up again for labour within 30 days. One wonders though whether he would have had sufficient authority to prevent abuses by the encomenderos.

The tribute in itself demanded much work, though it is difficult to determine exactly how much. Some indication is given in a Royal Ordinance of 1551, in which it is decreed that in levying a tribute the criterion should be that the Indian must keep enough over to be in a position to feed his children, tide his family over times of illness, and to cope with other unforeseen circumstances. Naturally, the question is to what extent these provisions were adhered to. Even toward the end of the period here under discussion—after attempts had already been made to lower the tribute—the Indians saw fit to complain about the exorbitant and completely arbitrary demands of officials and encomenderos. Sometimes matters were taken so far that Indians died as a result of the heavy labour, or fled their districts [1]. On the other hand, there were (in about 1550) also a few areas in which more tribute could have been levied without objection. Much depended on the character of the encomenderos individually. Although some were known to drive their Indians to the utter limits of despair, it seems that the situation was on the whole not intolerable toward the end of the period in which the encomienda system was the principal system of labour in Mexico.

However, we must examine a little more closely the manner in which the encomienda Indians were treated, and the conditions under which they had to labour. There is a marked difference to be found also here between the conditions in the early period of colonization on the islands, and the later developments in Mexico. On the islands the situation was inconceivably shocking; in Mexico, it was better in many respects.

Various reports out of the first period describe how the encomenderos provided their labourers with far too little food, and this in spite of the heavy work which was expected of them. Cursing had become so prevalent that a Royal Ordinance had to be issued, whereby it was forbidden to call an Indian a "dog". And abuses were

---

[1] W. V. Scholes, The Diego Ramírez visita, 1946, p. 47, 63.

rife. Later the situation actually improved in Mexico. The new system—more tributes than personal service—gave less opportunity for abuses and the various ordinances forbidding the bad practices did, after all, perhaps have some effect on the behavior of the colonists. Yet the situation there too was far from exemplary. Complaints of ill-treatment recur throughout the entire period.

There were a few practices which made the situation even worse for the Indians than it was already. Almost from the start of colonization of the Americas until long after the period here under consideration, the Spaniards made a continuous effort to bring the Indians together in great numbers in "cities"; the main intentions of this being that it would be easier to bring Christendom to the Indians and that there would be a larger labour supply at hand—of particular importance for the mines. On the islands this policy had tragic consequences for the Indians in the first period of Spanish colonization. It is not difficult to imagine how the life of these people must have been disrupted when they were ejected from their homes and made to live, sometimes far from their homes, in communities far more populous than they had ever been accustomed to—and, as a rule, in the neighbourhood of the mines. Their former dwellings had to be burned out, according to the laws of Burgos of 1512, so as to make them forget their attachment to them more readily. In Mexico, the process seems to have caused less difficulty, probably partly because the Indians there were already accustomed to living in large groups.

Those Indians who were not forced to live in the neighbourhood of the places where they were to work were often not much better off. They might be sent anything from 10 to 80 miles away to work, as a result of which a man and wife would not see each other for months, and—according to Las Casas—sometimes even for years. In this respect, the situation in Mexico later was not much better than that on the islands. The personal services here too had often to be performed at great distances from home, and the tributes delivered tens of miles away.

It was very unpleasant for the Indians when—as happened occasionally—they were exchanged, hired out, or sold by their encomendero, especially since this could involve them in extra work, further from home; and—if they were sold—the change of masters was usually disadvantageous. Moreover, in this respect the position of the encomienda Indians hardly differed at all from that of the slaves.

The many ordinances forbidding these practices were apparently of little help. When, on the death of an encomendero, his Indians were allotted to another colonist by the Governor or Viceroy, the Indians were more likely than not to have the worst of it. Sometimes they were divided among various encomenderos, and some of them sent to distant places without family ties being taken into consideration.

As regards the circumstances under which the work was done, much depended on the work which had to be done. Those who had household work to do in the residence of the encomendero, and those who worked on the land, usually had the best of the bargain, whereas it usually went very badly for those who worked in the mines and as porters. The work in the mines was most arduous and extremely unhealthy, the workers often having to stand deep in water while they worked. And the urge to become rich quickly made the encomenderos drive these people to their utmost. Initially, the authorities in Mexico put a ban on mine work for encomienda Indians because of the appalling mortality among the natives working in the mines on the Caribbean islands. The mine work was thus reserved for slaves. However, when enormous silver deposits were found a few years later a great demand for a labour force to work these deposits arose, and the ban on using the encomienda Indians was lifted.

The Indians also suffered much for having to portage freight. Later horses and donkeys were imported from Europe, but before that there were no tame animals which could be used for the purpose, and so the Indians became literally beasts of burden, having to carry loads which were far too heavy, for many hours in the day, and receiving far too little food. But, as if this was not enough, their life was even made more of a hell by the extreme ruthlessness of their Spanish task masters who exacted more out of them than was humanly bearable. Many fell by the wayside on the long journeys which could last months and months and would take them far from home. In this respect the situation in Mexico was little better than that on the islands. The many ordinances regulating the porters' labour or even forbidding it would appear to have had little effect.

Not only the encomenderos were guilty for the hard lot of the Indians. Many of the Royal functionaries in the Americas were not exactly above board. Bribery and corruption were rife, and naturally the encomenderos profitted. Also, many of these officials had encomiendas of their own, especially in the early days of colonization when they would be allotted these as payment for their services instead of a salary. Neither was it uncommon later for an official to be an encomienda-holder. As a result, their attitude was what could have been expected: practically always they favoured the encomenderos in their dealings at the expense of the Indians.

The attitude to this situation among influential circles in the mother country was quite different. As a rule, responsible people in Spain thought far more of improving the lot of the Indians than did official circles in America itself. This is not to say that they always favoured the natives. This would have been almost an impossibility in view of the fact that they themselves had a part interest in the encomienda system. The Crown presented gifts of encomiendas to people on whom it wished to shower favour, and these people, in turn, would appoint a task master to exploit the Indians allotted to them. Objectivity toward Indian matters was then no longer to be expected.

And the King was the greatest encomienda-holder of them all. In addition to which, a percentage of the profits made by the colonists ended up in the royal treasury. It is thus not surprising that the Crown rather tended to protect the interests of the encomenderos. It is indeed quite remarkable that honest efforts were frequently made to improve the lot of the Indian subjects, in spite of the profits to be gained by exploiting them. Proof of this is to be found in the truly impressive stream of ordinances regulating the treatment of natives to the smallest detail. We have already drawn attention to a few points from these protective measures; but we still have to add to this that special functions were created for the protection of the natives. It was not long before the office of "visitador" (inspector) was set up (first mentioned in 1512). This functionary was given the task of finding out whether the provisions passed for the well-being of the Indians were being carried out, and further to generally investigate whether the Indians were being badly treated or not. However there existed a ridiculous difference between the number of inspectors in relation to the size of the territories for which they were responsible, so that even with the best will in the world it would have been impossible for them to accomplish much. Further, the Crown experimented by creating the office of "protector", which functionary would supervise all matters pertaining to the well-being of the Indians. But the experiment would not seem to have had much success.

The good intentions of the Crown in regard to the Indians on the one hand, and the continual yielding to the interest of the encomenderos on the other, is well demonstrated by the conflict which arose over the abolition of the encomienda system. Even when the system was at its heights the Crown tried several times to abrogate it, but everytime allowed its opposition to peter out again. The attempt at abolition certainly carried with it the wish to strengthen the royal sovereignty over the encomenderos with their feudal leanings, but just as certainly its aim was often to improve the lot of the Indians.

All such attempts met with heavy opposition from the colony. The arguments of the encomienda-holders sounded fine in theory: in order to convert the Indians to Christianity it was essential that they should live in close contact with the Spaniards, and the encomienda system accomplished this end. Moreover, the Indians showed disturbing tendencies to indolence and: the encomienda system was the best way to train the Indians to an industrious life. However, the more practical reasons were also advanced: the labour of the Indians was indispensible. If they had to do without this they would be forced to return to Spain.

Indeed, it would seem to have been an impossibility to abolish the encomienda system while it still fulfilled its purpose, although there was a decision in 1530 toward gradually dismantling the system. Encomiendas whose periods of allotment had expired would not be again assigned to colonists, but the Indians belonging to them would come under the direct administration of the Crown. And in this way the encomienda system in fact slowly became of less importance; till it was finally done away with in the 18th century. Even more important, however, than the gradual transition from the encomiendas in the hands of the Crown was the change brought in the system, as far as it concerned Mexico, in 1549. It was then forbidden by Royal decree to demand labour in the mines in place of a tribute, while the Crown let it be known as its express intent that the personal services would be abolished as quickly as possible. This time the ruling was definitive. Naturally the personal services did not come to an end instantaneously, but this decree can be considered a turning-point in the history of labour relations [1]. The most essential aspect of the encomienda system was nullified by this measure.

[1] Silvio Zavala, op. cit., p. 85.

When it was at its heights the encomienda system yielded good results for the Spaniards. Economically speaking, there was great progress in the Americas after the first chaotic years. A few agricultural products could be exported in the course of years, and the production of gold and silver proferred great riches [1]. During this time, the Spanish Crown derived a substantial part of its income from overseas.

The Indian population, needless to say, had no share in this wealth. On the islands, the consequences of the contact with the Europeans were dire in the extreme; so dire in fact that the native population became almost completely extinct. On discovering Hispaniola [2], the islands were estimated to comprise from 200,000 to 300,000 Indians; by 1548 there were about 500 left [3]. Even if these figures are not accurate, they still say enough. Such a catastrophe is not to be attributed to forced labour alone; contageous diseases and the abuses of alcohol also took their toll. All the same, the arduous and unaccustomed labour together with the ill-treatment under the encomienda system, and the disillusionment of the natives when their traditional way of life was made entirely impossible for them, were certainly important contributory factors.

The native population of Mexico in the years 1519, 1540 and 1565 numbered $\pm$ 11 million, $\pm$ $6\frac{1}{2}$ million and $\pm$ $4\frac{1}{2}$ million respectively [4]. Here again, therefore, a shocking drop in the number of people, but still, a very much less unfavourable outcome than in the islands. And the remaining population was able to attain a certain degree of adjustment to the new conditions. Under the best circumstances, the life of the Indians became at least bearable; but this does not detract from the fact that the conditions in the first period of colonization were probably worse than slavery was anywhere at any time.

As has been seen, the Crown took a decisive step toward abolishing the encomienda system in 1549. On the one hand this measure was the outcome of a prolonged effort by the Crown; from both ethical and political motives (reduction of the power of the sometimes overly independent encomenderos) this had been the direction in which it had striven. On the other hand, however, it should be borne

[1] See Clarence H. Haring, America's Gold and Silver Production in the First Half of the Sixteenth Century. (Quarterly Journal of Economics, 29, 1915, p. 433-474).

[2] The Present Haiti, the first colonized territory in the Americas.

[3] John Collier, The Indians of the Americas, 1947, p. 99.

[4] Sherburne F. Cook and Leslie Byrd Simpson, The Population of Central Mexico in the Sixteenth Century, 1948, p. 38 ff.

in mind that the system was no longer really useful in the developing society of the mid-16th century, seeing that the labour-performing Indians were apportioned over a comparatively small number of Spaniards, which made it difficult for newly arrived colonists to obtain the necessary labour. In view of the economic development, a more flexible system was required, and this made it easier for the Crown to clamp down on the encomienda system.

After the reformation the colonists were encouraged to make use of Negro slaves to a greater degree than before; and further, it was hoped that the Indians would now be got to work as free wage-labourers. However, it very soon became clear that the labour supply problem was not going to be solved in this way. Negro slaves were not available in sufficient numbers, and they were far too expensive to be imported on a large scale. Nor were the Indians prepared to work voluntarily. The greater majority of them were not in the least inclined to work more than was necessary to provide for their simple needs. Thus it was found necessary to resort to a new system of compulsory labour, which took the form of a levy imposed by the authorities on the Indian villages, whereby a given number of labourers were to be made available to a stipulated organization or employer. The labourers were to be chosen in rotation by the head of the village, so that each individual only worked for a certain length of time, and at any given moment there would always be no more than a certain number of people absent from the village [1]. Wages were to be paid for this labour.

This system of labour was made possible in Mexico through the instructions of 1550 to the Viceroy of that time; and in Peru, where it was to develop on a much greater scale, this form of disposal of Indians for compulsory labour first occurred in 1575. In Mexico, the system acquired the name of *repartimiento* or *cuatequil*; and in Peru, *mita*, whereas the people labouring under the system were called *mitayos*. Although the Indians were thus still compelled to work, the conditions of labour were quite different from those under the encomienda system. In the first place, the administration now gave the orders and not the individual employers and enterprises. If labourers were required, requests had to be made to the proper functionaries, and the encomenderos also had to conform to this

[1] See for this labour system: Leslie Byrd Simpson, The Repartimiento System of Native Labor in New Spain and Guatemala, 1938. Also: Silvio Zavala, op. cit., Chap. 9.

pattern. They no longer had full control over the Indians of their encomiendas and were not allowed to make demands on them; so much so that these could even be ordered by the administration to work for others. In fact, the authorities regulated everything from the nature of the work which was to be done and the circumstances under which it was done, to the percentage of the Indian village community which could be subjected to this labour and for how long at a stretch, as well as the number of hours which were to be worked a day. And these things, according to the intention at any rate, were to be regulated in such a way that the Indians would not have to work over-long for the Spaniards, leaving them time over to attend to their own needs. Another important difference with the former system was that wages were to be paid now (the amounts of which to be determined by the authorities). In this way it was hoped to arrive at a point at which the Indians would come to work voluntarily for wages, and as such, the system was merely considered as an emergency measure to tide the colonists over a transitional period.

Moreover, it was the general intention that the Indians would only be assigned to labour which was imperative for the welfare of the country and its people. Obviously included in this category were the public works and also the labour performed for church or monastry; but also included were the private agricultural, animal husbandry and mining enterprises (the latter being the principal source of income in the colony). Industries (principally, sugar and textile) profited little by the system, while small artisans and merchants were practically certain not to be included for consideration.

Within 50 years, that is, by the end of the 16th century, mita and repartimiento had become the main sources of labour. A few changes were made in the course of the 17th century, but the main structure of the system remained unaltered and survived till the end of the colonial period. We shall now go on to examine how the system worked out in practice.

Not all Indians were considered for drafting for this compulsory labour. As a rule those tribes which had submitted voluntarily, and those tribes well disposed to the Spaniards and situated on the borders of the pacified territories, were excused. As were the heads of tribes committed to such labour, together with, as a rule, those persons already working in service of the church—for example, gardeners, cooks to the priests, and members of the choir. Further, there were age limits set—for example, 18 and 55 (Mexico, 1583).

Women were legally exempted from compulsory labour, but that is not to say that they were always spared. Leslie Byrd Simpson has listed many documents from the period in his book "The Repartimiento System of Native Labor in New Spain and Guatemala" and therein we read of Indians complaining that their women were forced to do housework or other kinds of labour, and also that they were made to substitute for their husbands when these were ill if they could not provide other substitute labour at their own expense [1]. This held good for Mexico, and in Peru such illegal practices occurred on a much wider scale. Juan and Ulloa report how women and very young children of the mitayos were also compelled to labour [2].

The percentage of the village community to be drafted at one time differed in the various territories, and also changed in the course of time. In Peru, the limit was set legally in most cases at one in seven; in Mexico the permissible percentage varied (except for the initial period) from 4 in the villages supplying mine labour to 25 where labour in agriculture was involved.

The periods to be worked at a stretch also varied in Mexico and Peru. In the first territory the period was set at one or two weeks, and in the latter as a rule four months were allowed. Not that these stipulations were always adhered to, however. Many complaints were heard from Mexico, even though the situation there was in many respects considerably better than in Peru. The one or two weeks sometimes stretched to two or three months, and it was not unusual for more villagers to be called up than allowed, especially if the population of the village had dropped in number as a result of an epidemic etc. The drafts were not adjusted to the new circumstances which meant that those remaining were sent out much more frequently.

Further, the fact that the Indians were made to labour far from their homes made the situation worse for them than was intended. In Mexico this was the exception, while in Peru it was the rule. There the trips would sometimes take months, so that the labourers would be away for at least twice as long as their period of employment. That these long journeys were a heavy burden on the population can be realized from Salvador de Madariaga's report of an eye

---

[1] P. 33.

[2] Jorge Juan y Antonio de Ulloa, Noticias secretas de América, London, 1826, p. 283.

witness who accompanied a caravan of Indians to the place where they were to work—in this case, the mines of Potosí [1]:

2,200 Indians departed, and all took their wives and children with them so that a total of 7,000 undertook the journey. Each Indian took lamas with him, at least 8 or 10, but sometimes also 30 or 40; and further, for food, some alpacas, so that a total of 30,000 animals accompanied the caravan. The lamas were used for carrying maize and other food, blankets, and so on. 100 miles were to be covered, and the journey took two months, since the children and the animals could not walk fast. Of the 7,000 who undertook the journey only 2,000 returned. Of the others, some had died, and a group had stayed in Potosí or thereabouts, not having sufficient animals or food for the return journey.

The number of hours to be worked per day was also carefully regulated. But here too, practice often differed from what was stipulated. A workday of 12 hours was common. But there are complaints, even from Mexican Indians, that they were frequently made to work till well into the night. As a rule, very hard labour was demanded; and the work in the mines besides being unhealthy as well was also doubly dangerous because of the poor arrangements made for getting underground. Many could not take the work, and either fell ill or died. At night, the labourers were locked up to prevent desertion; and to make it still more difficult to escape they would be made to sleep bound together in pairs. Every attempt was also made to prevent escape on the journeys; for instance, by tying their hands behind their backs. During work, any suspicion of insufficient industry was callously punished, particularly the overseers were notorious for this. Moreover, wages were usually low, often only partially paid, or given in goods instead of in money. Old hats, knives and trinkets would serve as wages.

Many natives tried to flee to other, more inhospitable areas in order to avoid repartimiento or mita, and all in all, the situation in some instances was probably as bad as anything experienced in the first period of the encomienda system.

Further, it must be remembered that repartimiento and mita were not the only systems of compulsory labour to which the Indians were subjected at this time. In the first place, they were also still expected to pay tributes—which required extra time, although it is

---

[1] Salvador de Madariaga, Cuadro histórico de las Indias, 1950, p. 139.

not easy to ascertain how much. We do know that there was a vast difference in this between Mexico and Peru. In a report from a Mexican functionary to Charles V in the year 1553, it is claimed that an Indian there could earn enough to pay the tribute for the whole year with from 12 to 15 days work [1]. Even though this estimate may be on the low side, it does indicate a favourable situation for the Indians. This was certainly not true of Peru. Juan and Ulloa give a description of the situation in the first half of the 18th century [2]. From this it would appear that the Indians had to spend a great deal of time on collecting the tributes levied on them by the authorities, and further, that the worst abuses accompanied the collection, with the result that both men and women were often compelled to work as hard as they could if they were to meet the obligations supposed to be imposed on the men only. One of the most common abuses on the part of the corregidores (the administrators of Indians subject to the Crown) was to make young boys below and older men above the obligation age deliver tributes, as well as the ill and infirm, who were officially exempt. Frequently they were hardly or not at all in state to do the work required, and then the other members of the family would have to come to their assistance so as to prevent them from being punished for insufficient tribute. It was also not unusual—according to Juan and Ulloa—for persons who had already delivered their tribute to be called on to do so for a second time in the same period. If they could not show a receipt for the first delivery, as was usually the case seeing that they were illiterate and quite ignorant of the importance of documents, they were put to work on the hacienda of the corregidor or elsewhere. For the Peruvian Indians of Juan and Ulloa's time the payment of tribute can thus be seen as having involved them in a considerable amount of compulsory labour.

It also repeatedly occurred that Indians were put to work outside the repartimientos, and thus quite illegally. Despite the ban on personal services, the encomenderos and corregidores still in a few cases continued to demand these from the natives entrusted to them, but more often Indians were simply taken at random and forced to work. A traveller, passing through a village, for example, might order a number of Indians to serve him as porters; and although some had

---

[1] Cited by Lesley Byrd Simpson, The Repartimiento System etc., p. 8.
[2] Juan y Ulloa, op. cit., p. 231 ff.

permission to do so just as many did not. In 1609 there was a ban on the use of repartimientos for portage (except in certain exceptional cases), and it is perhaps significant that pack animals were being imported at about this time, making it less necessary to use the Indians for portage. Nevertheless, travellers often went right on in their old ways. Thomas Gage, who was in the Americas between 1625 and 1637 describes how travellers would force Indians from one village to accompany them as bearers to the next [1].

The ecclesiastics were also guilty of wide-spread use of illegal labour. Repartimientos were allotted for building churches and so forth; yet the ambition of the clerics to be continually building more luxurious churches and cloisters knew no bounds; and to get anywhere near fulfilling such ambitions many more Indians were needed than supplied. Since many of the priests had great influence over the Indian villages, it was easy for them to call up extra help, and this, in fact, occurred regularly [2]. Many ecclesiastics themselves owned estates or sugar mills, and used their authority over the population to provide themselves with labour. Not that it stopped there either; for they loaned out—or hired out—people whom they had called up, to friends or relatives. And for all such labour there was often no payment at all.

Besides the ecclesiastics, the administrative personnel also often misused their power to have Indians do personal services for them. And even the ordinary colonists found ways and means of extorting extra services from the natives. The native population had therefore not a little labour to perform for the whites outside repartimiento or mita.

However, in this period too, the Spanish Crown endeavoured to protect the Indians against abuses. A series of decrees were issued designed to hold repartimiento and mita within certain limits, and obstruct the illegal demands for labour. In most cases these decrees made little difference, since their application depended on the administrative apparatus in the colonies, which was largely corrupt, and tended to favour the whites in relation to the Indians because of the advantages to be gained thereby.

The corregidores, under whose rule the Indians came when an

---

[1] Thomas Gage, A New Survey of the West Indies (1648), Edited . . . 1928, p. 233/234.

[2] See for example: Lesley Byrd Simpson, The Repartimiento System etc., p. 82 ff.

encomienda expired, were notorious for their scandalous treatment of the Indians. Even those officials whose special task it was to protect the Indians (i.e., the inspectors, "protector") were sometimes more of a burden to the Indians than a help. It was extremely difficult for them to carry out their duties as intended because of the opposition from the colonists. Juan and Ulloa describe how an inspector who took his job seriously and appeared to be incorruptable was threatened with assassination by those to whom his inspection was unwelcome, and was left no other choice but to resign his office [1].

On the other hand, it is noteworthy that the courts in this period, in Mexico at any rate, frequently discharged their duty in such a way that the Indians came to have some degree of trust in them, and occasionally went to them with complaints. Generally these complaints were thoroughly investigated, and the Indian was given due justice if he was found to be in the right. In this way, an end was sometimes put to the most serious abuses. Taken as a whole, however, the period of repartimiento and mita was a time of severe oppression for the Indians. This was particularly true of the mita in Peru, which — accompanied as it was by other forms of either legal or illegal compulsory labour— was just as hard for the Indians to bear as the encomienda system had been when personal services still formed the principal element of it.

Both repartimiento and mita underwent some changes in the course of time. Thus we find, for example, in Mexico repartimientos forbidden for all labour except mining, in 1632. In Peru, in the second half of the 17th century there was a temporary mitigation of the mita, but about 10 years later it was reinstituted in the old form. The repartimientos for mine labour came to an end toward the end of the 18th century in Mexico. Alexander von Humboldt found no trace of it when he visited the colony in 1803 [2]. In Peru, the mita survived somewhat longer, and came to an end with independence in 1821.

The disappearance of repartimiento and mita as systems of compulsory labour was partly the result of the fight against compulsory labour, from ethical motives, on the part of a section of the Spanish

---

[1] Juan y Ulloa, op. cit., p. 281/282.

[2] Alexandre de Humboldt, Essai politique sur le royaume de la Nouvelle-Espagne, 2me éd., 1825-1827, Vol. 1, p. 339.

population of the Americas. Many clerics were particularly active in pressing for the reform and abolition of compulsory labour; for although the upkeep of the clerics constituted a heavy burden on the natives as a whole, many individual clerics consistently defended Indian rights. Further, the influence of the slowly growing resistence of the Indians themselves to the abuses served as an added pressure. However, more important was the fact that the system was no longer worth preserving from an economic point of view. The repartimiento or mita Indians might have been excellent for use as unskilled labour, but they certainly had no place in the developing industries—particularly the mining industries—with their growing demand for skilled, permanent labour, which the continually changing gangs of compulsory labourers could not fill. In fact, the continual changing of labour supply in itself handicapped the proper development of the enterprises. In these circumstances other forms of labour supply made their appearance in the course of years, and the repartimiento and mita eventually became superfluous and unnecessary.

However, all this could not have happened if another factor had not been working in the same direction. This factor was perhaps more important than any of the other considerations and had to do with the land question. As time went by more and more Indians lost their lands, and consequently had to go to work for the whites since they had no other means of subsistence. This had the result that direct labour compulsion was no longer necessary. We will now go on to direct our attention more closely to the development of landholding [1].

In the period immediately following on the conquest the Spanish Crown planned to leave the Indians in possession of their land. Naturally some of the land was made over to the Spaniards, but —as we have said at the beginning of this chapter—the Indians—individually or collectively—retained possession of their land under the encomienda system. In time, however, this policy changed. Some encomenderos managed to have alotted to them not only the Indians but also the land on which they lived. But even where this was not the case, when in the course of a century after the conquest the duration of the encomiendas was continually prolonged by a generation, they began to consider the land as family property—

[1] The following is mainly taken from George McCutchen McBride, The Land Systems of Mexico, 1923, p. 42-61.

a situation which was later made official. Moreover, the colonists put more and more land into use as the economic development of the territories made great strides forward. The import of cattle, for example, meant that large areas had to be made available for grazing; and the discovery of mineral deposits in remote areas led to the growth of towns there, which in turn meant making use of land in the environs for the production of essential food crops. Because of this development in all spheres, there was eventually little good land left over for the natives themselves and many became landless. The encomienda Indians generally still had the right by custom to the use of small plots. The abolition of the encomienda system in the 18th century had nothing to do with the question of land ownership, which meant in effect that there was no change in the position of the natives in this respect.

The Indians who were landless had little choice but to work for the whites; although they did have one alternative, namely to withdraw to the wilderness to which the whites had not yet penetrated. And indeed we still hear in the 18th century of whole villages of Indians in Peru retiring to the mountains not yet occupied by the Spaniards so as to escape the oppression of the whites [1]. Nevertheless, this possibility was limited and by far and away the majority went to work for the whites.

In the first half of the 17th century there were already quite a number of Indians working on the Spanish estates, mines or the *obrajes* (places of textile manufacture) who were not included in the repartimiento or mita. Nevertheless, this labour could not be classified as really free, except for a section of the labourers on the mines; for here there were Indians who had spent so long working as mitayos that they came to prefer the new environment and could no longer reacclimatize themselves to their former way of life. The new way of life in the "cities" which sprang up near the mines attracted them, as did the higher wages which were later paid to those who settled down to their jobs and to those who did specialized work. However, in by far and away the most cases one cannot speak of free labour at all, but one can of a new form of compulsory labour; namely, debt bondage. Even when the land scarcity drove many people on to the labour market, there was still a wide margin between demand and supply of labour, and the consequent competition for

---

[1] Juan y Ulloa, op. cit., p. 343.

labour between employers caused them to do everything in their power to bind their workers to them. In the process of debt bondage, the employers gave an advance on wages, or paid their labourers' tribute debts, after which the debtor was obliged to work for the man who had loaned him money until such time as he was able to settle the debt. However, since the debt slaves always received very low wages, and since the employers provided them with essential commodities and possibly also tools at a very high price, the workers became more and more involved in debt the longer they worked—so that the system really in effect boiled down to lifelong compulsory labour.

We first hear of this method of binding labour power in the first decades of the 17th century [1]. After that the system gradually spread, to become the principal method of ensuring a labour supply by about 1800.

In the beginning, the transition to debt bondage was a natural process in agriculture. The Indians, whose land had been taken by the Spaniards, usually stayed where they were because of their attachment to their homes. Naturally they went to work for the landowner, who soon got them entirely in his power by advancing them money. In the mines, there was also an attempt to turn the repartimiento and mita Indians into debt slaves by means of a cash advance on their very meagre wages. The *obrajes* could only obtain repartimiento or mita workers in exceptional cases, and they therefore set about obtaining their labour by other means, such as through false promises, or even by force [2]. Once obtained, the natives were held by a speedily created debt. Working conditions were atrocious, and to prevent escape the doors in some establishments were kept locked all the time, even on Sundays when mass was said inside the *obraje*.

Indians deprived of their freedom by private entrepreneurs in this way were therefore no better off than before when they were forced by the administration to labour from time to time.

And not only private entrepreneurs resorted to debt bondage, for the corregidores were known to do the same. Juan and Ulloa describe [3] how the corregidores in Peru distributed exorbitantly

[1] See examples given by Simpson, The Repartimiento System etc., pp. 54, 78, 79, 99.

[2] Examples by Simpson, op. cit., p. 78.

[3] Juan y Ulloa, op. cit., p. 242-250.

priced goods to the Indians under their control, although the Indians could not pay for these, and in most cases did not want them anyway. For of what use were dying mules to them, or padlocks for their simple huts, or razors when they had no beards, or writing material when they were illiterate? But so be it, they were forced to accept these things, and as a result of the debts were made to do various jobs for the corregidores which sometimes took them months.

All such practices made repartimiento and mita superfluous. The time was ripe for a change in the situation; and this was brought about when the South American states became independent.

The constitutions of the new republics granted the Indians equal citizenship, the founders having experienced the influence of the ideas of the French Revolution. Repartimiento and mita were abolished. But the Indians profitted little. Debt bondage became the order of the day and persisted in spite of the fine sentiments expressed in the constitutions. Indeed, there was a marked worsening in the position of the debt slaves. This can be mainly attributed to the fact that the place of the patriarchal Crown—which had at least tried to attain a certain degree of protection for the natives—was now taken by the *laissez faire* ideas of the new era.

By about the mid-19th century humanitarian ideas had won even more ground. This led in various states to the abolition of Negro slavery—mentioned at the beginning of this chapter—and to the repeal of those ordinances requiring the Indians to pay obligatory tribute. But again this hardly effected the issue. The majority were still in debt bondage, and in debt bondage they remained. Until well into the 20th century this, and related systems of compulsory labour, remained of great importance to the economy. According to Turner, at the start of this century one third of the Mexican people, or 80% of all agricultural labourers were debt slaves [1]. Even in recent times, Indians on the great estates in Bolivia, for example, had the use of a small piece of land in exchange for labour: the head of the family had to work four or five days a week for the landowner, his children cared for the herds, and other members served as domestic servants. Since most of Bolivia is divided into these great estates—or *fincas*—one can imagine how many of the common people were involved in this system of compulsory labour. Moreover, if an estate was sold, the purchaser received the Indians as labour power with it. This was

[1] John Kenneth Turner, Barbarous Mexico, 1911, pp. 108, 110.

not provided for by law, but had become the custom [1]. The piece of land from which the Indian had to provide for his own needs in his spare time was sometimes good but more often poor, and the living conditions were frequently pathetic. These conditions repeated themselves in other parts of Latin America.

Even in the 20th century, with the continuous increase in labour demand, the methods by which the people were converted to debt slaves became more refined, and the pressure heavier. We see this, for example, in Mexico at the turn of this century [2]. Eighty per cent of the land workers were in debt bondage, and mostly that came about in the usual way. But in a few districts the situation was even far worse.

The agave farmers of Yucatan, for example, obtained their labourers from agents in the cities who made it their profession to incur people in debt—e.g., by offering them tempting articles— and then, once in debt, to turn them over to the planters for a substantial sum of money. The debtors then had to work for the planters until their debts were paid off. However, the conditions were such that this was an impossibility; hence, lifelong slavery. Municipal and district authorities, police and courts, were all in hands of the planter class, and they could therefore do as they pleased.

In the southern districts of Mexico—where much tobacco was produced—the authorities cooperated with the planters in not only a passive sense but also actively. Here people who had committed some petty misdemeanour were not sent to prison but turned over to the planters. In this way the district administrators stood to gain quite substantially, and so they went about arresting as many people as they could. More often, however, the matter was arranged somewhat differently. The labourers were supplied by professionals who worked hand in glove with the Government, which naturally received a cut in the profits. The methods by which the labourers were caught varied. Impoverished people would be enticed by promises of easy work for high wages with good living quarters, etc. On the strength of this they would accept an advance on wages, and as far as the agents were concerned, the deal was done. But it was not unusual for them to resort to kidnapping, and even children were

---

[1] S. E. Harris, Economic Problems of Latin America, 1944, p. 261/262. Labour Problems in Bolivia, 1943, p. 7.

[2] John Kenneth Turner, Barbarous Mexico, 1911.

taken in this way. Turner reports that 360 boys between the ages of 6 and 12 disappeared without a trace in the year September 1907 to September 1908—that is, according to the official statistics of Mexico City [1].

However, the worst is what occurred to the Indian Yaquis tribe who were condemned to deportation to the agave plantations of Yucatan—because some of them had refused to give up their land. Members of this tribe—men, women and children—were simply rounded up wherever they could be found, and taken to Yucatan where they were sold to the planters. The great portion of the proceeds of the "sales" went to the authorities responsible for the "business".

Once on the plantations, there was no hope for the labourers, and the atrociousness of the conditions they had to contend with is inconceivable. They had to go on working until they could no longer stand. Days of rest were practically never given, and even illness was seldom considered a reason for not working. Ill-treatment followed any suspicion of insufficient industry. Women and children were often made to work as well. Food and housing were extremely bad. At night all the labourers would be locked up in wretchedly small barracks. And wages were practically never paid. In theory, the debt slaves received a wage, but they had to buy everything they needed from the plantation owner who charged such exorbitant prices that nothing ever remained of the wage. On the contrary, the debt increased steadily, and was passed on from father to son. There was no escape. Moreover, the death rate among labourers was disturbingly high. All in all, the debt slaves in the worst districts of Mexico were far more badly off than the Indians in colonial times.

At least as bad was the situation in the regions of the rubber forests at the time of the expansion of the rubber industry. The situation of which we have heard most is that in the Putumayo territory, lying in the Amazon region in the territories of Columbia, Peru, Equador and Brazil. The whites first penetrated this territory in the eighties of the 19th century. The small settlements of these first Columbian visitors were later taken over by a Peruvian enterprise set up in 1903. About this time there developed an enormous demand for rubber on the world market, and this enterprise expanded rapidly.

---

[1] Turner, op. cit., p. 72.

Many British financiers invested in it, and within a few years it became known as the Peruvian Amazon Company, Ltd. The ruthless way in which this company set about victimizing the local natives soon became widely known, mainly thanks to an investigation set up at the instigation of the British Government.

The way in which the rubber company went to work was as follows [1]. The Indians of the district which the company controlled were forced to tap the rubber trees and to deliver the collected rubber to a depot of the company at set times. The company employed a number of people whose task it was to make certain that the desired amount of rubber came in regularly. These people were partly Negroes and partly Indians—usually caught young and trained to their task by the company—whereas the top jobs were all filled by whites. The Negroes, as a rule, played an important part in all this, and many of them were recruited without any foreknowledge of the kind of work which would be expected of them [2]. Once recruited, however, it was difficult for them to get away, since they were immediately trapped by debt bondage [3]. All essential commodities had to be bought in the company store, at prices anything up to and over 1000% above the normal price. On top of which they would often be forced to buy entirely worthless things. Thus the longer they stayed the deeper they got into debt; and they could not leave the company until such time as their debt was settled.

The Indians in the rubber district had a far worse time of it, however. The debt bondage to which they were also subjected was bad enough in itself, but made ten times worse by the terror in which they lived. It started innocently enough with offers of gifts by white dealers who asked for rubber in exchange; at first they were glad to oblige, but it was not long before they had been reduced to veritable slaves. The company had various depots scattered throughout the forest, and the managers of these—who were paid in relation to the amount of rubber they were able to deliver!—set the amount of

[1] Correspondence respecting the treatment of British colonial subjects and native Indians employed in the collection of rubber in the Putumayo district, 1912, Cd. 6266.

Slavery in Peru, Washington, 1913. (62nd Congress, 3rd Session, House Documents No. 1366).

W. E. Hardenburg, The Putumayo, the Devil's Paradise, 1912.

[2] They came mainly from Barbados, British West Indies, and it was because of the fact that these Negroes were British subjects that the British Government insisted upon investigating the situation in the rubber district.

[3] Correspondence respecting the treatment etc., Cd. 6266, p. 16-19.

rubber which each Indian in his territory was to collect in a given number of days. This quota was set so high that it was almost necessary to work day and night; and if, on delivery day, the full quota demanded was not complete, then the Indians responsible were beaten so frightfully that it was not unusual for some to die as a result. This manner of penalizing inadequate deliveries was so frequently applied that about 90% of the population, including women and children, bore the marks of it on their bodies [1]. Abuses of an even worse nature occurred as well, and not only the Indians were terrorized in this way, but also often the Negroes in the company's employ.

The transport of the rubber caused much suffering, not only on the frequent short trips to the company depots but also, especially, on the journeys from these depots to the company's headquarters, which took place several times a year. Long caravans were formed [2] of men, women and children, each carrying as much as possible, some of the men even taking a load of as much as 150 pounds. And thus they marched, the whole day, under the eyes of armed guards; and hungry, for no food would be distributed under way, and they themselves could never possibly take sufficient with them to last the whole journey.

Actually, hunger was not confined to these long journeys. For so much work was often demanded of the Indians in collecting the rubber, that they would be left no time to tend their fields, and as a result many starved.

The Indians received objects of diverse nature for the rubber which they delivered—if the delivery came up to quota, that is. But these objects were usually quite worthless to them; and such payment was called an advance given on the rubber to be delivered the next time. Thus the managers managed to maintain the lie that work was being done to pay off debts. Needless to say, the "advance" could not be refused so as to obtain release from the rubber collecting. In reality, this was a system of terrorization which brought the Indians again and again to renew their efforts. Each depot held control over its section of jungle with the help of armed personnel directly responsible to the company. Indians who took flight were tracked down and, if found, tortured or even killed. The natives

---

[1] Id., p. 34.
[2] Id., p. 36-37.

naturally only had primitive weapons and these were helpless against the guns etc. of the whites, and any chance of revolt was made all the more difficult by the fact that their most respected leaders—who were considered too dangerous—had been "removed" in the early stages of exploitation. Nor could they expect any assistance from the authorities. For insofar as there were officials in any way connected with the state of affairs in the Putumayo district, they were entirely in hands of the company [1]. However, the territory was so remote, and the question of the actual boundaries so far from settled, that there was no question of there being any workable authority.

The mortality among the Indians in the Putumayo district was indeed extremely high during the period of intense rubber exploitation—deaths being due to overwork, ill-treatment, and starvation. According to one estimate their number dropped from 40 to 50 thousand to less than 10 thousand in the space of a decade [2]; those who managed to escape into neighbouring territories are included in this decrease, however.

Profits were, of course, fabulous, the Peruvian rubber export rising from 15,863 kg. in 1900 to 644,897 kg. in 1906 [3]; and many of the managers of the company depots were able to amass great fortunes.

In time, opposition to the debt bondage spread over all Latin America and an end was made to it officially in many countries between 1915 and 1920. In most cases, however, the great land holdings remained intact, and this made it very difficult to root out the system entirely, so that cases of debt bondage still occur in some countries today [4].

The Indian in Mexico has attained a relatively favourable position.[5] Many of the great estates have been done away with there, and the land has come into the hands of the communities of Indians (and Mestizos). The Indians achieved this to a great extent themselves. The revolution of 1910/1911 was led by a progressive landowner, but it was an unlettered share-cropper—someone thus who had lived on the borderline of debt bondage—who designed the programme

---

[1] Hardenburg, op. cit., pp. 191, 197.

[2] Id., p. 16.

[3] Correspondence respecting the treatment etc., Cd. 6266, p. 48.

[4] Conditions of life and work of indigenous populations of Latin American countries, 1949, pp. 55/56 and 89-91.

[5] See John Collier, The Indians of the Americas, 1947, Chapter 8.

for land reform. The Indians first gave their support to the big landowner leader, but later, when he would not agree to the land reform, they sided with the peon designer of the programme. The land reform then got under way, though slowly at first; and was carried much further under President Cárdenas (1934-1940). By the end of 1938, a third of the agricultural land of Mexico had been put at the disposal of 13,000 Indian communities comprising 1,600,000 families. Thereby almost 8 million of the 10,632,000 Indians and Mestizos who made up the country population of Mexico in 1910 exchanged their dependence on the landlord for a free existence—thus, in this territory at least, the centuries-old tradition of compulsory labour was broken.

In conclusion, we have seen how, after the ban (except in a few cases) on enslavement of the Indian, various forms of compulsory labour appeared in succession in Latin America. Some systems were abolished—when they no longer suited the circumstances of the moment—to be replaced by other systems better able to meet the changing circumstances. And it was only on the awakening of the oppressed in one of the countries that the impetus was given to the abolition of compulsory labour.

LITERATURE

Barber, Ruth Kerns, Indian Labor in the Spanish Colonies, Albuquerque, 1931.

Chamberlain, Robert S., Castilian backgrounds of the repartimiento-encomienda, 1939.

Collier, John, The Indians of the Americas, New York, 1947.

Conditions of life and work of indigenous populations of Latin American countries, Geneva, 1949 (Fourth Conference of American states members of the International Labour Organisation).

Cook, Sherburne F., and Lesley Byrd Simpson, The Population of Central Mexico in the Sixteenth Century, Berkeley, Cal., 1948.

Correspondence respecting the treatment of British colonial subjects and native Indians employed in the collection of rubber in the Putumayo district, London, 1912, Cd. 6266.

Economic Problems of Latin America, edited by Seymour E. Harris, New York etc., 1944.

Erb, Konrad, Behandlung der Indier in Theorie und Praxis zur Zeit der Anfänge spanischer Herrschaft in Amerika (1492-ca.1565), Bern, 1906.

Friederici, Georg, Der Charakter der Entdeckung und Eroberung Amerikas durch die Europäer, Stuttgart-Gotha, 1925-'36, 3 Vols.

Gage, Thomas, A New Survey of the West Indies (1648). Edited with an introd. by A. P. Newton, London, 1928.

Hardenburg, W. E., The Putumayo, the devil's paradise, London, 1912.

Haring, Clarence H., American gold and silver production in the first half of the sixteenth century. In: Quarterly Journal of Economics, 29, 1915, p. 433-474.

Humboldt, Alexander von, Essai politique sur le royaume de la Nouvelle-Espagne, 2me éd., Paris, 1825-'27, 4 vols.

Juan, Jorge, y Antonio de Ulloa, Noticias secretas de América. Sacadas a luz por David Barry, London, 1826.

Labour Problems in Bolivia, Report of the Joint Bolivian-United States Labour Commission, Montreal, 1943. (International Labour Office).

McCutchen McBride, George, The Land Systems of Mexico, New York, 1923.

Madariaga, Salvador de, Cuadro histórico de las Indias. Introducción a Bolívar, 2a ed., Buenos Aires, 1950.

Nordenskjöld, Erland, Indianer und Weisse in Nordostbolivien, Stuttgart, 1922.

Pérez, Demetrio Ramos, Historia de la colonización española en América, Madrid, 1947.

Scholes, Walter V., The Diego Ramírez visita, Columbus, Mo., 1946.

Simpson, Lesley Byrd, The Encomienda in New Spain. Forced Native Labor in the Spanish Colonies, 1492-1550, Berkeley, Cal., 1929.

——The Repartimiento System of Native Labor in New Spain and Guatemala, Berkeley, Cal., 1938. (Studies in the administration of the Indians in New Spain, 3).

Slavery in Peru. Message from the President of the United States, transmitting report of the Secretary of State, with accompanying papers, concerning the alleged existence of slavery in Peru, 1913.

Turner, John Kenneth, Barbarous Mexico. London etc., 1911.

Zavala, Silvio, New Viewpoints on the Spanish Colonization of America, Philadelphia etc., 1943.

CHAPTER EIGHT

MADAGASCAR

When Madagascar came under French administration in 1896, one of the first official measures taken was the complete abolition of slavery [1], by which about 500,000 slaves obtained their freedom. This did not result in the hopeless confusion which accompanied slave emancipation in most other countries. Under the Hovas—a people of Malay origin who had ruled over the original population of Madagascar—the slaves had led a tolerable existence, and, with the inertia of habit, many remained in the service of their former holders after the date of abolition. It was, however, clear that it would be impossible for the white colonists—both those who were in Madagascar at the time of abolition, as well as the many still to come—to obtain sufficient labour unless exceptional measures were adopted to help them in this. As in other countries, the natives here showed little desire to work in the European manner; because of the climate their material needs were small and could be easily obtained with little work. If the colonists were to succeed they had to have labourers, however, and it is therefore understandable that measures to set the population to work (in the European sense of the word) were not long in coming [2].

Three months after slave emancipation, the obligation to work of every able-bodied male was proclaimed [3]. In a regulation of December 27, 1896, it was decreed that all healthy men between the ages of 16 and 60 had to be able to prove that they were executing work falling under any one of the categories listed in the regulation, and if this was the case they were to be issued with a special card or folder. Anyone not in possession of such a document would be considered a "vagrant", and as such convicted to from three to six months imprisonment, while at the end of that period he could

---

[1] In its "old" colonies, France had abolished slavery in 1848.

[2] We leave out of discussion the attempts made to provide for the demands of the labour market with foreign labour, particularly Chinese and Africans, since they were unsuccessful and were soon stopped.

[3] For a while this was only true for a part of Madagascar, Imerina, but the ruling was soon put into effect in other places as well.

be put to work on the public projects for a period equal to three times that spent in prison. In this way it was hoped that the natives would come forward to offer their services as contract labourers to the European colonists.

The question of these labour contracts was settled in the same regulation. Among other things, it determined that the maximum duration of a contract would be five years, that the maximum number of work hours a day would be ten, and that no work was to be performed on Sundays and public holidays. Furthermore, employers had to provide adequate housing to ensure that the health of their labourers would not be impaired. And employees had the right to request that the contracts be made invalid if the employer fell short of these conditions. The labourer, for his part, had to be at work at the prescribed times, and for absence of from one to five days he forfeited his wages for double that period, while he could be brought before a special court if he was absent for more than five days at a stretch.

This ruling of December 1896 did not have the desired result, however. Many natives succeeded in avoiding the labour obligations and, when contracts were concluded, they did not stick to these but deserted whenever they could. Nothing much ever came of convictions either, primarily because colonists—averse as they were to having anything to do with official red tape—did not keep their labourers works books up to date, and thereby lost the right to object legally to their deficiencies.

Because of the lack of success of this regulation, other means were sought, and the first step to finding a solution was through offering considerable advantages to those entering the service of Europeans. In August 1897, it was decreed that anyone concluding labour contracts for a term of at least one year would be freed from his otherwise compulsory obligation to labour on the public works—about which we will have more to say shortly. A good year later (October 1898) this decree was expanded upon by a regulation in which it was declared that anyone concluding a contract with a French colonist for a term of five years would be freed from military service.

Judging from the number of contracts concluded, this regulation was a huge success, but it soon became apparent that about half these contracts were fictitious, and that a number of colonists were doing a wonderful trade in mock contracts, since there were naturally many natives willing to pay a sum of money to gain an illegal release from military and labour services, which they hated. Indeed the regulations not only showed poor results but actually had a negative effect, because while the serious colonists still had a serious labour shortage to contend with there were also appreciably fewer men available for labour on the public works, so many of them having bought their way free.

The whole question of labour provision obviously had to be re-examined. In December 1898, the administration declared invalid those regulations providing an opportunity to be released from military and labour services; and the commission set up with the purpose of re-examining the situation came out with a proposal for a new ruling, which was rigorous in the extreme and rejected by the Government of the mother country; the opinion in France being that, after almost four years of colonization, it was about time for the appearance of a more liberal spirit in the colony. Before examining the system of labour that evolved out of all this, we will first take a look at the ruling pertaining to labour on the public works in the first years of colonization.

A start was made to the construction of roads etc. directly after the French took over the country. Naturally, the labour was to be supplied by the native population, which was, just as naturally, not inclined to work; thus, if the roads were to be constructed as planned, compulsion had to be resorted to. And so it was decreed in as early as October 1896 that all healthy men between the ages of 16 and 60 were to spend 50 days annually working for the administration. Only the military and members of the police corps were exempted, while certain native authorities and persons over 40 were given the opportunity of buying off their labour obligation. At the same time, there were certain provisions designed to protect labourers: not more than nine hours work a day could be demanded, labourers were to be paid a nominal compensation from which food could be bought, and the location of work was not to be further than 20 kilometers from where the labourers lived. If the distance was more than five kilometers, then the time required to travel to and from work had to be subtracted from the working hours. Unfortunately the provisions regarding the distance were reduced to nothing a few months later when the authorities concerned with the recruitment of labour were granted broad powers.

In the following year, a few of the provisions mentioned above were made lighter. The duration of labour was reduced to 30 days, and labourers contracted to French employers were excused altogether—an encouragement, as we have seen, to promote contracting. Moreover, all natives were given the opportunity of buying off their time. Here it should be remarked that the work referred to remained unpaid except for the compensation allowed for the costs of food.

The obligatory labour on roads and other public works was a very heavy burden on the population of Madagascar at that time, for, although the demand of 50 days a year to start with was heavy enough in itself, matters were made much worse by the way in which the labour was conducted, malpractices being rife.

Firstly, the labourers were frequently taken to places far removed from their homes, involving them in long, frequently arduous, journeys, sometimes to regions of a different climate. Usually all the men from a number of neighbouring villages would be called up at the same time, and, since their wives and children customarily accompanied them on long trips, entire districts would often be left deserted. As a result, the native agriculture would be neglected: labour for road building was needed throughout the year, and it was not sufficient to call up labour only in those seasons in which the natives did not need to work their own land.

Also, it was not unusual for the native functionaries, responsible for ensuring that a village supplied its quota of labourers, to be very arbitrary in recruitment. Some natives would be called up several times while others, in the headman's favour, would entirely escape service. The weak and the sick, greybeards and children would also be sent, even though they were exempt according to the regulation. At the location of work, the stipulated duration of the period was not adhered to; force and intimidation being used time and again to keep them at work after the expiration of the service period.

The death-rate among obligatory labourers was shockingly high —due to the change of climate often involved, the lack of hygienic conditions, and the unaccustomed nature and long hours of the labour — in fact so high that the colonists grew worried that there might soon be no potential labour force left for them, so high that public opinion in France was disturbed and began clambering for the abrogation of the system.

Compulsory labour, both for the administration and for the planters, was only really intended for the first difficult years of transition. It was hoped that there would eventually be sufficient free labour. And so the labour system was put on an entirely different basis in the course of the year 1900. By January of that year compulsory labour, which had been instituted in 1896 [1], was entirely repealed. The natives would from henceforth be free to choose for themselves whether they wished to work for the European colonists or not. But the penal sanctions covering the contracts concluded would be retained: now absence from work without good cause, and unwillingness to carry out orders, was punishable with a fine as well as imprisonment of from one to five days. There were fewer provisions for the protection of employees than in the previous regulation, although the maximum duration of contracts was limited to 2 years.

To encourage natives to work for Europeans, the regulation reintroduced a clause decreeing that a contract for a period of at least one year gave the right to release from, this time, half the obligatory labour on public works. As of December 31 of that same year, however, obligatory labour on the public works was repealed altogether. In future the administration was to obtain its labourers in the same way as did private employers, and the labourers were to be paid for their efforts. When penal sanctions on contract labour were also dispensed with a few years later (1905), labour on Madagascar therefore became entirely free—in theory. We will now, however, examine, how the system developed in practice.

Firstly, it is significant that the head tax which already burdened the natives was considerably increased in the same regulation proclaiming the abrogation of obligatory labour on the public works. In some areas this head tax was doubled, and in others increased to four and even six times the original amount, which, if we take into account the circumstances of the native population, must have brought many of the natives into dire difficulties. These tax increases were certainly not primarily intended as a boost to the treasury income. No, the main intention was to indirectly compel the natives to go to work for the colonists, now that the direct compulsion, incubent in the (partial) freedom from labour service, was removed.

But since this measure in itself might not have sufficient effect, a more direct attempt to promote native labour was attempted simultaneously. Labour bureaus were set up [2] for the purpose of

[1] See page 107.

[2] Léonce Jacquier, La main-d'oeuvre locale à Madagascar, 1904. p. 183 ff.—The recruiting of labour in colonies and in other territories with analogous labour conditions, 1935, p. 73 ff.; 138 ff.; 249.

in the first place (according to the relevant rulings) bringing those seeking work and those supplying work together. However, in view of the fact no one ever turned up to say that he was seeking employment, the labour bureaus were able to devote themselves entirely to another of their tasks; namely, to promote the recruitment of labour for both the colonists and the administration (public works). It is difficult to define their terms of reference exactly [1], but it is certain that they played an important part in the provision of labour [2]. Instituted at the end of 1900, these labour bureaus were done away with in 1906, only to be set up again in 1925; and in a ruling of April 1938, whereby native labour was regulated anew, their task was described in almost exactly the same words as before, in 1900 [3]. Only in very recent times does an end seem to have been put to this assistance on the part of the administration in the recruitment of labour [4]. But during the many years it was in force, it may, on the basis of the already cited report of the International Labour Conference of 1935, be considered to have been the most virulent form of governmental activity in the recruitment of labour which has ever been seen in any colonial territory [5].

This does not mean that the authorities did not assist in the recruitment of labour in the period in which the labour bureaus ceased to function; on the contrary, they kept up their assistance even then, albeit in a less official way [6]. And in view of the tendency of the natives to take a hint from the white rulers as an order, it is hardly surprising that mere urging by officials as such was enough to accomplish a great deal.

Even though the freedom of the natives to enter or not to enter the service of the Europeans was more or less fictitious—because of the high taxes and the pressure exerted on them by the authorities, usually *via* the labour bureaus—it still seemed impossible to do without direct compulsion. We see penal sanction—dropped in 1905—reappear in the same wording as before in new regulations later (a fine plus one to five days imprisonment for breach of contract

[1] The recruiting of labour in colonies etc., p. 75/76.
[2] Id., p. 75.
[3] A new decree in Madagascar. In: Industrial and Labour Information, Vol. 67, 1938, p. 289.
[4] Hildebert Isnard, La vie rurale à Madagascar. In: Cahiers d'Outre-Mer, Oct./Déc. 1950, p. 314.
[5] The recruiting of labour in colonies etc., p. 138.
[6] Id., p. 139/140.

without valid reason). And even in the most recent times deserters could, on the request of their employers, be tracked down and returned to their work [1].

However, even the principle of freedom for the native was in reality reduced to nothing by a regulation of August 1921, whereby it was decreed that those who could not demonstrate that they had any means of support (de moyens réguliers d'existence), or had no place of fixed abode, would be liable to imprisonment of from three months to one year [2]. The Governor General on issueing this regulation said that he hoped to see the existing labour shortage reduced by the ruling. Actually it closely corresponds to that of December 1896 [3], whereby the entire male population were obliged to labour.

But we must see whether the supply of labour for the public works really took place on a voluntary basis after the obligatory labour service was done away with on December 31, 1900. Firstly, it should be noted that it was made possible in as early as the beginning of 1901 to pay the very high taxes levied right after the abolition of the labour service in work instead of in money; which, in actual practice, meant the reinstitution of the labour service.

It should further be borne in mind that although the labour service for the higher authorities was repealed, at least in theory, the local authorities retained the right to call up natives over whom they had jurisdiction and make them perform work on projects of general importance in the neighbourhood. This local system of labour could be considered as a direct continuation of the pre-French policy, when the *fokon'olona* (the clan or village community) provided for the carrying out of work of general interest, or even arranged groups to work the lands of the members [4].

Within bounds, this system was quite tolerable; after all, the labourers had direct interest in the results and the work was usually not too long in duration. But when the labour service was abrogated and no one could be called up for labour on the large public works, use was indeed often made—with payment—of manpower called up by local heads, which invariably would lead to unfavourable circum-

---

[1] Isnard, op. cit., p. 317.

[2] Livre gris du travail forcé, rapport supplémentaire, p. 11, cited by: René Mercier, Le travail obligatoire dans les colonies africaines, 1933, p. 82.

[3] See page 107.

[4] Guillaume Grandidier, Ethnographie de Madagascar, 1928, p. 29-30.—Madagascar. Étude économique, publ. sous la direction de M. Loisy, 1914, p. 112.

stances, and in every case involved the labourers in compulsory labour.

It must also be taken into account with regard to labour on public works that to the native an official summons was as good as an order; and in this way many were brought to perform labour which they would never have undertaken voluntarily.

Finally, straightforward compulsory labour was instituted again in the end. The Governor General considered himself qualified to do this, when it was decided in 1925 to construct an important railroad which would require tens of thousands of labourers over the course of several years. To obtain these by voluntary means alone was quite out of the question, neither would it have been easy for the village chiefs to supply such numbers, and anyway—so wrote the Governor-General [1]—if they could not be obtained without compulsion it would be better to have the force organized from above than leave it to the village heads who were usually most arbitrary. And so the "service de la main-d'oeuvre pour les travaux d'intérêt général" (usually referred to as SMOTIG) came into being in 1926.

The regulations included provisions for the employment on public works of a portion of those doing military service. From 1919, a yearly draft had been called up to do three years military service but, seeing that only a small proportion of those called up were really needed, a great number remained quietly at home, only holding themselves available in case of emergency. And from now on these would be used on the railway construction projects etc. as part of their military service. At those times when not all men would be required, the labourers would be chosen by lot, while married men would only be chosen when all the bachelors had had their turn, and if married men were called up they would be allowed to take their wives and children with them. Frequently the projects on which the natives had to work were far from their homes, and the period of three years was only relieved by one month's leave. In 1929 the period was shortened to two years (without leave). Negligence, laziness, etc. could be penalized, and imprisonment could be applied to cases of absence from work without good cause and insubordination. The regulations concerning social provisions were sound—an eight hour work day six days a week; adequate camp arrangements—and as it turned out the death rate among the men in

[1] M. Olivier, Six ans de politique sociale à Madagascar, 1931, p. 107.

the labour service was very low in the first few years. Nevertheless, even with all these provisions, SMOTIG still meant to the natives a long period of compulsory labour, usually far from home, and for objectives which had a purpose only for the ruling class and not for themselves [1].

Having seen which measures were adopted to provide a supply of labour for the administration after the abrogation of the obligatory labour service in 1900, we will now go on to examine, in conclusion, how these measures worked out in practice. The following information is taken from "Erreurs et brutalités coloniales" (1927) by Victor Augagneur, who was Governor General of Madagascar from 1905 to 1910 and in this book describes the situation in the years immediately preceding 1905.

We have already stated that after the abrogation of the labour service in 1900, the local chiefs were still empowered to call up the population for work in the interests of the community, and also that the higher authorities were able to draw on this supply by means of a form of contract entered into with the chiefs. But besides this many French officials of lower rank quite arbitrarily had all sorts of work done for them by the natives in their neighbourhood. If one of them for example had need of wood, he ordered it cut, at a distance of a day and a half's walk, and brought to his house. If an official's home was destroyed by a heavy storm, he had it rebuilt by natives. Moreover, labourers called up by officials would be loaned out to others; for example, to missionaries for the building of a church. And of the methods of "calling up" labour by higher and petty officials we are told the following. Men who had nothing on hand in their village at a given moment would be forcibly carried off. If not enough men could be found, women would be taken too and put to work. Village chiefs, not responding readily enough to a call for labour, would be thrown into prison. If anyone was convicted and jailed for being overdue with tax payments, or if anyone was held as hostage because a member of the family or—if it concerned the chiefs—the people of the village had not yet paid, he was used as labour. Indeed, if labour was particularly needed, it would even happen that prisoners convicted because of tax debts were, when the debt was finally paid, held on as labourers for a period at least as

[1] The "deuxième contingent" for public works was also used in Afrique Occidentale Française, but on a smaller scale. In Madagascar the system was dispensed with in 1936.

long as that which they had already spent in prison. And this when the original imprisonment itself was in many cases illegal.

Most of the labour was unpaid, or as good as unpaid, although payment for work in the general interest became obligatory in 1900. The amounts made available for these wages were ludicrously low, and were divided among the overseers, village chiefs and so on.

To avoid compulsory labour and the veritable manhunts undertaken to collect taxes, great numbers of natives would go into hiding in the forests or make their way to other provinces in the belief that the compulsory labour would be less severe there. Sometimes whole villages would take flight, and in such instances the authorities would not hesitate to open fire on them.

The native population did not register complaints since this was made very difficult for them and also because they had absolutely no faith that their complaints would be justly considered, and not without reason. Thus they were completely at the mercy of those who ruled over them.

Finally, attention must be paid to another system of labour current in Madagascar which also contains an element of compulsion; namely, the *métayage*, a system of share-cropping [1], whereby the native is given the use of a small piece of land by the landowner in exchange for a share of the harvest—usually a half—added to which is frequently the commitment to work a certain number of days annually for the landlord. In some cases only labour is demanded in exchange for the use of the land. Since the natives are hardly ever in the position to lay out capital expenditure, invariably the landowner supplies the tools, seeds, etc., besides handing out loans for tax payments, and so forth. The money value of all this has to be repaid with interest at the end of the season when the crop is sold.

The *métayage* appeared directly after the abolition of slavery, many of the former slaves remaining with their former holders on these terms. And because the natives have always been inclined to show very little enthusiasm for taking on wage-earning jobs, the *métayage* has, in a later period also, often been the only system whereby the colonists could be sure of a labour supply, consequently it is still practised today, at any rate on the West coast of Madagascar [2].

Because of the inequality between the parties involved, many

---

[1] See for this especially: Isnard, op cit.

[2] Isnard, op. cit., p. 314, 317.

abuses have always accompanied *métayage*. Sometimes the cropper will receive less than his share of the harvest, but the especial danger is in the indebtedness resulting from advance payments. The landowners have in the past frequently shown themselves all too willing to provide their tenants with money and goods in advance because a) the tenants will then be forced to sell their share (often directly to the landowner) right after the harvest when prices are low, and because b) there is a provision that the *métayer* cannot leave his landlord's service without first having settled his debts. With which condition the labour ot the *métayer* falls under the category of compulsory labour. As a result of the inspection of the labour systems in Madagascar in 1938, *métayage* was roundly condemned. An attempt was then (1939) made to put an end to the abuses, an earlier attempt at regulating the system in 1932 having shown little result. But even today some colonists manage to bind their tenants to a sort of serfdom [1], the never ending difficulties of obtaining sufficient labour creating the temptation to do so.

In Madagascar, to conclude, compulsory labour can be said to have occurred for both the authorities and private persons. And even though particular forms of it were abolished from time to time, the practice as such did not change much; as a former Governor General (1924-1930) M. Olivier put it [2]: "If appearances changed, at bottom everything remained the same". Yet the worst forms of excess undeniably occurred in the beginning period (if this is taken in the widest sense). However, where a shortage of labour has persisted, certain forms of compulsory labour have been imposed on the population even in recent times.

LITERATURE

Augagneur, Victor, Erreurs et brutalités coloniales, Paris, 1927.

Cherrier, R., La législation concernant le travail indigène à Madagascar, Paris, 1932.

Galliéni, J. S., Neuf ans à Madagascar, Paris, 1908.

Grandidier, Guillaume, Ethnographie de Madagascar, Paris, 1928. (Histoire physique, naturelle et politique de Madagascar, publ. par A. et G. Grandidier, vol. 4).

Isnard, Hildebert, La vie rurale à Madagascar (1er article). In: Les cahiers d'Outre-Mer, oct./déc. 1950, p. 301-318.

Jacquier, Léonce, La main-d'oeuvre locale à Madagascar, Paris, 1904.

---

[1] Isnard, op. cit., p. 315.

[2] M. Olivier, Six ans de politique sociale à Madagascar, p. 78.

Madagascar, Étude économique, publ. sous la direction de M. Loisy, 1914.
Mercier, René, Le travail obligatoire dans les colonies africaines, Vesoul, 1933.
A New Decree in Madagascar, In: Industrial and Labour Information, publ. by the International Labour Office, vol. 67, 1938, p. 287-290.
Olivier, Marcel, Six ans de politique sociale à Madagascar, Paris, 1931.
The recruiting of labour in colonies and in other territories with analogous labour conditions (International Labour Conference, 19th session, report IV), Geneva, 1935.
Roubaud, Louis, L'organisation du service civil obligatoire à Madagascar. In: L'Europe nouvelle, année 14, 1931, p. 850-854.
Sabatier, Fernand, Le problème de la main-d'oeuvre à Madagascar depuis la suppression de l'esclavage, Toulon, 1903.
You, André, Madagascar, Histoire, organisation, colonisation, Paris, 1905.
You, André, et George Gayet. Madagascar colonie française 1896-1930, Paris, 1931.

CHAPTER NINE

BELGIAN CONGO

The territory today known as the Belgian Congo [1] has only been a colony of Belgium since 1908. Before that time it was an independent State—the Congo Free State—which may be called the creation of one man, Leopold II of Belgium, and which was also as it were his private possession. He alone was responsible for this vast country, and, free from all parliamentary control, he could do with it what he pleased. In the first years he was also responsible for defraying all expenses.

The expressed intentions with regard to the natives in this new country were especially fine. At the conference in Berlin in 1884/85, when the Congo Free State was recognized as a sovereign State, it was declared that the Crown would watch over the preservation of the native tribes and care for the improvement of the conditions of their moral and material well-being, and help in suppressing slavery, and especially the slave trade; and protect and favour . . . . all religious, scientific or charitable institutions and enterprises created or organized for these ends or which aim at instructing the natives and bringing home to them the blessings of civilization [2]. And Leopold himself in 1876 voiced the inspired sentiment that "to open to civilization the only part of our globe where it has not yet penetrated, to pierce the shadows which envelop entire populations, is, I am bold to say, a crusade worthy of this century of progress" [3]. This was indeed fine rhetoric—made to look silly in practice, however.

In 1891, a few years after the creation of the new State with its humanitarian ideals, there began an era of terrorization of the African population that is one of the most horrifying chapters in the history of the meeting of white and dark skinned peoples. Between 1885 and

---

[1] The mandated territory of Ruanda-Urundi is left out of consideration in the following.

[2] An English translation of the Berlin Act is to be found in: Raymond Leslie Buell, The Native Problem in Africa, Vol. 2, p. 891-907.

The words cited here are from Art. 6.

[3] Recueil usuel de la législation, Etat Indépendant du Çongo, Vol. 1, p. 1. (Cited in Buell, op. cit., Vol. 2, p. 415).

1890, the new State had cost the king some 20 million Belgian francs [1]. Understandably enough, this worried him; and thus it was that he issued his momentous decree (in 1891) that: the State was the owner of all the products of the vacant lands. This decree was to be the horror of the population of the Congo for many years, and to it thousands were to succumb. True, it was modified—as a result of outspoken protest from Belgian businessmen who rallied against it—on October 30, 1892—to the extent that the State would not exercise its ownership to the products of *all* vacant land; but this made little difference. A large part of the territory was still to be assigned to private exploitation.

There was a subtle difference between these decrees of 1891 and 1892 and the one issued in 1885 which determined that *vacant lands* were the property of the State. Yet the difference was fundamental enough, for the natives were little affected by the first, whereas they most certainly were by the later ones. To secure the products of the land which the State had declared to be its property, a labour force was required; thus, the natives were of course needed: they had to collect the products—primarily rubber and ivory. To ensure that they would do so, a tax was levied on them, which had to be paid in rubber (or other products). And certain labour obligations were imposed for the benefit of the Europeans. Nor was this all. Since it was clear that the State could not exploit the products of this enormous territory without the help of private entrepreneurs, a solution was found in a form which was to be of decisive significance for the development of the Congo: Business corporations which obtained a concession from the State were given the exclusive right to exploit particular products (primarily rubber) from the area assigned to them—frequently of fantastic size. And the State further delegated to these concerns the right to collect the levied taxes, as well as the right to demand a supply of labour, and, if necessary, the right to use compulsion to get the natives to fulfil these obligations.

Until 1903 there existed absolutely no regulations to cover the nature and extent of the labour that could be demanded, or concerning the amount of compulsion which could be inflicted on the population—thus, in effect every official and agent of a company could do exactly as he pleased. The first decree to restrict such unbridled liberty was issued on November 18, 1903, and stipulated

[1] Buell, op. cit., Vol. 2, p. 425.

that the tax to be paid by the natives was to be equivalent of 40 hours of work per month—a ruling to which no one adhered and which brought no improvement in the situation. Hardly surprising considering that the decree was swiftly followed by a circular letter from the Governor General on February 29, 1904, notifying the District Commissioners that they were to ensure that not only the results thus far obtained were to be maintained, but that there was to be a continual rise in the income of the treasury.

The system here sketched in brief was in force until 1906 and led to unimaginable abuses, which became known mostly through British consular reports of the years between 1904 and 1908 and through a report made by a Committee of Enquiry set up by King Leopold in 1904 as a result of agitation from both inside and outside his country.

The compulsory labour which used the most people was that relating to rubber exploitation [1]. Every 14 days they would have to make a journey of one or two or more days to reach a location where there were sufficient untapped trees, and there they would have to stay several days under the most unfavourable circumstances. When they had collected enough rubber together they had to bring it to a Government or company depot, and on returning to their villages they would remain there only two or three days before setting out on the next collection. They felt that they were the slaves of the white overseers, and considered that they had been much better off in the time of the Arabs who had at least left them in peace occasionally, whereas the Europeans pursued them unceasingly [2]. Whole villages would sometimes be left deserted as countless Africans crossed the Congo River into French territory to escape the rubber collecting [3].

The supplying of food was another heavy burden [4], not made any easier by the great distances—sometimes 100 miles there and back which had to be covered to turn in the produce. Also the obligatory services —such as cutting wood for the steamboats on the Congo River services and its tributaries, building roads, and even clearing land for new

[1] The following is from the description in Rapport de la Commission d'enquête, p. 513.

[2] Correspondence respecting the Independent State of the Congo, 1907, p. 49, 65.

[3] For example, Correspondence and Report from H. M.'s Consul at Boma respecting the Administration of the Independent State of the Congo, 1904, pp. 28/29, 30.

[4] Rapport de la Commission d'enquête, p. 508 ff.

plantations—took much time; often so much that the population in the neighbourhood of a white post had to work ceaselessly. The worst burden the population had to bear, however, was the providing of bearers for the Europeans [1]. The first twelve years after 1891 were the worst for this. An unending caravan of heavily laden Negroes plied between Matadi and Leopoldville, and the route was marked with the countless skeletons of those who had not survived the journey. (The population was decimated within a few years by this work). When after twelve years the railway line between these two settlements was finished—we will not go into details at what expense in suffering for the natives—there came an end to this one horror but, for the one route which disappeared several new ones sprang up as the territory was opened further. And for years after this portage labour was so gruesome that for many in the tribes on which it was imposed it meant certain death, if only because there was hardly ever sufficient food taken with on the caravans.

It is quite obvious that all this work could not have been wrung from the natives without compulsion and violence. And these took many forms [2]. Armed Negroes were stationed in the villages to supervise the rubber collecting, and these behaved like complete despots. If, in spite of their efforts, the quantity of rubber (or other products) collected was too small, penalties were imposed. One of the most common of these was to take a number of the villagers prisoner; often women because it seemed the best way of exerting pressure on the men. But worse still, the places in which the people detained were locked up were often completely unsuited for the purpose. The mortality was extremely high since "prisoners" lacked all amenities and were further subjected to the ill-treatment of the guards. Those that survived could consider themselves lucky if they were released when their fellow-villagers had made up the quota, since it was also very common for "prisoners" to be taken off and never heard of again. They were put to work at remote posts or made to serve as soldiers of the *Force publique*. Another penal measure was to levy excessive fines. In this way a village could be reduced to complete poverty, and women and children would be sold for a chance of survival. However, all this was as nothing compared to the sufferings caused by the military expeditions to "remind"

[1] Id., pp. 511, 512.

[2] The following is taken from Correspondence and Report from H. M's Consul at Boma etc., 1904, pp. 31, 35, 39, 40, 46/7, 52/3.

the Negroes of "their delivery obligations", or to hunt down and return groups who had fled to escape the rubber levy. Whole villages were destroyed by such expeditions; men, women and children captured, mutilated, or killed off in great numbers.

In principle, the labour thus obtained from the Africans was to be paid, but it was left to the officials and agents to decide the amounts, and so they were in effect paid practically nothing, a mere fraction of the value of the products delivered [1]. It would happen that those on whom demands were made did not themselves have the product in question, and would have to buy it from some other village—and this was especially true of those areas in which poverty had become widespread; then it was quite common for them to have to pay double, sometimes even thirty times the price they could hope to obtain from the authorities for these products. Sometimes they would not be paid at all, or payment would be made in commodities which were practically or completely worthless to the recipients—for example, reels of cotton or buttons, when the people to whom these were given were not accustomed or wont to wear clothes at all. Frequently such commodities would be distributed in advance, which was taken to mean that the recipients were responsible for delivering a certain quantity of rubber etc. by the end of the month. Nor were the natives permitted any choice in the matter. If they objected the articles were simply left in front of their huts, and they were still responsible for seeing that the rubber was delivered, whether they accepted the articles or not. Finally, it was not unusual for a chief to demand for himself the payment made to the villagers, so that these received nothing at all for the work which they had done.

The native population was completely powerless in the face of all this injustice. In theory, there were institutions to which they could take their complaints, but, in the first place, these were few and far between, and, if the natives took the trouble to travel the tremendous distances involved, they would find that the functionaries responsible for their welfare were the very same who collected the taxes and planned the work-parties; and thus the very people who were the cause of most of the Negroes' woes! [2] For the most part the crimes committed by the Europeans and their African helpers went

---

[1] Rapport de la Commission d'enquête, p. 505. Also: Correspondence and Report etc., pp. 28, 31, 32, 38, 39, 48, 49, 59/60, 70.

[2] Rapport de la Commission d'enquête, p. 537, 539.

unpunished [1], whereas the prisons were overcrowded with natives who had landed there as a result of a simple order of the administrative authority. For most of these, their only crime had been that they had fallen short of their delivery quotas, or as labourers had committed some petty misdemeanour, such as insubordination [2].

We see therefore that the natives were entirely at the mercy of their rulers, and in a situation which differed from slavery in name only. One of the immediate results was a great decline in prosperity, something which was noticed by all travellers who had known the Congo before and after 1891. These were alarmed at the growing poverty of the people, and the state of decay of their villages. The natives no longer had time for their own work; huts were not kept in repair and new ones were not built because for all they knew a troop of soldiers might turn up at any moment and destroy them. The death rate during the period here under discussion was fantasticly high—partly as a result of sleeping sickness—which was on the increase—but also of the excessive work demanded and the victimization under the reign of terror [3].

But these were not the only forms of labour to which the natives were subjected in the period up to 1908. They had, for example, also to supply a certain number of men per year for the *force publique*, the military power used to ensure the delivery of rubber and other products for the whites, and from which the police services were drawn. In 1930 the *force publique* comprised 18,000 men [4] (of whom some were volunteers). Initially, the period of service was five years, but in 1900 it was lengthened to seven years. In the early years it was customary to use about half the natives conscripted for the military as labourers, especially on fortifications—although this was not provided for by law [5].

There were also natives serving as contract labourers for the State, and their labour could not be called free either [6]. In the first

[1] E.g., Corresp. and Report from H. M's Consul etc., pp. 44, 50, 54, 55, 68; Correspondence respecting the Independent State of the Congo, 1908, Cd 3880, p. 8.

[2] Rapport de la Commission d'enquête, p. 540/541.

[3] Rapport de la Commission d'enquête, p. 527/528. Correspondence and Report etc., pp. 22, 25, 27, 31, 36, 64, 70.

[4] Correspondence and Report etc., p. 30.

[5] We shall discuss later the so-called "second section" of the recruits officially meant for labour in 1906.

[6] All details from the following paragraph can be found in the Rapport de la Commission d'enquête, p. 533-536.

place they were subject to penal sanction, which made their labour in a sense compulsory, and was especially objectionable in view of the fact that the conditions of labour were atrocious. The pay was often insufficient to keep a family, housing was bad, and the abuses by the European superiors were not punished as they should have been because no one wished to question the authority of the whites. Moreover, the workers often did not know the conditions of their contracts, while the period of contract was from three to seven years —even children of seven or eight years of age were taken in service by District Commissioners for such a period! It is hardly surprising that only a few natives volunteered for service with the Government. Therefore compulsion had to be resorted to: the native chiefs were charged with delivering a given number of labourers, or a given number of labourers were demanded as a fine. Nor was it unusual for natives to be taken as labourers when they made their periodic visits to the post to bring provisions. When it was simply a question of finding sufficient people to man the posts, recruitment by force did not take on such large proportions. But recruit labour was needed and "found" for every big project which had to be undertaken. The Commission of Enquiry came to the conclusion that only a few of the 3,000 labourers working on the construction of the railway line near Stanleyville had been contracted in a manner consistent with the regulations; and the Commission consoled itself with the thought that the Negro's fatalism helped him to adapt himself to the circumstances.

However, news from the obscure Congo Free State began to leak out to the rest of the world, especially England, and people were shocked to the core. First official protest came from England and took the form of a resolution passed in the House of Commons in 1903, and the formation of the Congo Reform Association in 1904. Other countries also made known their protest, and the question was debated in almost all the Parliaments of the world. The governing body of the Congo Free State retaliated by denying that things were not as they should be. As was said in the Bulletin officiel de l'Etat Indépendent du Congo [1], the natives were free to seek by work the remuneration which contributed to the increase of their well-being. Although it was, so the text went on, naturally one of the aims of the State to regenerate the natives by impressing them with the high

[1] Cited in Correspondence and Report from H. M's Consul at Boma etc., p. 20.

idea of the necessity of work. True, tax was being levied on the Negro; but no one could object to that, because through it the natives carried their share of the public burden as a return for the protection afforded them by the State. Moreover, their share was very light. The Negroes were in fact much better off than before the coming of the whites [1].

The true state of affairs was, however, incontrovertibly given in other documents such as the Report of the British Consul in Boma, Roger Casement. And critics were to be found in Belgium itself. Eventually King Leopold could not do otherwise than name a Commission of Enquiry (1904)—which submitted its report on October 31, 1905; the report from which some of the above material is taken.

As a result of the findings of the Commission a period of reform was indeed inaugurated, which, after further agitation both inside and outside the country, was finally consummated in the annexation of the Congo by Belgium in 1908. This marked the beginning of a new era. The first radical change came in 1910 when an end was made of the State monopoly. From henceforth any European could, on payment of a certain sum, obtain a license to collect wild products, and natives could do so without license, even if only on the unconceded lands. The second great reform came a short time afterward when it was decreed that the labour tax was to be replaced by a money tax. And with these two measures the former system of exploitation of the Congo Free State came to an end. The natives were no longer obliged to labour for a State playing the part of a merchant.

But of course this did not mean that compulsory labour was to be no more. Labour was still required for all forms of exploitation of the country, and therefore the Negroes were still obliged to work, even if compelled to do so by other means.

In the first place, the natives had now to work to secure the money to be able to pay taxes [2]. The principal tax was a head tax; initially from 5 to 12 Belgian francs per head of the male population—the amount varying in relation to local circumstances—and gradually raised. In 1926, for instance, the maximum was set at 50 francs.

---

[1] Cited in same source, p. 19/20.

[2] L. Guebels, Relation complète des travaux de la Commission Permanente pour la Protection des Indigènes, p. 82, 323, 324. Buell, op. cit., Vol. 2, pp. 495, 496.

Relatively speaking, this tax was high, as is illustrated by the fact that in 1912 it amounted to four times the tax paid by the natives of South Africa [1]. The obligation to pay began at the age of 14; and failure to pay meant imprisonment for a maximum of two months during which forced labour on public works could be imposed. This tax had the desired result. To get the necessary money the natives in the first period did the same work as they had done before: primarily, collecting rubber and other forest products, which they sold to the traders now making their appearance in the district.

Besides this indirect compulsion the natives were also subject to a direct obligation to labour. In accordance with a decree of May 2, 1910—which was later replaced by a decree of December 5, 1933—the natives could be called up for various activities of local importance and in emergencies, such as at times of epidemic or famine [2]. This labour was to be partially paid, partially unpaid [3]; and, as of 1918, it was decreed that anyone failing to respond to such a call-up would be liable to imprisonment for a maximum of seven days with hard labour and/or a fine of 200 francs (later reduced to 100 francs). The maximum period which could be imposed for this labour was, except in unusual circumstances, 60 days a year, or 5 days a month; and only able-bodied male were eligible—except for work involved in keeping the village clean and clearing the grass, for which work women could be called up.

The period of 60 days a year was, however, often prolonged. The Commission Permanente pour la Protection des Indigènes reported in 1923 that sometimes 90 and sometimes 104 days were demanded, and added that as a result there was a genuine impoverishment in food crops necessary to village subsistence [4]. In 1925/1926 natives were obliged to work for four months consecutively—October to February—on the construction of a 60 kilometre road near the capital of the Equator Province, constructed only for the pleasure of Europeans who wish to go for an automobile ride in the evenings [5]. Women as well as men were compelled to work, with the

---

[1] Corresp. respecting the affairs of the Congo, 1913, p. 108.

[2] Forced Labour, Report and Draft Questionnaire, Geneva 1929, pp. 139/40, 26/27.

[3] By decree of December 29, 1955, it is stipulated that the labour in the public cause has to be paid in every case. See: Bulletin Officiel du Congo Belge, 48me année, nr. 24 bis, 31 Déc. 1955, p. 1752-1756.

[4] Guebels, op. cit., p. 245.

[5] Buell, op. cit., Vol. 2, p. 499/500.

result that the Christian natives with only one wife complained that they had no one to work their plots for them. More often than not it was women who were used for work relating to the maintenance of roads and bridges [1]. In 1928 the Commission pour la Protection des Indigènes suggested the desirability of completely forbidding the use of women, old men, and children for road construction and maintenance [2]. But in 1947 the Commission still felt compelled to draw attention to the fact that young mothers and pregnant women were being made to work on the road projects. These projects were often far from home, and the work which had to be done was not exactly light [3]. And then, all too frequently the chiefs pocketed the pay of the labour gangs, little to none of it reaching its destination [4].

This labour on public projects (of "local importance") and in times of emergency was not the only obligatory labour the natives were subject to. A decree of December 26, 1922 (concerning civil requisitions) stated that able-bodied adult males could also be called up to serve as guides, porters or paddlers for public officials, or, in certain cases, other persons [5]. Conscripting for this work could only be done in cases of real urgency, and the duration of the work could only be a maximum of 25 days a year. Furthermore, the work had to be paid.

Evidently the diverse obligations have been felt as a heavier and heavier burden by the population, and this has been one of the main reasons for the mass migration to the cities in the Congo, a trend which has reached alarming proportions in recent years [6]. The villagers were liable to be called up for conscription at any time for some public project or other, and thereby they were prevented from properly pursueing their regular activities as farmers, fishermen and so on. As a result they were less prosperous than they might have been, and, especially, they felt repressed, *taillable et corvéable à merci*, and consequently disillusioned [7].

---

[1] E.g., Correspondence respecting the affairs of the Congo, 1913, p. 95, 100.
[2] Guebels, op. cit., p. 378.
[3] Id., p. 640.
[4] Id., p. 378. Also, e.g., Correspondence respecting the affairs etc., 1913, p. 100.
[5] Forced labour, Report and Draft Questionnaire, Geneva 1929, p. 25.
[6] Rapport de la Mission Sénatoriale au Congo etc., p. 14; L. Guebels, Aperçu rétrospectif des travaux de la Commission Permanente pour la Protection des Indigènes . . . 1949, pp. 103, 106.
[7] Guebels, Aperçu rétrospectif etc., pp. 106, 121.

Another form of compulsory labour was to be found in the military service. In 1906 it was determined that a section of the *force publique*[1] could be used for labour on public works. The total duration of such work—which could be broken up into several shorter periods—was not to be in excess of 5 years. Later, in 1910 this was brought down to 3 years. This system of labour was particularly hated by the population[2]. Soldiers had to be sent out to round up natives in the forests, and those caught were shackled as criminals and brought to their destination. This means of providing a supply of labour to meet the needs of the State would appear to have been abandoned fairly soon, however. And by 1919 the system was abrogated completely by a decree which provided for the reorganisation of the *force publique* and made no reference to the existence of a body of soldiers allocated for labour on public works. The military service as such (which strictly speaking falls outside the scope of this book) kept its old term of seven years—and remained a great plague for the population[3]. Partly because of the meagre wages there were very few volunteers; and conscription was very unsatisfactorily arranged. The native chiefs were charged with the delivery of a certain number of men, and they normally chose either poor villagers, slaves or people against whom they had a grudge. If a chief could or would not cooperate it was still worse, for in that case the European administrator would do the recruiting himself, and this turned out to be more like a manhunt, through which the whole village was thrown into panic, the population to rebellion, and the general consequence was hatred and distrust of the adminstration. Once recruited, the soldiers were usually sent far from their own section of the country—which is understandable in view of the fact that they frequently had to take part in police actions against the native population, and they could hardly be expected to be severe against their own tribesmen. However, many did not take well to the transfer. In the instruction camps to which the recruits were first sent for training, the mortality was unusually high: In 1924 the death rate was 106.4 per thousand in the Congo-Kasai, and 153.6 per thousand in the Katanga[4].

---

[1] See page 124.
[2] Correspondence respecting the Independent State of the Congo, 1907, pp. 60, 63.
[3] Buell, op. cit., Vol. 2, p. 496-498. Guebels, op. cit., p. 177/178.
[4] Buell, op. cit., Vol. 2, p. 571.

The indirect compulsion to work by means of taxes, and the imposed obligatory labour for public purposes was still not the end of the story for the natives. Whenever circumstances made it desirable a new form of compulsion was used—whether or not in official guise.

In 1917, the so-called obligatory undertakings were set up—a system which was not, or at least not in such proportions, used anywhere else as in the Belgian Congo. In accordance with an ordinance of the 20th February of that year [1] natives could be obligated to cultivate certain alimentary and/or industrial plants—which were, in practice, primarily (but far from exclusively) rice and cotton.

Actually one can trace back this system to the days of the Free State when the Negroes were ordered to provide the posts settled by the Europeans with foodstuffs, and, if the normal native cultivation proved inadequate with the gradual expansion of the posts, the natives in the neighbourhood could further be ordered to expand the amount of land they already had under cultivation. The obligatory cultivation in the form instituted in 1917 was first thought of in the years after 1910 [2]. As already stated, in that year an important step was taken toward putting an end to the Free State system, whereby the natives were compelled to deliver rubber and other forest products for the benefit of the State (or concession companies). The immediate result of this was an appreciable drop in the income of the colony. And in the same year, 1910, the price of rubber collapsed on the world market. All this led to speculation as to how best the colonial treasury could be replenished. Thoughts first went to the development of native agriculture through which, among other things, the native taxes could be increased. Before anything was done about it a new element stimulated the development; namely, the outbreak of World War I. Suddenly rice and other food crops were needed in great quantity to provide the troups which had to be sent to the Eastern border of the Congo, and at the same time there was a great demand for cotton for the manufacture of munitions. This led to the ordinance of February, 1917, whereby obligatory cultivation

---

[1] Later the compulsory plantations were regulated by the decree of December 5, 1933.

[2] The principal sources of information in what follows are: E. Leplae, Histoire et développement des cultures obligatoires de coton et de riz au Congo Belge de 1917 à 1933, in Congo 1933 I, p. 645-753; and id., Méthode suivie pour le développement de l'agriculture au Congo Belge, in Congo 1930 II, p. 386-418. Leplae was the originator of the system of obligatory cultivation.

could be imposed on the native population. When the war came to an end the administration did not feel much for abolishing the system, which had yielded such fine results. Besides, there now existed another factor making it desirable to maintain the system. In the years after the war a start was made to the industrialization of the Congo, and there were especially big developments in mining. As a result, new centres were established, sometimes in areas where there was as yet almost no agriculture, and this naturally led to another increase in the demand for foodstuffs. Also, these years brought about a great revival in the economic life of Europe and America, which increased the demand for Congolese raw materials. Needless to say, under these circumstances obligatory cultivation was not abolished. On the contrary, everything possible was done to expand native agriculture, and there were indeed results. Rice production rose from 15,000 tons in 1918 to 71,240 tons in 1928 (to drop somewhat after that) and the area cultivated with cotton increased in extent from 112 HA in 1917 to 67,068 HA in 1931.

Concerning the time to be spent on all this agricultural development, the ruling on obligatory cultivation was appendixed to the articles in the decree of May 2, 1910 regulating obligatory labour in the public interest (on roads, bridges etc.) [1], and the obligatory cultivation therefore went coupled to the obligatory labour—both together not to take more than 60 days a year of the native's time. However, it is quite obviously difficult—according to E. Leplae who planned the scheme—to apply such a rule to agricultural work. The same penalties applied here as had for the obligatory labour on public projects; i.e., a maximum of seven days hard labour and/or a fine not exceeding 200 francs [2]. Leplae writes [3] that these penalties were not often applied, but Lord Hailey (An African Survey, 1st. ed. 1938, 2nd. ed. 1945) states to the contrary that "in recent years there have been many convictions in some districts for non-compliance with the obligation to grow cotton" [4]. And a Commission from the Belgian Senate, which in 1947 reported that 10 per cent of the male population were convicted to a prison sentence annually,

---

[1] See page 127.

[2] Forced Labour, Report and Draft Questionnaire, 1929, p. 26/7. The fine was later reduced to 100 francs. See: Codes et Lois du Congo Belge . . . , 6th. ed. des Codes Louwers, Bruxelles etc., 1948, p. 779.

[3] Leplae, Histoire etc., p. 730/1.

[4] P. 634.

cited as the principal offences leading to this high percentage, the breaches of the regulations governing cotton planting [1].

In theory, the obligatory cultivation was instituted for the exclusive benefit of the native population, and the educative element was highly praised, especially by Belgians. This praise was to a certain extent justified, for once contact has been established between primitive peoples and Western civilization, one of the best solutions is to train the natives to farm crops for export; in this way they can share the advantages of the new way of living while retaining as close a contact as possible with their former way of life. But this must not lead us to lose sight of the fact that obligatory cultivation was largely instituted and developed for the white population and not so much for the benefit of the natives; and that there were many questionable aspects to the way in which it was implemented. The *Commission pour la Protection des Indigènes* repeatedly criticised the way in which the system was handled in practice. In 1919, it objected that the culture obligation was too heavy, so heavy that it seriously disrupted the economic life of the Africans [2]. And the prices the natives received for their produce, especially foodstuffs, were often very low [3]. The Commission reported in 1938 [4], that the natives had to sell their rice at a five day's walking distance from where it was grown, and that the price they received for it was less than what they would have earned for carrying such a load for someone else. Finally, it should be noted here that it was not exactly an encouragement to the natives that the tax—which constituted a quarter or a third of their production—was continually raised as the area under cultivation expanded [5].

Where conditions were good, obligatory cultivation yielded good results, also in as far as the natives developed a growing interest in agriculture on a large scale—so that one can assume that they would have continued with it even should the obligation be removed [6]. In general, however, compulsion and continuous control remained absolutely indispensible if the progress of cultivation was to be

---

[1] Rapport de la Mission Sénatoriale au Congo et dans les territoires sous tutelle belge, 1947, p. 68.

[2] Guebels, op. cit., p. 217/220.

[3] Buell, op. cit., Vol. 2, p. 500.

[4] Guebels, op. cit., p. 557.

[5] Leplae, Histoire etc., p. 727.

[6] Lord Hailey, An African Survey, 2nd ed., 1945, p. 634.

ensured [1]. The compulsion in fact has been retained up to the present day—and is still felt as a burden by the majority of the population.

Great numbers of labourers were required when the expansion of the railway network was undertaken on a large scale, and particularly for the widening of the Kinshasa-Matadi line. To ensure a labour force, the Government took over the recruiting. In this way labourers were obtained who were free in name, although in reality it would have been difficult to find any voluntary element in their labour. In 1922 a Labour Bureau was established and from it recruiters were sent to the various provinces to assist the district commissioners in their work of assembling the number of men stipulated by the governors of the provinces. Before 1925, however, it would appear that many officials remained aloof, preferring to leave the work primarily to the recruiters; but in this way, the required quotas were not met. Then followed an instruction from the Governor General to the Governor of the Equator Province that "the recruiting of this labour should be the first duty of the administration and that no effort should be spared in obtaining men". The subsequent course of events can easily be imagined [2]. Resistance to the "persuasion" of the officials was hardly possible, and the Negroes were transported, sometimes over a distance of more than a thousand miles, to the place where they were to work. The conditions under which they had to travel were described as "simply infernal". Wages were not paid on the journeys which sometimes took months, and the provision of food was such that they would arrive at their destination literally famished. They rarely knew ahead of time that such distances were involved. And sometimes they were deliberately deceived in this respect. Some areas were robbed of all their young men in this way. That the care of the men was good as a rule once they arrived at their destination can not make up for the abuses during recruitment.

The abuses were so extreme, that the Minister of Colonies submitted a proposed decree in 1926 for a regular, legal conscription of labourers, and he included the recommendation that not more than 5% of the adult males could be recruited at any one time for this work. The Colonial Council agreed, also feeling that compulsion under legal control would be better than the illegal unsupervised conscription which was taking place on such a large scale. The Belgian

[1] Leplae, Méthode etc., pp. 397, 408; Leplae, Histoire etc., pp. 659, 704.
[2] Buell, op. cit., Vol. 2, p. 504-506.

Cabinet, however, rejected the decree, being, in principle, against the use of compulsion in this field. With the result that the unofficial conscription continued just so long as the railway was still being constructed.

Use was also made of unofficial compulsion for the supply of labour to private citizens when an increasing labour shortage was experienced by private entrepreneurs in the years following after World War I. The labour shortage was particularly acute in the developing mining industry (copper mines in the Katanga, diamond mines in the Kasai, and the Kilo-Moto gold mines). The following figures, showing the number of native labourers in the service of European enterprises from 1916 to 1930 (when the world depression slowed things down considerably), illustrate the continual and rapid growth of activities [1].

1916	45702
1922	157000
1924	278104
1930	409665

To obtain the required labour, recruitment was (to a large extent) put in hands of the *Bourses du Travail*, established by a number of combined enterprises. The territory was divided into zones, each of which was assigned to a European recruiting agent with a native helper. Unfortunately these agents were paid in proportion to the number of "boys" they supplied, which of course led to scandalous practices. Later it was said that only fixed salaries would be paid, but even in 1938 the Commission Permanente pour la protection des Indigènes was still urging the abolition of the commissions paid to agents and/or native chiefs [2]. However, the strong element of compulsion in recruitment was above all due to the attitude of the Government. For many years the Government gave its support—to a greater or less extent, but always perceptibly—to the recruiting, and to this end exerted pressure on the native population [3]. It must be borne in mind that the Congo Government had a direct interest in the growth of industry. In 1926, it received 30 million francs from its "portfolio" representing the Government's share in companies, most of which

[1] The recruiting of labour in colonies and in other territories with analogous labour conditions, Geneva, 1935, p. 20.

[2] Guebels, Relation complète etc., p. 613.

[3] The following is principally taken from Buell, op. cit., Vol. 2, pp. 538-543.

operated in the Congo, and in addition, 2,660,000 francs from the Kilo-Moto mines, a Government enterprise [1]. A strictly unprejudiced attitude was hardly to be expected under such circumstances.

In 1922 the Governor General published a circular letter in which it was, among other things, stated: "It is a mistake to believe ..... that once taxes are paid and other legal obligations met, the native may remain inactive. Under no circumstances may magistrates or officials express this opinion. In every case I should consider this to be a lack of discipline violating the recommendations of the Government and our most positive duties toward our black subjects". The natives had to be made to work through the moral authority of the magistrate and administrator, persuasion, encouragement, and favours. And if that did not help marks of displeasure were to be imposed. Later in the same year the Governor General expressed himself even more forcibly. Each Government official, so he stated, must be penetrated with the idea that his reason for existence was to favour and develop the occupation and that this duty consisted in supporting every enterprise. "You will put yourself to work to aid agriculture, commerce and industry. You will be apostles of labour, which you will preach constantly everywhere, not of an accidental labour which is content with paying taxes, but a persevering labour, which is the basis of all prosperity, development and civilization". And some time later he expressed it even more severely: Anyone who told the native that his obligation to work stopped when he had enough money to pay his taxes, was "an enemy to the colony". The native chiefs were to cooperate with the system. If they did not make enough effort to secure labourers the administration could reduce their status of a "very good" to that of a "good" or "mediocre" chief, which also meant a reduction in their salaries. And if this had no result they could be removed.

The administration officials certainly discharged their duties to the letter. They exerted pressure on the chiefs to help the recruiting agents or joined them in "encouraging" the population. Some of the results of this were described in a letter from a local official to a district commissioner (September 1925) as follows: The population was profoundly discontented, and began even to wish they were still under the old Arab regime. In those days people were carried off as slaves, but what the recruiters did was worse. The

[1] Buell, op. cit., Vol. 2, p. 533.

villages emptied at the approach of a Government official. Often the recruits did not know for what sort of work they would be used or where they were going. Sometimes they were deliberately given false information. There were legal provisions to which the recruiters were supposed to adhere, on pain of penal servitude for a maximum of six months (1922), but this did not always have the intended effect, because, among other things, in the Katanga the judicial officer responsible for the enforcement of the provisions was also for a long time the manager of the Bourse du Travail. The recruited Africans were sometimes sent very far from home, and the mortality en route to places of work was very high [1]. But even in the industries and enterprises where they had to work the mortality figures were excessively high, despite the fact that the treatment of labour in the Belgian Congo, once actively employed, was as good as in any other part of Africa. The high death-rate among the Negroes was probably the result of their having been recruited forcibly, and brought to the industries under compulsion. Natives from Rhodesia who worked in these same mines, but in whose recruitment no force had been used, showed a considerably lower mortality figure [2]. The recruitment was actually so hated that to escape it great numbers of Congo Negroes migrated en masse to Ruanda and Uganda [3].

Disturbed by these developments, the Belgian Government in 1924 named a Commission to study the problem of labour supply in the Belgian Congo. When the attempts at improvement, following the indications of this report, bore too little result, two other commissions followed, in 1928 and 1930. It is gratifying to be able to point out with respect to this question that in no other colony in Africa in those years was so serious an attempt made to solve the problem of native labour. In general, it can actually be said that the interest in colonial questions was greater in Belgium than in any other country [4]. It was difficult to arrive at a satisfactory solution in practice, however. As soon as the Government ordered the administrative officials to stop the direct recruiting of labour for private employers (December, 1925) such strong protests were made from

[1] Hailey, op. cit., p. 645.
[2] Buell, op. cit., Vol. 2, pp. 536, 570. Later, after 1930, the mortality figures dropped sharply. See, e.g., Hailey, op. cit., p. 681.
[3] Buell, op. cit., Vol. 2, p. 543; Hailey, op. cit., p. 648.
[4] Buell, op. cit., Vol. 2, pp. 550, 457.

interested and influential industrial quarters that the instructions were so diluted as to be rendered useless [1].

Thus the Committee of 1928 came to the conclusion that only subordinate officials should assist directly in recruitment. The higher officials should, in general, limit their activities to propaganda of a general nature. The Commission of 1930 went further. This felt it to be imperative that the role of all officials should be limited to an energetic and continuous propaganda. It should only be permissible to temporarily intervene in favour of satisfactory undertakings when dealing with backward tribes, and then only in pursuance of a definite ordinance by a Governor of a province.

Then came the economic depression of the thirties, and the repercussions were severely felt in the Congo—which suddenly brought about a complete change in the situation. The demand for labour was considerably reduced. In the economically important province of Katanga, the number of African wage-earners dropped by 50% between 1929 and 1933, while the percentage for the industrial region of upper Katanga was even as much as 70%. In such circumstances it was not difficult to proscribe (as was done in 1932 in instructions from the Minister of Colonies to the Governor General) that, except for general propaganda, any intervention by the Administration in recruiting was to be forbidden, and that the practice by which recruiters in the service of undertakings were accompanied on their recruiting journeys by an officer of the Administration could no longer be tolerated.

When the crisis was over, the views of the Government seemed to have changed again somewhat. In his instructions of October 15, 1934, the Minister of Colonies stated that the official who forcefully persuades the native to work for an employer who provides acceptable working conditions etc. is accomplishing one of the duties of his post [2]. Nevertheless there soon came further change—because the situation changed. From about 1940 there began literally an exodus from the rural areas toward the industrial centres. Then the problem was no longer one of, as Davidson says [3]: "to find means wherewith to bully and bamboozle Africans into employment; it was to house and feed these huge new urban populations, and to bring succour to a

[1] Id., p. 550/551.
[2] Hailey, op. cit., p. 650.
[3] Basil Davidson, The African Awakening, London, 1955, p. 99.

deserted countryside". In such circumstances it is no wonder that in the Report of the Ad-hoc Committee on Forced Labour of 1953 [1] the conclusion was come to that there was no longer any forced recruitment in the Belgian Congo. For a long time, however, it had survived at least to some extent, as witnessed by Lord Hailey who says in his "An African Survey" published in 1938 that "there appears to be some evidence of the continuance, despite official condemnation, of the system which permits administrative officers to interest themselves in recruiting for private employers" [2].

The labourers in the service of European enterprises were, and are, subject to penal sanction, an institution which in itself renders the labour to some extent involuntary; but begins to take on a very abusive character if it concerns labourers who signed their contracts to a large extent unwillingly. The question of penal sanction is regulated in the decree of March 16, 1922 (last modified on June 30, 1954) which to a great extent advocates the protection and control of native labour in the Belgian Congo. The penalty for breach of contract or desertion was originally [3] a fine of 50 francs and/or two months hard labour, which period could be extended to three months if the labourers had received advances from his employer and if he was a porter. This penalty is much less severe by the way than the equivalent sanction in British East Africa. There is further a penalty (originally a fine or a fortnight's hard labour) for a serious offence or repeated offences against labour discipline. The number of natives convicted for failing to respect their contracts of employment in 1949 was 34,066 [4]. And the Commission chosen from the Belgian Senate which in 1947 published its report on the Congo, itself came to the conclusion that 10% of the male population had been convicted to penal labour, among which by far the most frequent offences were breaches of the regulations governing cotton planting and breaches of labour contracts [5].

The International Labour Convention No. 65 (adopted in 1939), and in which (Art. One and Two) it is stipulated that penal sanction

---

[1] P. 27.

[2] Hailey, op. cit., 2nd. ed., 1945, p. 698.

[3] According to the decree of June 30, 1954, the punishment is one month hard labour and/or a fine of 500 francs; see: Bulletin officiel du Congo belge, 1954 I, p. 1462.

[4] Report of the Ad hoc Committee on Forced Labour, Geneva, 1953, p. 191.

[5] Rapport de la Mission Sénatoriale au Congo etc., 1947, p. 68.

for breach of contract should be abolished as soon as possible, has not yet been ratified by Belgium (1958).

In conclusion, we have seen that compulsory labour has also been introduced in the Belgian Congo wherever and whenever this seemed necessary or desirable. And even today it has not entirely disappeared from the picture, although many important changes have been made in recent years, whereby the application of compulsory labour has been minimized.

LITERATURE

Bourne, H. R. Fox, Civilisation in Congoland, a story of international wrong-doing, London, 1903.

Bruhat, Jean, Léopold II. In: Les politiques d'expansion impérialiste, Paris 1949 (Colonies et empires, sér. 1, t. 5), p. 73-122.

Buell, Raymond Leslie, The Native Problem in Africa, New York, 1928, Vol. 2, section 13: The Belgian Congo.

Cattier, F., Étude sur la situation de l'État Indépendant du Congo, 2me éd., Bruxelles-Paris, 1906.

Codes et lois du Congo Belge . .. 6me éd. des codes Louwers . . . Bruxelles etc., 1948.

Correspondence and report from His Majesty's consul at Boma respecting the administration of the Independent State of the Congo, London, 1904, (Africa no. 1, 1904, Cd. 1933).

Correspondence respecting the Independent State of the Congo, London, 1907, (Africa no. 1, 1907, Cd. 3450).

Correspondence respecting the affairs of the Congo, London, 1911, (Africa no. 2, 1911, Cd. 5860).

Correspondence respecting the affairs of the Congo, London, 1913, (Africa no. 1, 1913, Cd. 6606).

Davidson, Basil, The African Awakening, London, 1955.

Forced Labour, Report and draft questionnaire, Geneva, 1929, (International Labour Conference), p. 23-28, 139-140, 190-193.

Further correspondence respecting the Independent State of the Congo, London, 1908, (Africa no. 1, 1908, Cd. 3880).

Further correspondence respecting the Independent State of the Congo, London, 1908, (Africa no. 2, 1908, Cd. 4079).

Further correspondence respecting the affairs of the Congo, London, 1913, (Africa no. 3, 1913, Cd. 6802).

Guebels, L., Aperçu rétrospectif des travaux de la Commission Permanente pour la Protection des Indigènes d'après les rapports des sessions, Edité par le Centre-d'Etude des Problèmes Sociaux Indigènes, C.E.P.S.I., Elisabethville, 1949.

Guebels, L., Relation complète des travaux de la Commission Permanente pour la Protection des Indigènes. In: Bulletin trimestriel du Centre d'Etude des Problèmes Sociaux Indigènes, C.E.P.S.I., nr. 20-23, Elisabethville, 1953.

Hailey, Lord, An African Survey, a study of problems arising in Africa South of the Sahara, 2nd ed., London etc., 1945.

Halewyck, Michel, La charte coloniale, commentaire de la loi du 18 octobre 1908 sur le Gouvernement du Congo Belge, Bruxelles, 1910-1919, 4 vols.

Heyse, Th., Le régime du travail au Congo Belge, 2me éd., Bruxelles, 1924.

Labour problems in the Belgian Congo. In: International Labour Review, vol. 40, 1939 II, p. 364-374.

Leplae, Edm., Histoire et développement des cultures obligatoires de coton et de riz au Congo belge de 1917 à 1933. In: Congo, revue générale de la colonie belge, 1933 I, p. 645-753.

Leplae, Edm., Méthode suivie pour le développement de l'agriculture au Congo Belge. In: Congo, revue générale de la colonie belge, 1930 II, p. 386-418.

Leplae, Edm., Résultats obtenus au Congo belge par les cultures obligatoires alimentaires et industrielles. In: Zaïre, revue congolaise, 1947, p. 115-139.

Mille, Pierre, Le Congo léopoldien, Paris, 1905 (Cahiers de la Quinzaine, sixième cahier de la septième série).

Mille, Pierre, et Félicien Challaye, Les deux Congo devant la Belgique et devant la France, Paris, 1906, (Cahiers de la Quinzaine, 7me série, no. 16).

Morel, E. D., Great Britain and the Congo, the pillage of the Congo basin, London, 1909.

Morel, E. D., King Leopold's rule in Africa, London, 1904.

Morel, E. D., The story of the "Crown domain". In: The nineteenth century and after, vol. 69, Jan.-June 1911, p. 674-691.

Rapport de la Commission d'enquête. In: Recueil usuel de la législation etc., (État Indépendant du Congo), par O. Louwers et G. Touchard, t. 5, 1904-1906, Bruxelles, 1909, p. 495-542.

Rapport de la Commission pour l'étude du problème de la main-d'oeuvre au Congo belge. In: Congo, revue générale de la colonie belge, 1925 I, p. 693-714, 1925 II, p. 1-12.

Rapport de la Mission Sénatoriale au Congo et dans les territoires sous tutelle belge, Bruxelles, 1947.

The recruiting of labour in colonies and in other territories with analogous labour conditions, Geneva, 1935, (International Labour Conference, 19th session, Geneva 1935, Report IV, first discussion).

Report of the Ad hoc committee on forced labour, Geneva, 1953 (United Na tions—International Labour Office).

Twain, Mark, King Leopold's soliloquy, a defence of his Congo rule, London 1907.

Vandeputte, R., Toestanden en misstanden in Kongo, Antwerpen etc., 1950, (Katholieke Vlaamse hogeschooluitbreiding, jg. 44, nr. 1).

Vandervelde, Emile, La Belgique et le Congo, le passé, le présent, l'avenir, Paris, 1911.

Vermeersch, Arthur, La question congolaise, Bruxelles, 1906.

Waltz, Heinrich, Das Konzessionswesen im Belgischen Kongo, Hrsg. von der Kolonialabteilung der Zivilverwaltung in Belgien, Jena, 1917, 2 vols.

CHAPTER TEN

KENYA

In Kenya—formerly known as the British East Africa Protectorate—colonization by Europeans only really commenced on any marked scale in about 1903. From 1904 to 1914 the European population rose from 886 to 5,438, and stood at 17,997 in 1935 [1]. The main activities of the colonists have been in the field of agriculture, the leading crops being coffee, corn, maize and sisal. The main European settlements are situated on the upper plateaus because the climate is most favourable for whites here. In spite of the favourable climate, however, the colonists have never shown themselves prepared to do manual work themselves. The early colonists were not accustomed to it at home either, since those with less than £ 5,000 capital were advised against immigrating and people with such a sum of money at their disposal do not generally come from circles accustomed to working with their hands [2]. The colonists were therefore dependent on African labour but, just as in the other colonies, the natives showed little inclination to work for foreigners. They could provide for their simple needs and be self-sufficient with very little labour. Moreover, the export market for native agriculture developed favourable in the course of years, and as a result one can hardly speak of any growing enthusiasm to work for Europeans, notwithstanding the growing needs of the natives through years of contact with Western culture. Therefore it was necessary for the colonists, if they wished to succeed, to find ways and means of compelling the natives to work for them. But public opinion in England flatly refused to tolerate the imposition of undisguised compulsory labour for private persons, and it was for this reason that other measures were resorted to.

The most important of these has been "persuasion", i.e., the exertion of a continuous moral pressure, mainly *via* the native chiefs, on the native population to go to work for the colonists. The Africans were mostly not in a position to tell the difference between an "in-

---

[1] Max Salvadori, La colonisation européenne au Kenya, 1938, p. 63, 106.

[2] Raymond Leslie Buell, The Native Problem in Africa, 1928, Vol. 1, p. 329.

citement" and an order when given by the governing officials, and the chiefs were, as a rule, prepared to cooperate—since their salaries depended largely on the impression they made on their white superiors. This measure of "persuasion" can therefore be seen to have given fairly good results; in fact, in Kenya more Africans in proportion to their population were got to work for the colonists than in any other central African territory [1].

Already in the first years the colonists put pressure on the Government to gain its assistance in the recruitment of labour, but the question only really became a major issue in 1907 and 1908. As the Government had not as yet expressed itself clearly for or against the measure of "persuasion", officials followed their own ideas. Many sided with the colonists and used their influence over the native chiefs to persuade these to call up their subjects for work. But quite a few officials had ideas of their own and refused to comply with the colonists' requests. Dissatisfaction among the colonists was all the more aggravated when the Secretary for Native Affairs visited the Kikuyu reserves, and declared to the natives at several gatherings that they were not obliged to work for the Europeans, and that they need only do so when they themselves felt like it. A counter-action on the part of the colonists led to the declaration by the Governor that officials would assist planters in as far as they could with their labour requirement problems, on provision that they treated their labourers in accordance with the prescribed standards; i.e., provided them with the stipulated quantity of food, certain other necessities, medical attention if necessary, and decent huts [2]. Although this provoked another storm of dissatisfaction—colonists claiming that the fulfilment of these conditions would make the labour far too expensive [3]—a period of comparative peace followed. Actually by this time the most serious labour crisis was already a thing of the past.

Another crisis arose in 1919, however, when there was a sudden influx of settlers—mainly ex-servicemen on the financial backing of the Government—and when many labourers were required for the construction of a railroad. Steps were taken to deal with this

[1] Buell, op. cit., p. 412.

[2] Correspondence relating to affairs in the East Africa Protectorate, 1908, Cd. 4122, p. 28/29.

[3] Correspondence etc., in various places.

situation in a Kenya Government publication, "Labour Circular No. 1", which *inter alia* determined the following [1]:

a) Governing officials were to exert all influence permitted by law to get the male population to work for Europeans.
b) Where the agricultural estates were situated close to an African settlement, women and children were to be encouraged to perform work for which they were suited.
c) Native chiefs were to cooperate as best they could. They were to be continually reminded that it was their duty to advise all the young men under them who had no work to go to work on the estates.
d) District Commissioners had to make a list of the names of chiefs not cooperating properly, and report on this matter to the Governor from time to time.

To end with, other measures were threatened if "persuasion" did not produce adequate results.

These regulations aroused much indignation in England, not because they contained anything new—although perhaps less harshly worded, similar regulations had been issued by Governors from time to time, and the practice had always been consistent with what was now being said—but because they were made generally known on this occasion through a protest signed by the Bishops of the Anglican Church in Kenya and Uganda and the oldest representative of the Scottish Church in Kenya. The protest was called the "Bishops' Memorandum", and the conclusions drawn by the ecclesiastical functionaries were in fact extremely conservative [2]. It was not that they were against the principle of persuasion; not at all. They were only objecting to the way in which it was to be effected, as stated in the Labour Circular. Making use of the native chiefs they considered as fatal since, in their experience, this could lead to nothing but serious abuses. "Advice" and "encouragement" they claimed, would in this case only be words used to cloak the imposition of force of the worst order. They were also opposed to the inclusion of women and children in the labour force. And, finally, they thought it would be far better to speak openly of an obligation to work than to shelter behind such words as "advice" and "encouragement".

---

[1] Despatch to the Governor of the East Africa Protectorate, relating to Native Labour, and papers connected therewith, 1920, Cmd 873, p. 6/7.
[2] Despatch etc., p. 8-11.

They were not opponents to the use of compulsory labour as such, provided it was honestly acknowledged and well regulated. The Bishop of Zanzibar, Frank Weston, was the only one to attack the system fiercely. In his book, "The Serfs of Great Britain", he called what amounted to the compulsion on the Africans to labour for the Europeans a "sacrifice of the weakest race to the financial interests of the strongest" [1].

As already stated, the "Bishops' Memorandum" raised a stormy controversy in England. The "Anti-slavery and Aborigines Protection Society" went into action and after a debate in the Upper House the Government promised that a supplementary "circular" would be issued. This indeed appeared in Kenya [2], with several mitigating provisions; namely, that there was to be supervision that the native chiefs were just in their choice of labourers, and in particular, that they exercised no pressure on those whose labour was required for the cultivation of their own land; and, further, that women and children who were employed had always to return home at night. The principle that native chiefs were to apply all legal means to convince their people to work was emphatically restated, however. Nevertheless, the Minister of Colonial Affairs now declared that he was well satisfied. His successor—Winston Churchill —who took office in 1921, was the first to attempt to put a stop to this form of labour coercion by decreeing that officials were in no way whatever to assist in the recruitment of labour [3]. According to McGregor Ross, who was Director of Public Works in Kenya from 1905 to 1923, the practice was too deeply rooted for that [4], and a few years later the Governor, on whom the colonists exerted tremendous pressure, issued a declaration once again permitting the use of "persuasion" to work. Yet all this seemed not to have been taken so far in later years [5].

This measure of "persuasion" was not the only one taken. There were many more. In the first place, there was the application of a proven method; namely, high tax levies. The main tax—and certainly not the only tax which the natives were made to pay—was the so-

[1] Cited in: W. McGregor Ross, Kenya from Within, 1927, p. 107.
It was not possible for me to procure a copy of Weston's book.
[2] Despatch etc., p. 7-8.
[3] Despatch to the officer administering the Government of the Kenya Colony and Protectorate, relating to Native Labour, 1921, Cmd. 1509.
[4] McGregor Ross, op. cit., p. 110.
[5] Salvadori, op. cit., p. 102, 205.

called "head tax", which in about 1937 amounted (for the whole family) to from 28% to 35% of the average income of a native farmer [1]. Needless to say, only very few could afford to pay such a high tax from the yield of their small farms. The majority were forced to enter into labour contracts with the Europeans, and then, as a rule, it would take the entire earnings of three to four months labour to pay the tax for the labourer himself, his family, and possibly other family dependents [2]. It is interesting to note how the rate of the head tax increased in the course of years [3]. There was a fairly regular, continual increase from the first years of colonization till the end of World War I. Then, in the period of great labour scarcity, the head tax suddenly jumped to a level more than twice as high as it had been before. However, this, together with the imposition of a pass system and compulsory labour for women and children (about which, more shortly), only served to cause a revolt. Consequently, the head tax was reduced by about a quarter, but, the import taxes on native truck were then raised; some commodities by 20% to 30%, and a few even by as much as 90% [4]. The natives did not realize the full implications of these indirect taxes, and the overall effect remained the same; they were still forced to work for the colonists because of the raised cost of living.

It is difficult to determine exactly in how far the land policy, whereby the natives were by degrees deprived of their land and pushed back into reserves of very limited size, actually was intended to affect the supply of labour for Europeans; but it is certain that it was with this in view that the colonists agitated for a policy of limiting the land set aside for the natives [5], and it is equally certain that the land shortage which soon developed in these reserves did drive many Africans on to the labour market.

The same effect was obtained by banning native production of certain products, to wit, coffee and tea. According to McGregor Ross, the natives would easily have been able to pay the high taxes

---

[1] Id., p. 202.

[2] Norman Leys, Kenya, 3rd ed., 1926, p. 215.

[3] See the graph in: McGregor Ross, op. cit., p. 150.

[4] McGregor Ross, op. cit., p. 108.

[5] Correspondence relating to affairs in the East Africa Protectorate, 1908, Cd. 4122, p. 16. See also the opinions of the colonists heard by the Native Labour Commission in 1912-1913, and cited in McGregor Ross, op. cit., p. 92/93. In 1895 all land, whether or not in use by the original residents, was declared to be the property of the British Crown.

levied on them if they had been given scientific information, and had been allowed to cultivate the indigenous crops [1]. But this was, of course, not the intention, which explains the ban on the most profitable products.

A measure of an entirely different order, implying no direct or indirect compulsion but merely encouragement, was provided in a regulation decreeing that those who had worked three months of any year—the meaning being of course for a European—would in the following year be exempt from the 24 days compulsory duty on the public works (see below).

The above measures were principally directed at the population of the reserves. However, there were many Africans living as "squatters" on the European estates—because of the overcrowding in the reserves—and as such they were given the use of a small piece of land in exchange for a part of the harvest or cash rent. This system was condemned by the Native Labour Commission in 1913, because, among other things, it had a negative effect on the labour supply [2]. And on the advice of this commission, it was decreed by the Resident Natives Ordinance of 1918 that any native wishing to live with his family outside the reserves had to conclude an agreement with the landlord on whose land they settled; whereby, in exchange for the use of a piece of land, he and all the male members of his family above the age of 16, would work 180 days per year for the landlord. This labour was to be paid, and the agreement was to be for not less than one and not more than three years. It is very difficult to concede that such agreements were voluntarily entered into if we take into consideration that many Africans were forced to live outside the reserves because of the very little land which had been assigned to them. All these agreements had to be submitted for approval to a magistrate or another official appointed by the Government, and these were empowered to veto the agreements if, for example, they considered that the wages agreed upon were too low. However, since the Government appointed European farmers to these posts, this provision had little practical value.

Having discussed the measures taken to get the African population to work for the Europeans, it would now be interesting to see how much further the colonists would have liked to have gone, since

[1] McGregor Ross, op. cit., p. 195.

[2] The data concerning the squatter system are taken from Buell, op cit., Vol. 1, p. 325-328.

we know that they have right from the beginning of colonization always found the Government too slow in introducing more rigid legislation, and were always exerting pressure to obtain more. To their way of thinking, the assistance by the officials in recruitment was never sufficient [1]. Many a colonist thought it a crime for a European not to drive the African to work [2]. "By the sweat of your brow shall ye work" it was said, and if the African through his labour aided in bringing about prosperity in the country it would be to his advantage too [3]. If an African should have the audacity to refuse to work after being "advised" to do so, then he deserved to be whipped for having been so shameless as to think that he knew better than the European Government what was good for him [4]. The natives had to be kept poor so that they would all the more be forced to work. To achieve this the taxes should be set very high and the wages kept very low [5]. If the colonists had had their way, the best time to have collected taxes would have been at the very moment when the demand for labour was at its greatest, and the fact that this might coincide with the time of the African ceremonial celebrations was of absolutely no import [6]. And finally, there should have been very strong measures against those who deserted their work [7]. Fortunately, the Government strongly opposed the most excessive of the colonists' demands; unfortunately this perhaps explains the repeatedly expressed desire of the colonists for self-government.

We will now go on to examine the conditions under which those Africans who had signed contracts worked, and how they were treated.

Mostly recruited by professional agents who relied on the good offices of the native chiefs, the labourers would be brought to the nearest magistrate for the contracts to be signed in his presence—the period of contract usually ranging from three to twelve months. Then there would follow the journey to the employer's estate which could be hundreds of miles away; these journeys were almost always made by foot and might take several weeks. To make matters far

---

[1] Correspondence etc., p. 11.
[2] Id., p. 12.
[3] Id., pp. 12, 13.
[4] McGregor Ross, op. cit., p. 94/95.
[5] Id., p. 99. Correspondence etc., pp. 16, 17.
[6] McGregor Ross, op. cit., p. 194.
[7] Correspondence etc., p. 17.

worse, the rest camps along the routes taken were invariably in a most unhygienic state, causing many to fall ill.

Employer-employee relations were regulated in the Masters and Servants Ordinance of 1910 [1], although a few modifications were introduced later. Included in it were provisions for the feeding and housing of native labourers, as well as the penalties to cover breach of contract. The provisions benefiting the labourers, however, had very little effect on the practice. In fact, the employers would do more or less whatever they pleased with them, and what they did do was often so improper that the Chief Native Commissioner gave it as his opinion (in 1919) that if things went on much longer in the same irresponsible manner there would soon be no more natives left to work [2]. Generally speaking, nutrition was shocking, even worse than in other parts of Africa, and housing quite inadequate [3]. Abuses occurred most often in the early colonial period [4]. On the other hand, wages have always been extremely low. After World War I taxes and prices rose considerably, but wages were kept at their pre-war level [5]. This was naturally more than directly advantageous to employers since it meant that more Africans would have to work for longer periods for the Europeans. But these low wages were often not paid at all. Various devices were used to achieve this end. For example, some planters would treat their labourers so badly just before payday that they deserted in great numbers. Or otherwise they would give them so heavy a task toward the end of their term of service that it was impossible for them to finish it, and on that basis they received no wages [6].

Labour inspection was instituted in 1919 with a view to improving the conditions of labour. Buell describes the activities of the four labour inspectors assigned to Kenya in his time [7].

Two of these had the task of controlling the labour on the construction of the railroad and other large projects. A third was put in charge of the office in Nairobi, the capital. Which left one official

---

[1] Despatch to the Governor of the East Africa Protectorate relating to Native Labour, and papers connected therewith, 1920, Cmd. 873, p. 13-29.

[2] Buell, op. cit., Vol. 1, p. 351.

[3] Id., Vol. 1, p. 353.

[4] McGregor Ross, op. cit., p. 98, 114.

[5] See a quotation from a letter of the Bishop of Zanzibar, Frank Weston, in McGregor Ross, op. cit., p. 89.

[6] Cited from an official report by McGregor Ross, op. cit., p. 91.

[7] Buell, The Native Problem in Africa, 1928, Vol. I, p. 352.

to inspect the 2,000 odd agricultural enterprises, and one can imagine with what results.

We still have to discuss the question of penal sanction, which was not left out of the picture in Kenya either. The Masters and Servants Ordinance of 1910 contains the following stipulations concerning it [1]. For absence from work without good cause, negligence and insubordination toward the estate owner or other superiors a fine to a maximum of a month's wages or—if payment was not possible—imprisonment with or without forced labour to a maximum of one month could be imposed. For desertion the maximum fine was the equivalent of two months' wages and the subsidiary imprisonment was put at a maximum of two months, and increased to six months in 1916 [2]. The time of illegal absence from work could be added to the contract period.

These regulations, however, were not enough to prevent the frequent desertions from the plantations; and this is why the planters —who had been clammering for a pass system for many years— eventually had their way. The pass system was decided upon in 1915 but, because of the war, was not put into effect until 1920. From henceforth all Africans had to carry on their persons a pass issued by the district officer. The dates of entering and of leaving the employment of a European had to be shown on the pass, and it was illegal to enter new employment if the pass book had not been signed by the previous employer. Naturally such a regulation was bound to make desertion far more difficult, since a desertee could no longer offer his services to another planter without his offence being spotted. And it had now become impossible, in most cases, to avoid working for a European once in a while. Indeed there was a very marked drop in the number of desertees after the institution of the pass system. All in all, the system was a great burden for the natives, even aside from the fact that they were completely bound to the European whom they happened to be working for. If a native could not produce his pass when accosted by the police and told to do so, he was liable to arrest, even though he might have left it at home by mistake, and prosecution could follow. And both the police and the courts sometimes fell far short of reasonable flexibility. Frequently the maximum penalty would be demanded for desertion without any attempt to

[1] Despatch etc., p. 13 ff.
[2] Despatch etc., p. 24.

investigate whether the African had good cause to desert or not. The occasional magistrate who refused to favour the interests of the planters in his verdicts would more than likely find himself soon transferred to some inhospitable district far in the interior of the country [1].

The events accompanying the expiration of contracts are of great importance in examining the contract labourer's position. Occasionally employers would refuse to sign their labourers' pass books [2], but a method more frequently adopted was to withhold a portion of their wages. The labourer then had the choice of going on working for the same employer or losing a part of his wages [3]. Under certain circumstances employers could even resort to legal methods; for example, if any of their labourers were in debt to them, since the Masters and Servants Ordinance of 1910 contained a clause decreeing that an employee who had accepted an advance from his master could, if he left his service before the debt was settled, be convicted to a maximum of three months imprisonment [4]. In general, however, it did not frequently happen that contract labourers were held on the estates against their will on the termination of their contract.

Finally, we must discuss the obligatory labour for the benefit of the Government. African men could be called up for unpaid work on roads, bridges, and so forth in their immediate neighbourhood for a maximum of 24 days a year [5], as well as for paid labour, in any district, for a maximum of 60 days a year [6]. Labourers called up for paid work were used primarily as bearers for government personnel on travel connected with their function, for employment on roads, railways, government buildings, telegraph and telephone installation projects, etc., and in the last place for emergencies of various sorts. Exempt from such labour were *inter alia* those whose time was completely taken up in some other employment, and further, those who had worked three months (for a European) in the previous year. Any native shirking his obligation would be

---

[1] McGregor Ross, op. cit., p. 280.
[2] Report of the East Africa Commission, 1925, Cmd. 2387, p. 170.
[3] McGregor Ross, op. cit., p. 91.
[4] Despatch etc., p. 18.
[5] Buell, op. cit., Vol. 1, p. 370.
[6] Compulsory Labour for Government Purposes (Kenya), 1925, Cmd. 2464, p. 6-8.

liable to a high fine, with the alternative of imprisonment for a maximum of two months.

In 1921, however, provisions were made in London which severely restricted the drafting of labour for public works. From henceforth special permission for its imposition had to be obtained from the Minister of Colonial Affairs, except when it concerned the conscripting of bearers [1]. In fact, abuses of a serious nature had frequently occurred, especially on railway projects, seeing that often hundreds of natives had to live together in labour camps situated far from their homes. Partly because of this, the death-rate among the labourers was very high for a number of years [2]. However, abuses also occurred on the obligatory labour projects in the neighbourhood of the native labourers' own homes. Sometimes they were made to work longer than was permitted by law [3]. And sometimes not only the men were drafted, as proscribed, but also the women and children [4]. Besides, apart from abuses and aggravating circumstances, three months compulsory labour on public works is a great deal, the more so since neither the telegraph and telephone installations (and other such projects) nor the tours of government personnel could be expected to hold very much interest for the average native.

In time, however, compulsory labour decreased in extent. As far as the labour on the public works is concerned, a new regulation was introduced in 1932, whereby the drafting of labour was only permissible if there were no ordinary labourers available [5]. And it would appear that the exerting of official pressure on the population to get them to work is a thing of the past [6]. Nevertheless, penal sanction remains in force, as does the pass system [7]. And a new ordinance—the "Voluntarily Unemployed Persons (Provision of Employment) Ordinance" of 1949—could, according to the Ad hoc committee on forced labour of the United Nations, when broadly applied lead to a system of compulsory labour not without significance to the economy of Kenya [8]. This ruling decrees [9] that all

[1] Id., p. 6.
[2] Buell, op. cit., Vol. 1, p. 354/5.
[3] McGregor Ross, op. cit., p. 110.
[4] Buell, op. cit., Vol. 1, p. 370.
[5] Lord Hailey, An African Survey, 2nd ed., 1945, p. 618/9.
[6] J. D. de Roock, Sociaal-economische aanpassingsproblemen in Kenya, 1953, p. 121.
[7] Id.
[8] Report of the "Ad hoc Committee on Forced Labour", 1953, p. 111.
[9] Id., p. 110/111, 540-542, 572/573.

persons without work must present themselves within seven days at a labour bureau where they will be offered suitable work, and that those who are "voluntarily unemployed", if they refuse to accept this offered work, must either seek work for themselves or would be put to work by the proper authorities. Failure to comply with the ordinance is punishable wih a maximum of three months imprisonment and/or a substantial fine, increasable for recidivists to 12 months imprisonment with a fine.

From the first arrival of the colonists up to the present time the Government has in various ways attempted to make labourers out of the Africans. That these attempts have succeeded to a large extent can be seen from the increase in the course of the years of the number of Africans working for Europeans. Buell gives a review of this [1]. In 1912 they numbered 12,000; in 1920, 90,000; and by 1927 the number had risen to 185,409. We have established that this labour has been for the most part compulsory. Thus also in Kenya, a colony of that country that has always led in the fight against slavery, widespread compulsory labour has occurred, and even into the 20th century.

LITERATURE

Compulsory Labour for Government Purposes (Kenya), London, 1925, Cmd. 2464.

Correspondence relating to affairs in the East Africa Protectorate, London, 1908, Cd. 4122.

Despatch to the Governor of the East Africa Protectorate relating to native labour, and papers connected therewith, London, 1920, Cmd. 873.

Despatch to the officer administering the government of the Kenya colony and protectorate relating to native labour, London, 1921, Cmd. 1509.

Report of the East Africa Commission, London, 1925, Cmd. 2387.

Report of the Ad hoc Committee on Forced Labour, Geneva, 1953. (United Nations—International Labour Office).

Report on slavery and free labour in the British East Africa Protectorate, London, 1903, Cd. 1631.

Buell, Raymond Leslie, The Native Problem in Africa, New York, 1928, Vol. 1, section 4: Kenya.

Church, Archibald, East Africa, a new dominion, London, 1927.

Hailey, Lord, An African Survey, a study of problems arising in Africa south of the Sahara, 2nd ed., London etc., 1945.

Huxley, Elspeth, White Man's Country, Lord Delamere and the making of Kenya, London, 1935, 2 vols.

Leakey, L. S. B., Mau Mau and the Kikuyu, London, 1952.

[1] Buell, op. cit., Vol. 1, p. 345.

Leys, Norman, Kenya, 3rd ed., London, 1926.
—— A Last Chance in Kenya, London, 1931.
Roock, J. D. de, Sociaal-economische aanpassingsproblemen in Kenya, proeve ener toepassing van de dualistisch-economische theorie op een Afrikaans gebied, Haarlem, 1953.
Ross, W. McGregor, Kenya from Within, a short political history, London, 1927.
Salvadori, Max, La colonisation européenne au Kenya, 1938.

CHAPTER ELEVEN

HAITI

Up to now in this study we have concerned ourselves solely with countries in which slavery was abolished by whites, who thereupon set about compelling other races to work for them under new systems of compulsory labour. Now we shall examine the labour situation in a country where the Negro slaves themselves made an end to slavery, and then found themselves obliged to seek new paths; namely, in Haiti, the first independent Negro State in the world, and the second free State in the Western Hemisphere.

In what later became Haiti (the western part of the island of that name), a French colony till the end of the 18th century (Saint Domingue)—and the most prosperous of her colonies—the slaves rebelled in 1791. The revolution came as a complete surprise, for although relations in the colony had been strained for some time, the slaves were actually hardly involved. Toward the end of the 18th century, the population was made up of 40,000 whites, 28,000 half-castes and 452,000 Negro slaves [1]; of these the free half-castes—mostly mulattoes—had in part attained a high degree of prosperity. They owned plantations and held slaves, and like the whites sent their children to be educated in Paris. In the last decades of the 18th century, however, there was a marked increase in the discrimination against this group; consequently, the situation between the European and half-caste groups became exceedingly tense. All at once the French Revolution broke out. The free half-castes heard with enthusiasm the Declaration of the Rights of Man and considered that the time had come to regain their dwindling rights. It were the Negro slaves, however, who unexpectedly availed themselves of the opportunity to revolt. All the Europeans fled the island. The half-castes and Negroes at first joined forces, but later they split, and in the resulting struggle for supremacy the Negroes won—thus, eventually, West Haiti came under the leadership of a Negro, the ex-slave Toussaint Louverture. The years that followed were full of unrest and it was only under Louverture's successor, Dessalines, himself a former slave, that

[1] James G. Leyburn, The Haitian People, 2nd printing, 1945, p. 18.

Haiti was proclaimed an independent republic, in 1804. There were no more Europeans in the country and the Negroes and half-castes could begin to create a new society.

By 1793 slavery had been declared abolished. A few years later —in an interim period of comparative peace—an energetic attempt was made to get the estates producing again: former slaves were ordered to return to their work and to commit themselves to remain on the same plantation for a period of at least five years. The Negroes willingly obeyed their leader, and the consequent economic recuperation was startling. However, this short period was followed by years of strife against the Napoleonic army and by the time of the declaration of independence the country had been reduced to a state of complete chaos. The plantations had been destroyed in the war, the population had completely lost the habit of work; and this was the situation in which the new leader had to create order.

He did this by imposing compulsory labour [1]. Every citizen of Haiti had to become either a labourer or a soldier. Idleness was forbidden in the new State. The obligation to work also held for women who, since they could not become soldiers, automatically fell under the first category and became labourers.

It was decreed that all labourers (with the exception of a few artisans) were to be bound to work on a plantation. To leave that plantation was strictly forbidden, and to shelter a run-away labourer was a crime.

The work was to be supervised by a hierarchy of officials, each of whom had to report periodically to his superiors. And the military was also involved in this work. It was necessary to maintain a large army for fear that the French might endeavour to recapture the country—but this army could also be used to maintain order on the plantations.

Thus the majority of the population were compelled to cultivate the land. The only exceptions to this system were the half-castes who had owned plantations before the abolition of slavery. They were allowed to keep their plantations, and remained independent. All land formerly belonging to the whites was made the property of the State (i.e., more than two thirds of the plantations in 1806 [2]).

To distinguish the situation of the labourers from the earlier

---

[1] Leyburn, op. cit., p. 34-37.
[2] Leyburn, op. cit., p. 39.

conditions under slavery, it was forbidden to use the lash—the consummate symbol of slavery—on the plantations; and the working day was shortened by a third. Further, it was declared that labourers could obtain a transfer to other plantations if they were able to show good cause for wishing to do so.

However, in practice these qualifications had little effect. The overseers were charged with the completion of a given amount of work on the plantations, and they knew of no way of meeting their obligations other than by resorting to physical force—though this was perhaps not as ruthless as it had been in earlier times. Also, often they felt they could ill afford any postponement on the agricultural programme that was set them — hence, little came of the shorter working day stipulations. Nor were labourers ever granted formal permission to leave their plantations.

All in all therefore, the common people were hardly any better off than they had been in colonial times, and dissatisfaction was rife not only among the Negroes but also among the half-castes who saw little scope for their ambitions.

Dessalines, after having ruled the country for two years, was assassinated in 1806. On his death, the country was divided in two parts: a State in the north, first a republic but soon afterwards a monarchy under the rule of a former slave; and a republic in the south where most of the half-castes lived—thus the president here was a half-caste.

In the northern State, compulsory labour was imposed [1]; and the mass of the people were again obliged to labour on the plantations, it being decreed that anyone whose mother or kin had been born on a plantation had to return to that plantation. The remaining town and village inhabitants had to become artisans. If they did not wish to do so the only choice that remained open to them was to become plantation labourers. Even the handicapped were put to work in agriculture; anyone unable to do physical labour being charged with minor duties such as carrying to the field what the field-workers required. And to maintain the plantation labour force as best as possible, it was forbidden for anyone employed in agriculture to marry anyone not living and working in agriculture. This was to prevent departures from the plantations for family reasons, especially by women—the mothers of future field-hands.

---

[1] Leyburn, op. cit., p. 44-51.

The labourers were strictly bound to their particular plantations, changes only being allowed under very exceptional circumstances. The daily work was also stringently regulated: no one could leave his work during working hours except in cases of emergency; laziness could be punished with whip and fetters; and for refusal to work one was liable to be convicted to forced labour.

On the other hand, it was decreed that Saturday afternoons and Sundays were to be free. Also, a quarter of the yield of the plantation was to be set aside for the labourers—which meant for them a much higher income than they had ever enjoyed before.

The new Government maintained the land policy of the previous one, which was to rent large tracts of country to the wealthier citizens. But there was vigilant government supervision with military backing, and an inspector in every district, charged with seeing that the cultivation went according to plan.

This labour system was a great success from an economic point of view. Within a few years the production of sugar and coffee increased enormously, and the prosperity of the colonial days returned to North Haiti.

In the southern republic matters were arranged quite differently [1]. Where in the north the policy was to rent out large tracts of land, in the south it was to break up the land into small holdings for the benefit of the little man. Soldiers were presented small holdings as a gift, and other citizens could buy land very cheaply. The President probably assumed that the people would work harder and more efficiently as small landowners. Every form of compulsory labour was abolished and the system of agricultural inspection was done away with. From henceforth there was to be no more supervision from above over the amount and efficiency of work performed.

The larger landowners naturally objected, especially to the creation of small holdings, fearing that this would only lead to insufficient labour for their plantations.

And in that they were right; a lot of difficulty was experienced in hiring labour—partly because the planters were not wealthy enough to offer decent wages. A system of share cropping now developed on the plantations; small pieces of land being given in exchange for a half share of their yield. And the relations between landlords and tenants were indeed strictly regulated. Breach of contract was made

---

[1] Leyburn, op. cit., p. 51-64.

a penal offence. Any tenant leaving a plantation without written permission—even if only to pay a visit elsewhere—was liable to eight days imprisonment the first time, a month the second time and three months the third time. During his term of imprisonment he could be put to labour on the public works. Further, anyone found guilty of inciting another to commit a breach of contract could be convicted to a year's imprisonment. And finally, it was decreed that the District Commandants were to take charge at any sign of disorder. However, the mildness which marked the Government of the southern republic was expressed in the provisions for the protection of labourers and tenants: physical punishment was abrogated, planters had to provide medical attention for their tenants, and those no longer able to work through age or illness had the right to keep their huts and gardens.

As opposed to the northern State, the system followed in the southern republic led to acute economic deterioration. Now that compulsion had been made an end to, field-hands on the plantations tended more and more to abandon the cultivation of sugar which required such hard work, and instead grew only what was necessary for their own immediate needs; for example, maize, yams, potatoes, bananas and so forth. But the attitude of the planters themselves contributed to the decline of the big plantations. Not knowing of a way to drive people to work other than the use of brute physical force, they did not know what to make of the provisions for the protection of labourers and tenants, so they switched by degrees from the cultivation of sugar, now renting their land divided into small holdings; and, needless to say, the people who held these holdings soon gave up any idea of becoming rich through sugar and grew only what they required for their own needs.

The economic deterioration was complete. Exports collapsed, the national income dropped. But the President was revered by his people; and many from the northern kingdom, with its forced labour, fled to the southern republic where life was easy.

North and South Haiti were re-united in 1820, after the death of both heads of State [1]. The new President was against the use of compulsion, just as his predecessor in the south had been. It reminded him too much of the earlier days of slavery, and he set out by ruling leniently in the hope that his people would take to working hard of their own volition. But after a few years it became clear that

[1] See for the ensuing period especially Leyburn, op. cit., p. 64-74.

his hopes were ill-founded; practically no one volunteered to work on the sugar plantations and people were taking more and more to a carefree existence. Authority went into action again. In 1826 the "Code Rural" was published, reinstating compulsory labour in Haiti. The provisions of the Code closely resembled those in force earlier. People with no means of their own, and all those who were not employed as officials, artisans or soldiers, were obliged to work in agriculture by concluding contracts with plantation owners for periods of from three to nine years. Breach of contract was a penal offence. For a first conviction for absence from work, a labourer was liable to 24 hours' imprisonment; thereafter, on relapse, he could be put to labour on the public works. Disobedience and insolence were also made penal offences; and the system of inspection was instituted again. Also, as before, the military was made responsible for maintaining order on the plantations.

The Code contained severe provisions against those who did not conclude contracts when they were supposed to do so. If such a person refused to yield to persuasion he could be sentenced to imprisonment, and if he still refused after that he was to be convicted to labour on the public works until such time as he reformed. And for those once working in agriculture, it was made very difficult to change to another category of work. A certain authority had to be applied to for permission to do so, but such permission was only granted in exceptional circumstances. This same authority was also responsible for granting special permission for children of field-hands to go to school or to learn a trade in the towns.

Even though this system closely resembled that which had been in force in the former kingdom of North Haiti—and which had led to good economic results there—nothing came of it in practice.

The islanders were now too used to indolent living—particularly those in the south—and they sabotaged the new system en masse. This was made easier by the fact that a large section of the population were already small landowners, and for many others it was not difficult to become so. All these were excused from plantation labour, provided, that is, that their plots were larger than the stipulated minimum size—but many found it easy enough to evade the law on this point. Eventually even the big landowners turned against the system after their initial enthusiasm. They thought the stipulated payment to the labourers—a fourth to a half of the annual yield—

excessive. Since it could hardly be enforced against the will of the whole population, the system was soon abandoned.

And from then on the economy of Haiti steadily declined. Labour shortages meant smaller harvests, and as a result the big planters felt compelled to break up more and more of their land into small holdings, on which only crops of immediate importance were grown. Apparently in 1842 there was not a single plantation left in the country comparing in size to those common in the colonial days [1]. As a result of all this the export of sugar, once the most important product, dwindled to nothing, while there was also a marked drop in the cultivation of other products. No attempt was ever made again to impose compulsory labour on the people of Haiti, and the country never recovered from its decline. Rather, it became poorer and poorer.

In summarizing therefore, we find that although compulsory labour was resorted to in the Negro State of Haiti it was soon done away with. After the French left there was no longer a landowning class of any significance, since the few halfcaste planters were not very powerful as a group. Consequently, the leaders of the State could hardly be expected to have been able to enforce compulsory labour on the people indefinitely, and as soon as there was no longer any compulsion to work the population fell back into their older, more primitive ways, only producing for their own use and not for a market.

The history of Haiti is interesting in that it shows the contrast between a period of prosperity with compulsory labour and a long period of freedom in which the country went under economically.

LITERATURE

Gerling, Walter, Wirtschaftsentwicklung und Landschaftswandel auf den westindischen Inseln Jamaika, Haiti und Puerto Rico, Freiburg i. Br., 1938 (Thesis Würzburg).

Leyburn, James G., The Haitian People, 2nd printing, New Haven etc., 1945.

[1] Leyburn, op. cit., p. 75.

CHAPTER TWELVE

LIBERIA

We will now turn our attention to Liberia, the second independent Negro State, which became with Haiti the only two such states in the world.

The State of Liberia owes its origin to the American effort to establish Negro settlements in West Africa for liberated slaves. These freed slaves were not so welcome in the United States at the start of the 19th century, since it was feared that they would bolster the agitation for emancipation. In 1816 the American Colonization Society was founded, under the leadership of which the settlement of freed Negroes on the West Coast of Africa principally took place. The first group of Negroes to be brought over by them (under the direction of white agents) arrived at Cape Mesurado in 1821, and many other groups followed later—mainly in the second quarter of the 19th century, but also after. In all, 15,000 liberated Negroes from the United States were re-settled in the Liberia to be—to which were added 5,000 freed at sea by the American navy. The United States had put a ban on slave *trade*, and whenever an American slave ship was captured on the high seas the slaves aboard were immediately taken to Liberia. Thus various Negro settlements sprang up along the Coast, which—with one exception, Maryland—joined to form the Commonwealth of Liberia in 1839; and later, in 1857, Maryland joined too. The Government of the Commonwealth was under the control of the American Colonization Society, and the first Governor was a white man. As time went by, however, it became apparent that it was not desirable to have a private society run a country—and it was not long before the Colonization Society gave preference to withdrawing. The settlers held a convention on the advice of the Society in 1847, and it was decided that the Commonwealth should break its ties with the United States and become an independent State; thus, on July 26, 1847, the Republic of Liberia was born. From that day on the Negroes were left to manage their own affairs.

Freedom was very dear to the Liberians, as is expressed in the name they gave their country; and in their first constitution, adopted in 1820, it was declared: "There shall be no slavery in the settlement" (Art. 5) [1]. (England, the first Western country to abolish slavery, only did so in 1834). In the Constitution of the Commonwealth of Liberia drafted in 1839, and in the Declaration of Rights and in the Constitution, which were both drafted when Liberia became an independent republic in 1847, the ban on slavery (*mutatis mutandis*) was repeated, and strengthened with a ban on slave *trade* [2]. Moreover, the Declaration of Independence adopted as the motto of the Republic the phrase: "The love of liberty brought us here".

It would appear, however, that the immigrants in Liberia only had the freedom of their own group in mind. The native population of the territory (which far outnumbered the newcomers) they treated in a way reminiscent of the colonial practices of white peoples. The Declaration of Rights (1847) actually begins with a sentence which throws significant light on the attitude of the immigrants toward the natives. The opening words run: "We, the people of Liberia, were originally the inhabitants of North America"!

We see this attitude expressed, for example, in the political field: the Government of the country remains firmly in hands of the descendants of the 20,000 original settlers (now numbering approximately 12,000 [3]); and there has never yet been a serious attempt to raise the natives out of their backward condition [4]. In various parts of the country the natives have even been robbed of their land, just as in the white colonies [5]. But particularly the African population has been forced to work for the benefit of the minority group of immigrants (and their descendants). We will now consider how and to what extent this happened.

To start with the native population was obliged to work on public projects, especially roads and public buildings. The obliga-

---

[1] Charles Henry Huberich, The Political and Legislative History of Liberia, New York, 1947, Vol. 2, p. 896, 1263. (The text of the Constitution of 1820 is given on p. 1263/4).

[2] Id., pp. 895/6, 1457. Raymond Leslie Buell, The Native Problem in Africa, New York, 1928, Vol. 2, p. 855. (The text of the Constitution of 1839 is given in Huberich, op. cit., Vol. 2, p. 1454-1458; that of the Constitution of 1847 in Buell, op. cit., Vol. 2, p. 855-864.

[3] Raymond Leslie Buell, Liberia: A Century of Survival 1847-1947, Philadelphia, 1947, p. 7.

[4] Id., p. 10.

[5] Buell, The Native Problem in Africa, Vol. 2, p. 736. Henry Fenwick Reeve, The Black Republic, Liberia; its political and social conditions to-day, London, 1923, p. 46.

tion to construct and repair roads dates back to the early days of the Republic, but never attained serious proportions until in the twenties, when it was planned to extend the road system—formerly confined to the coastal areas—to the interior. And from that moment on very heavy demands were made on the native population for this objective; although they need not have been so heavy if the work had been reasonably planned in advance. They set to work, however, without calling in engineers or surveyors; in fact, without even making topographical studies first; as a result, suffering an enormous loss of money and labour [1].

The arrangement was as follows [2]: The District commissioners ordered the native chiefs in their district to supply a certain number of men to work every other week (or possibly two successive weeks out of four). If the number called for was not too high, each male member of the village had only to work one week a month, and in this way their own work would not be jeopardized. But the numbers asked for were often very high. No census had ever been taken, so they went by estimates of the village populations, which meant in practice that the District commissioners had a free hand and made excessive demands—thus in fact the way of life of the natives was certainly disrupted. In some districts such heavy demands were made that a rebellion threatened (in 1926) if they were not reduced. A presidential decree then ordered that the natives be given 3 months freedom a year for the cultivation of their lands [3], which meant that the demands which could be made for the public works were still excessive. And nor was this work paid; though the chiefs were occasionally given gifts. The labourers had to provide their own implements and food, which caused many difficulties. Often they were badly treated. Sometimes they were driven to work harder by soldiers who were stationed over them; and soldiers were also used to round up sufficient men in the villages. Fines were imposed for failure to fulfil specifications of any kind; thus, if a labour gang arrived late at the place of work, if the stipulated tasks were not finished in time, if tools were missing, etc. etc. If the labourer himself could not pay the fine imposed on him, his chief was held respon-

[1] International Commission of Enquiry in Liberia: Communication by the Government of Liberia dated December 15th 1930, transmitting the Commission's Report, Geneva, 1930, pp. 49, 50, 51, 52.

[2] Id., p. 52-68.

[3] Buell, The Native Problem in Africa, Vol. 2, p. 749.

sible; and sometimes the combined fines of a labour gang would accumulate to such an extent that the villagers were forced to sell their cattle or resort to pawning. Moreover, sometimes the chiefs were made to pay substantial sums of money to buy off their people from this work in seasons when they had to cultivate their land—whereas by law the work on the roads should have been brought to a standstill automatically without it! All these factors could only have led to general impoverishment.

The native Liberians were not only drafted for work but also had to pay money taxes. The principal (sometimes the only) tax was the hut tax, which was initially 1 dollar, but later 2 dollars. The amount in itself was not so very high, but the manner in which it was collected and the many abuses which went with the collection, made of it a real plague. The collecting frequently took place with the help of the military, who then over-taxed and behaved in the most brutal fashion [1]. Moreover, everything was so badly organized that it could happen that persons who had nothing whatever to do with tax collecting would go round taking considerable sums of money from guileless natives simply by saying that it was for taxes [2]. Even worse perhaps was the fact that the money collected as taxes was not used for the benefit of the natives, but always only for the Americo-Liberians—as was stated by a United States Congressman in 1933 [3].

Besides the labour on public projects and the cash taxes, the natives also had to deliver food to the District commissioners and the military posts [4]. Usually these consignments had to be brought monthly, and they consisted of rice and palm oil. This in itself involved a considerable amount of work, which largely fell to the women. But here too, the complete arbitrariness of the demands made the situation almost unbearable for the population. One month the functionaries would order chicken or cattle, and the next might order a portion of the harvest for the soldiers. If the President or any other high official made a tour of the interior, the natives had to provide him and his entourage with all they required. Buell tells of a case when 200 goats, 585 hampers of rice, 40 tins of palm oil, 400 chickens, and other food to the value of $ 1600 was required for a visit by the

---

[1] Charles Morrow Wilson, Liberia, New York 1947, p. 77/78.
[2] Buell, The Native Problem in Africa, Vol. 2, p. 747.
[3] Cited in Buell, Liberia, p. 10.
[4] International Commission's Report, p. 53, 60, 69. Buell, The Native Problem in Africa, Vol. 2, p. 745.

President [1]. When the visit was canceled, the food was not returned. In this particular case the native commissioners were found to be the guilty party, and they were penalized—but then that was the first time in 16 years that the Liberian Legislature undertook to investigate the Administration. However, if the natives were one or two days late with their monthly consignments of food, they were made to pay a fine, and the chiefs would be held hostage until the desired quantity of food was delivered.

Since they could be commandeered to give up their cattle and their agricultural produce at any moment, the natives lost all interest in their farming. In addition they were being steadily impoverished by the taxes—which perhaps should not have been high by law, but worked out so in practice—by the fines imposed on them for any petty matter, and also by the fact that the work on the roads, etc., left them too little time for their own work. The decline of many districts was especially noticeable in the twenties; and many tried to escape the excessive demands made on them by trekking into the bush, or going into voluntary exile.

Yet we have only spoken thus far of the demands made—at least in theory—in the public cause. Besides this, however, the natives were exploited in various ways for the benefit of private individuals. In the first place, government officials would use some of the men called up for road work on their own plantations or farms [2]. The natives in their ignorance thought that this too was work for the State and therefore did not expect wages—and naturally did not receive any. This form of labour supply was not infrequently used by the high officials who almost all owned rubber, coffee or cocoa plantations, or farms on which rice and vegetables were grown. The report of the International Commission of 1930 contains many examples of instances when half or more of the men of a particular village or district were sent to a farm instead of to the road project for which they had been called up.

But this was by no means the only way in which government officials got labour for their own enterprises. For example, if a native was sentenced to pay a fine by a court and he was not able to pay, the magistrate or another functionary would let him work on their own farms—although the official alternative to a fine was imprison-

---

[1] Buell, The Native Problem in Africa, Vol. 2, p. 748.

[2] International Commission's Report, p. 74-77.

ment [1]. Nor was it unusual in such cases to charge the luckless "convict" with some trivial breach of the regulations toward the end of his term of sentence, and then to condemn to a fine or imprisonment all over again. This would occur particularly in the busy agricultural season; but it has been known to happen that a native lost his liberty for 20 years in this way, and for an offence which might, at most, have cost him a suspended sentence of 30 days in the United States [2]. According to quite a few authors, the Bench in Liberia was incredibly corrupt and biased [3].

But there was yet another way in which the use of an even larger number of labourers might be obtained. Here advantage was taken of the customs of the natives themselves. These had slavery in their own society, especially of prisoners taken in tribal wars, and further it was their custom to "pawn" members of their family, mostly children, if they were in need. Such forms of slavery and "pawning" were known among many Negro peoples, and most ethnologists are in agreeance that these "slaves" were generally well treated, that they did not necessarily have a low social status, and that therefore this form of slavery as such is in no way comparable with the Negro slavery in America where the slaves and their masters were of different races. The Americo-Liberians were quick to avail themselves of the opportunity of buying up the slaves belonging to the natives of the territory and using them for labour [4]—which immediately gave this slavery quite a different character. In some cases apparently the majority of the plantation workers and house servants were bought "boys". Often they would be called apprentices; and a law was passed decreeing that native boys could be taken into the service of Americo-Liberians as apprentices. It should be noted though that a true apprenticeship system developed under this law as well, and the results of this were truly beneficial to the natives. It would even appear that many native fathers were glad to apprentice their children to the settler families, believing that they would at least get some general education in this way. However, this does not detract from the fact that a real trade in native boys and girls existed, and not

[1] Reeve, op. cit., p. 86.

[2] Arthur Hayman and Harold Preece, Lighting up Liberia, Toronto, 1943, p. 52. (Cited in Buell, Liberia, p. 13. I was unable to obtain a copy of Hayman and Preece's book).

[3] Hayman and Preece, op. cit., p. 54. (Cited in Buell, op. cit., p. 56/7). Reeve, op. cit., pp. 96, 99.

[4] Reeve, op. cit., p. 132-141.

always under the guise of apprenticeship either; indeed, this trade did not differ much from genuine slave trading, and provided the Americo-Liberians with a substantial labour force. In a similar manner the ruling class made use, or rather misuse, of the native custom of pawning individuals. In the hands of the Americo-Liberians—who were not of the society in which this usage served a purpose—this system also became something which can only be described as genuine slave trade [1].

However, perhaps the native Negroes were exploited worst in quite another field of activity; namely, the recruitment of labourers to be sent abroad. Throughout the entire history of Liberia natives have gone to work outside the borders of their own country for certain periods, and right from the start this movement was attended by abuses. In the 20th century it became notorious, especially with respect to the shipment of natives to the Spanish island of Fernando Po. Labourers were also recruited for the Portuguese islands of St. Thomas and Principe and for the French Congo, which recruitments often went coupled with equally shocking irregularities, although these migrations were on a much smaller scale.

The International Commission of 1930 established [2] that in most cases the labourers who went to Fernando Po did not do so voluntarily but under compulsion; and as far as the Commission was concerned, it was difficult to distinguish the whole business from slave trade; nor, to their minds, would it have been so tragically effective if there had not been active cooperation on the part of the Government. Indeed, the Government was involved to the hilt. It even went so far as to make troups of the Frontier Force available to assist in the recruitment, and not as an exception but regularly. Quite a few of the upper hierarchy of public functionaries were directly involved in recruiting. Moreover all those concerned in the business could do more or less as they pleased since there was seldom or never any danger of prosecution seeing that the Government was already so implicated that to take action against any of its officials might have proved acutely embarrassing; besides which, the business was also a very profitable one: a certain sum of money had to be deposited in the Government treasury for every labourer recruited—which fact once led a Liberian statesman to remark, no doubt with justification, that

---

[1] Huberich, op. cit., p. 905. See also: International Commission's Report, p. 14.
[2] International Commission's Report, p. 16-46.

labour power was the principal export commodity of his country. Needless to say, those who concerned themselves with recruitment earned generous rewards in the process.

The usual procedure was for a District Commissioner (or some other functionary) to order his staff to round up a certain number of people. But as a rule this was not sufficient in itself, and soldiers would have to be called in—who then mostly went about creating a veritable reign of terror in the area. Ill-treatment, not only of men but also of women and children, was in no way unusual. If all who could have been consigned to Fernando Po had fled into the bush, then it was customary to take some of the remaining older members of the village community, or even the village chief, and hold these as hostages until a sufficient number of men returned to offer themselves up. Another method of gaining control over a village that resisted was to levy fines under all sorts of pretexts until the chief was forced to give in and cooperate. In the same way a village not cooperating willingly enough in the recruitment for Fernando Po might be charged to deliver an extra large number of labourers for the road projects as punishment [1]. In short, the authorities stopped at nothing in their rule of despotism; and when they had obtained enough people—by no matter what means—these were escorted under armed guard to the coast, to be forcibly put on ships taking them to Fernando Po and elsewhere.

This recruitment by force was followed by a life of hell on the plantations to which the native Liberians were sent. Reports of labourers being flogged, sold and exchanged by their masters were made known right from the start (shortly after 1900). Wages were seldom paid, and the mortality figures were exceptionally high. To this was added that they were forced to work after the expiration of the period for which they had been contracted. In 1929, the situation of labourers on Fernando Po was officially described as: "A state of peonage, hardly distinguishable from slavery. They were only to return to their homes, if they returned at all, when broken in health or wasted by disease" [2].

No wonder then that the Liberian natives were terrified at the prospect of being forced to go to Fernando Po. Thousands fled into the bush or across the borders to escape recruitment. The results for

---

[1] Id., p. 59, 69.

[2] Cited in Azikiwe, Liberia in World Politics, p. 197.

the country itself can be imagined. The villages became sadly depleted, especially of men. Where there had once been well-being there now ruled poverty and decay.

For all the compulsory labour discussed thus far the responsibility lay with the Americo-Liberians, the ruling class in the country. In 1926, however, a new element appeared in Liberia, for in that year the Firestone Plantations Company, an American corporation, began rubber exploitation activities in the country. They had obtained a 99 year lease from the Liberian Government for a maximum of 1 million acres of land—the biggest rubber concession in the world—and it was agreed that the Liberian Government would give reasonable cooperation in securing the necessary labour force for the efficient operation of the plantations. In many quarters [1] it was feared that the natives would be exploited, as had been the case with such concessions in other countries. Certain of the Company's statements seemed indeed to justify this concern. It was said that 200,000 tons of rubber would be produced annually (half the world production of the time), that there was practically an inexhaustible supply of labour in Liberia, and that the enterprise would need from 300 to 350 thousand labourers. This while the total able-bodied male population of Liberia was hardly 400,000! Also the way in which the Company first set about procuring labour appeared to give reason for concern. The Government, having promised to lend a helping hand, now set up the labour bureau which it had passed a law for as early as 1912, the object of the labour bureau of that time having been to "regulate and supervise the labour situation, to procure labourers and to protect the rights of such labourers . . . .". Now only, with the advent of the Firestone Company, did they take the matter in hand. The bureau sent out requisitions to the District Commissioners who in turn divided up contingents among the chiefs. And the company paid for this recruitment to the extent of one cent to the chiefs and the same amount to the Government Bureau for each day's work performed by each man supplied. Thus, a system which had led to widespread compulsory labour in other countries.

But in Liberia things were not taken so far—among other things, because the development of the company was not nearly so fast as the directors had at first expected. Of the 1 million acres to which the company had a right, 80,000 were under cultivation in about 1946.

---

[1] See for example Buell, The Native Problem in Africa, Vol. 2, p. 831-836.

Instead of employing 350,000 native workers as was first predicted, it employed about 30,000. And instead of producing 200,000 tons of rubber a year it produced about 17,000 tons, which still made them the leading rubber producers in the world [1]. The same authoritative writer, Raymond Leslie Buell, who had in 1928 shown great disquiet over the results which the activities of the company could have for the natives stated indirectly in a publication in 1947 that the Firestone Company had not exercised labour compulsion [2]. This was also the conclusion of the International Commission of 1930 [3]. The company was evidently successful in securing sufficient labour without compulsion. From the very beginning they took the matter of recruitment into their own hands, and even in 1927 the percentage of labourers supplied by the Government was not more than 10% [4]. Buell also records that the Firestone Company has the reputation of treating its workers well [5]. And, what is even more important, it has done something to encourage independent rubber production in Liberia. A few years ago there were 140 independent producers [6], of which a few were native Africans although the majority were still Americo-Liberians. In 1943, these farmers together exported about 100 tons of rubber [7].

Whatever advantages and disadvantages the company may have had for Liberia—and as disadvantages one should in the first place note that some tribes seem to have been robbed of their land for the benefit of the company [8]—it did not bring compulsory labour with it. For that the Liberians have only their own ruling Negroes to thank. It were the Americo-Liberians and especially their descendants who exploited the natives, and that in a manner closely resembling the practices of the whites in colonial territories. If it has not been as extreme as in other territories, it would only have been less so as a result of the more limited economic development of the country, so that less labour was required than elsewhere. The attitude of the Americo-Liberians was the same as that of the whites in the colonies: they did not wish to do manual labour themselves but to be served

[1] Buell, Liberia, p. 49.
[2] Id., p. 52.
[3] International Commission's Report, p. 83.
[4] The recruiting of labour in colonies etc., p. 91.
[5] Buell, Liberia, p. 49.
[6] Wilson, op. cit., p. 156.
[7] Buell, Liberia, p. 49.
[8] George Brown, Firestone-Libéria. In: Le travail en Afrique noire, p. 344.

by others. And thus wherever there was manual labour to be done the native population was compelled to do it.

The Government did not entirely disregard the protection of the natives. Its attempts, however, were mainly confined to the emigrating labourers, with whom the situation was quite different from that of the labourers in Liberia itself. The Liberian Government was not primarily responsible for what happened in Fernando Po as such, and, moreover, the departure of Liberians was a drawback to the labour supply in the country and was therefore looked upon with mixed feelings. In 1903 severe restrictions were put on the "exportation" of labour, the main provision being that recruiting agents had to obtain a special licence (at a high fee). In 1908, there was a ban in some parts of the country on the shipment of labourers to foreign countries; this because of agitation by Liberian farmers who complained that these "exports" were injuring their labour supply [1]. In 1914, there followed an agreement between Spain and Liberia, whereby it was attempted to protect the emigrating labourers against all the abuses to which they were exposed. From now on there was to be Government supervision, and all sorts of questions concerning this labour were regulated in detail [2], so that the agreement read like a sort of Magna Charta for migrating labour. However, in actual practice, all this had very little effect: the planters of Fernando Po went on treating their "imported" labourers just as badly as before [3].

Attempts were also made—for example, in 1917 and 1921—to put labour relations in general with the natives on a better footing; and here pressure was certainly exerted by the United States, under whose protection Liberia had in a sense remained. But once again, the results were unsatisfactory.

However, the situation was to change, in 1930. Strong accusations by Americans of the existence of forced labour and a veritable slave trade in Liberia led to a visit—at Liberia's own request—of an international commission of inquiry. And on the recommendations of the commission, the Liberian Government instituted various reforms. Pawning was abolished by a law of December 19, 1930, and recruiting for shipment overseas was forbidden by a law approved on December

[1] Buell, The Native Problem in Africa, Vol. 2, p. 777.

[2] A summary of the provisions can be found in the International Commission's Report, p. 35/36; Buell, The Native Problem in Africa, vol. 2, p. 778/9; Azikiwe, op. cit., p. 172/173.

[3] Huberich, op. cit., p. 912; Azikiwe, op. cit., p. 174.

15, 1930—one of the reasons being (as actually stated in the first lines of the law [1]) that there was a growing demand for labour in Liberia itself. But Liberia seems to have put through the reforms even without immediate economic motivation—and concern for its reputation in other countries may have played a part in this. According to an official communication in 1933 [2] as of that moment approximately 84 per cent of all pawns were already free. And as regards the Convention on Forced Labour, made by the International Labour Conference of 1930, and demanding the immediate abolition of forced labour for private individuals, Liberia (with Ireland) was one of the first two countries to ratify [3]. The International Slavery Convention of 1926 was also ratified by Liberia.

All this, however, was not sufficient to repair the damage already done; and native uprisings, which had been a feature in Liberia from the very beginning, did not cease, but have been known to have occurred even in comparatively recent times [4]. One writer reports that fighting against the "Americans" is the daily occupation of some tribes [5]; and in a work published in 1943 we are told that the tribes hate their Negro rulers in a sullen, restless fury [6]. This has been the outcome in a country which in its Constitution wrote that the improvement of the native tribes was a cherished ideal of the Government [7]. And in all this, compulsory labour has played a very important part.

LITERATURE

Azikiwe, Nnamdi, Liberia in World Politics, London, 1934.

Brown, George, Firestone-Libéria. In: Le travail en Afrique noire, Paris, 1952, p. 342-347.

Buell, Raymond Leslie, Liberia: a Century of Survival 1847-1947, Philadelphia 1947, (African Handbooks 7).

Buell, Raymond Leslie, The Native Problem in Africa, New York, 1928, Vol. 2, section 14: The Liberian Republic.

Forced labour, Report and draft questionnaire, Geneva, 1929 (International Labour Conference, 12th session, Geneva 1929, first discussion), p. 136, 188/9, 225-227.

---

[1] Cited in Huberich, op. cit., p. 914.
[2] Cited in Azikiwe, p. 196, note 2.
[3] Report of the Ad hoc committee on forced labour, Geneva, 1953, p. 146.
[4] See for example Buell, The Native Problem in Africa, vol. 2, p. 737-743.
[5] Henry Fenwick Reeve, The Black Republic etc., 1923, p. 47.
[6] Hayman and Preece, op. cit., p. 52. (Cited in Buell, Liberia, p. 13).
[7] Sec. 15 of Art. 5 of the Constitution of 1847. In Huberich on page 863.

Harris, John H., Liberian Slavery: The essentials. In: The Contemporary Review, vol. 139, 1931 I, p. 303-309.
Huberich, Charles Henry, The Political and Legislative History of Liberia, New York, 1947, 2 vols.
International Commission of Enquiry in Liberia: Communication by the Government of Liberia dated December 15th 1930, transmitting the commission's report, Geneva, 1930 (League of Nations.—Official number: C. 658. M. 272. 1930. VI).
The recruiting of labour in colonies and in other territories with analogous labour conditions, Geneva, 1935 (International Labour Conference, 19th session, Geneva 1935, report IV, first discussion).
Reeve, Henry Fenwick, The Black Republic, Liberia: its political and social conditions to-day, London, 1923.
Schuyler, George S., Slaves Today, a Story of Liberia, New York, 1931.
Sottile, Antoine, Documents divers sur la Commission Internationale d'Enquête concernant l'esclavage et le travail forcé dans la République de Libéria. In: Revue de droit international, de sciences diplomatiques et politiques, 8me année, 1930, p. 289-347.
Wilson, Charles Morrow, Liberia, New York, 1947.

CHAPTER THIRTEEN

SOVIET RUSSIA

We will take Soviet Russia as our example of a European country in which compulsory labour has recently appeared on a large scale.

The establishment of the Soviet regime brought with it an attitude toward labour differing greatly from that current until then. The new rulers adopted Marx's and Engels's principles, as stated in the Communist Manifesto, that everyone who was able to work had the right to as well as the obligation to work. Art. I, § I of the first Soviet Labour Law Code (1918) reads as follows: all citizens of the USSR, with exception of the categories mentioned below shall be subject to compulsory labour [1]—the categories being a) all persons under 16 and over 50, b) the sick and infirm, and c) women from 8 weeks before to 8 weeks after a confinement. The idea underlying this proclamation was that the community should provide all its members with the means of subsistence, just as each member of a family is supported from the family income. But this obviously implies, according to the official commentary in the American edition of the Code [2], that all who are able must participate in the work necessary to render the community capable of supporting all its members.

The principle of a universal obligation to work is still upheld. The following statement is to be found in art. 12 of the present constitution: In the USSR, to work is the obligation and pride of every able-bodied citizen, in conformity with the principle that "he who does not work, does not eat". The text goes on to say that this principle is the basic principle of socialism: "From each according to his ability; to each according to his effort". Here we might hesitate to suggest that the principle thus formulated is definitely not in conformance with orthodox socialism; socialist theoreticians in general putting it this way: "From each according to his ability, to each according to his needs"; which makes quite a difference.

The significance of the labour law just discussed was primarily abstract and political in so far as it expressed the rejection of the old

---

[1] The Labor Laws of Soviet Russia, 3rd ed., New York, 1920, p. 15.

[2] Id., p. 5.

class differences, and stressed present social equality. The extent to which the principle was applied depended in the first place on the economic circumstances, which fluctuated quite considerably in the course of years.

The way in which labour was regulated was, in fact, dependent mainly on quite another circumstance, namely the unique role of the State in Soviet Russia, whereby it takes upon itself almost entire control of the economic life, and almost absolute power over the individual; and it is this factor which has led to largescale compulsory labour being imposed, in some periods less so, in others more so.

From the very start, the State began to exercise most rigorous control over the work of its subjects [1]. Everything was subordinated to the reconstruction. Industries were nationalized, and labour distribution was also controlled by the State. This applied to the privately-owned enterprises as well, now regarded as auxiliary forces in the nationalized economic life. Free contracting between employers and employees was no longer permitted. Various provisions made it possible for workers to be taken on for temporary or periodic work, or to be directed to a specific, permanent place in the production system. Personal preferences were generally not taken into consideration in such distribution, and to object in any way was punishable, even with the death penalty.

In practice, however, these provisions seemed to result in a very inadequate labour supply. It seemed unavoidable that often professional people were taken from their place of work and told to perform unskilled labour elsewhere. In general it turned out that unfamiliar work performed against the worker's will was unproductive and a drain on State funds. The least satisfactory of all was the situation with regard to the farmers. Generally speaking, there were no regulations covering their labour on behalf of the State; thus nobody knew for how long he could be conscripted or whether he was to be paid for extra work etc. This naturally led to some extremely serious abuses. Farmers would be called upon to do anything up to 120 days compulsory labour in a year, without advance warning and regardless of whether they could be spared on their own farms or whether these would go to ruin. The location of work to which they were sent would be some distance from where they

[1] Industrial life in Soviet Russia 1917-1923, International Labour Office, Geneva, 1924, Chapter 5.

themselves lived, sometimes even in another province; and frequently they had to work with inadequate tools and without sufficient to eat, so it is hardly any wonder that their work on the whole gave scant results.

Because of the limited success of the legal provisions most were repealed (in 1921 and 1922). Another reason for this was that there was actually widespread unemployment in Russia at the time, making such strict measures unnecessary because of the availability of labour. Workers and employers were now granted considerably more freedom with regard to the concluding of individual contracts, and conscription for extra duty of a temporary nature could only be resorted to in cases of emergency.

Russians now lived for a few years in comparative freedom, at least in as far as their work was concerned. Workers could, if they felt thus inclined, give up their jobs and look for new employment themselves, or even not work at all for a time if their means permitted this.

However, with the first of the five year plans introduced in 1928, all this changed. Now suddenly there was a gigantic programme of work which had to be carried out, and which was to alter the entire economic life of Soviet Russia. The first objective was the complete collectivization of agriculture by degrees. It was hoped that a vast amount of labour power would be liberated in this way, which labour could then be transferred to the large industries which were to be created. Other objectives were the construction of roads and canals throughout the country and indispensable to the growth of the economy. And finally, the as yet unexploited expanses in the North and East were to be developed.

To obtain the labour force necessary for this, the State again began concerning itself actively with labour legislation [1]. The Peoples' Commissariat for Labour was assigned the task of distributing the country's available labour supply to the various undertakings. From henceforth it was strictly forbidden, except in special cases, to re-

---

[1] A selection of documents relative to the labour legislation in force in the Union of Soviet Socialist Republics, 1931, Cmd. 3775.
David J. Dallin and Boris I. Nicolaevsky, Forced Labor in Soviet Russia, 1948, p. 191-199.
Frédéric Eccard, Le travail forcé en Russie soviétique. In: La revue hebdomadaire, avril 1931, p. 457-472.
Solomon M. Schwarz, Labor in the Soviet Union, 1952, Chap. 3.
Report of the Ad hoc Committee on Forced Labour, 1953, p. 95-97.

cruit workers through any channels other than those officially recognized.

In the first place, all unemployed individuals were to be put to work immediately, the only acceptable reason for refusing to work being one of illness, and the payment of benefits to the unemployed was completely suspended.

It was, moreover, necessary to determine where a smaller labour force could serve as adequately as the one in use. Superfluous labour was to be transferred to undertakings which were short of labour. One of the most serious labour supply problems occurred in the lumber production schemes in the North and various regulations were passed especially pertaining to this case. In the villages, radical measures had to be taken to promote recruitment for this purpose, and the cooperation of the village authorities was obligatory. However, it was especially the collective farms which were to supply superfluous workers for the lumber industry and other seasonal work.

Not only superfluous workers were to be transferred. Whenever trained workers and people with special qualifications were used for work other than that for which they were already qualified, they were to be assigned work of more direct benefit to the State. In such transfers, the personal wishes of the workers were of no account, and only women with families could not be moved to another location without their agreement. All other persons could expect to be severely punished if they in any way refused to carry out official orders. The managers of the undertakings were compelled to release workers designated for (temporary or permanent) transfer, within a stipulated time. Finally, any official concerned with recruitment who did not show himself active enough in the performance of his duties could be punished.

Everything possible was done to prevent workers from leaving their work. Strict measures were taken against "deserters" and those who frequently changed employment in order to better their position. It was a culpable offence for managers of undertakings to try to attract labourers or other personnel from other undertakings to their own, and they were also forbidden to employ workers who had left their previous employment without permission. Wide use was made of the press. In the years immediately after 1928, papers were full of accounts about persons "depraved" enough as to "desert" their work. However, all this still proved inadequate, and therefore the State resorted to the pass system, as has been used in all the colonial territories to gain more control over the labourers. From now on all citizens were obliged to carry on their persons a pass in which the management recorded the date of entering employment and, in cases where this was lawfully allowed, the date of departure. Naturally, this made it still more difficult for workers to change employment; but apparently not difficult enough, for by 1940 control was even stricter. From henceforth, all those committing a breach of contract were to be prosecuted under penal sanction—just as we found in colonial countries—and sentenced to imprisonment.

Measures were also taken to combat absenteeism, and on this point too regulations were intensified in 1940 when it was decreed that a worker found guilty of "absence from work" could be convicted to a maximum of six months forced labour in the place where he had been at work; meaning in effect that he would work under police supervision during the day but would be free outside working hours. As a rule, this sentence carries with it a 25% reduction in wages during the period of conviction. A worker can be considered guilty of "absence from work" when he wastes 20 minutes of the working time in one day—either through coming too late, leaving too early, or taking an extended lunch hour--or when he wastes time on three occasions in one month or on four occasions in two months, even though the loss of time on each occasion may be less than 20 minutes.

Negligence connected with work is also heavily punished, especially when related to the transport industry, which is regarded as a very important part of the national economy. In Art. 59 of the Russian Code of Penal Law we find for example that whenever errors made in the regulations of train traffic and inadequate repair of rolling stock or of the rails result or could result in damage or accident, a maximum of ten years imprisonment can be imposed on the guilty party. But not only errors which could be of serious consequences are punished so severely since the same sentence of 10 years' loss of liberty is applicable to those responsible for the late departure of trains or boats, allowing empty freight trucks to pile up at unloading points, or other "crimes" holding up the transportation schedule as determined by the authorities. And this has nothing to do with there being any deliberate attempt on the part of the guilty parties since in that case the death sentence can be applied, with, further, the confiscation of the convicted man's property. In addition, any mistakes or negligence can be punished as counter-revolutionary sabotage, defined as the deliberate failure to fulfil, or adequately fulfil one's duties with the object of injuring the State. Since all labour falls under the jurisdiction of the State in Russia, this charge is always applicable, and in fact often used in cases of petty negligence [1].

All in all therefore we see that workers in Russia are allowed little freedom in the choice of their work, and that they are bound down to this work through rigorous penal sanction.

Moreover, a regulation was passed in 1940 [2], whereby boys of from 14 to 17 could be conscripted—to the number of from 800,000 to 1,000,000 a year—for training in trade schools, to be followed by an assignment to work for a period of four years where it is most needed. This is clearly a case of compulsory labour since neither the boys nor their parents have any say in the matter of conscription or assignment, and their consent is not required. But what makes it even more a case of compulsory labour is the fact that the boys are still not free to leave their work after four years without special permission from a higher authority.

The State has been able to accomplish a great deal in the way of economic development by all these measures, but all that can be considered as having been truly ambitious was not accomplished in this way since an appreciable proportion of the bigger projects, especially the exploitation and clearance of the practically uninhabitable areas in the north of Russia and Siberia, have been executed by labourers drawn from another source. Large-scale use has been made of prisoners in Russia. The performance of work by prisoners is of course a common and universal phenomenon. As a rule, however, it is intended purely for the well-being of the prisoners, and the work as such has little or no economic significance. Not so in Russia. In the first place here, as frequently happens in countries with a dictatorial government, the number of prisoners was enormously increased by the flood of political prisoners. And further, the number of arrests was deliberately increased to provide labour for government projects, especially in places where living is difficult. It is this factor which justifies us in terming such labour "compulsory labour", in the sense in which it is used in this study.

It is in a sense tragic that it should be precisely in Soviet Russia that we find such an inhuman system of convict labour, for after

---

1 Silvestre Mora et Pierre Zwierniak, La Justice soviétique, Rome, 1945, p. 23.

2 Schwarz, op. cit., p. 76-83.
Report of the Ad hoc Committee on Forced Labour, 1953, p. 96/7.

all it were the communists who started out with much idealism with respect to crime and punishment [1]. In their eyes, crime was the natural consequence of the capitalistic system; to their way of thinking, moral degeneration resulted from a rotten social system in which hunger, poverty and other evils were tolerated. And it was they who were confident that the new social system would swiftly put an end to the phenomenon of crime. Those who were already criminals before the Revolution were to be cured rather than punished, for after all, they had not been the guilty ones, but the society in which they had had to live. Thus it was that the terms "guilt" and "punishment" were dropped from official terminology together with the word "prison". Prisons were survivals of the capitalistic era; all that was now needed was for a short time to have "places of internment" where those who had strayed for no fault of their own would be transformed into good citizens. Work was to be the tool of accomplishing this—the communists have always believed in the corrective influence of work—but this work would be performed under congenial conditions, and would be solely for the benefit of the detainees themselves. Exploitation of prison labour was to be found in capitalistic countries but had absolutely no place in the communist scheme of things; or at any rate, so they said directly after the revolution. And they even instituted a new form of punishment, which was a source of great pride to them, and went under the name of "compulsory labour without imprisonment". By it, convicted persons were to do the labour to which they had been sentenced at a somewhat lower than normal pay while living at liberty in the community.

However, to the great disappointment of the communist leaders, under this system and under their regime, crime did not decrease. On the contrary, it rose to a disturbing degree. Dallin gives some official figures concerning the number of prisoners before and after the revolution [2]:

In the year	1901	84,632
	1903	96,005
	1908	171,219
	1912	183,949
	1913	169,367

[1] See, for the historical development of the present system of forced labour, especially Dallin, op. cit., Chapters 7-14.

[2] Dallin, op. cit., p. 159/160.

1924	87,800
1925	148,000
1926	155,000
1927	198,000

And these figures are mainly in respect of criminals in the ordinary sense of the word, and do not include the many thousands of political prisoners. The Soviet Government was after all a minority government, and to stay in power they had to ruthlessly suppress opposition, therefore holding in abeyance humanitarian considerations. As a result of the enormous increase in the numbers of political prisoners, the prisons and concentration camps in which they were mainly impounded became overcrowded, and in the end other solutions had to be found.

Practically nothing had ever come of the system of corrective labour. Due to the prevalent unemployment at the time there was little need for prison labour which only tends to reduce the available opportunities for free workers. Also, there was not much to do in the prison areas as such, and no material to do it with. So before the Government really required prison labour, this form of labour was not utilized anymore than it is in other countries.

The change came in 1928 with the institution of the first five-year plan. Vast numbers of workers were needed and the State was quick to avail itself of the potential labour force in the overcrowded prisons. Now all humanitarian ideals about the reeducation of the misled were thrown overboard, and the misled were introduced to forced labour under the most difficult of circumstances. New proclamations were issued decreeing that from henceforth penal servitude was to be replaced by forced labour, and judges unwilling to comply with these regulations would themselves find out what forced labour was like [1]. The number of concentration camps, now fitted out as work camps, increased enormously, new camps being constructed there where labourers were most needed. And where first use was made of the working capacities of already convicted persons, later there were widespread convictions because labour was needed [2]. In about 1934, it looked almost as though the regime would become more clement, but forced

[1] See, for example: A selection of documents relative ro the labour legislation in force in the USSR, p. 138-140; Dallin, op. cit., p. 206/7.

[2] See, among others, the report of the second session of the „Ad hoc Committee on Forced Labour" of the U.N. In: Bulletin de L'Organisation Internationale du Travail, E/AC. 36/4, Add. 1, 27 juin 1952, p. 3.

labour had become such an essential part of Russian economy that it was now almost impossible to do away with it, and the threat of a new war, making an extra national effort necessary, tipped the balance in favour of retaining the system and even utilizing it to a greater extent [1]. The number of forced labourers has understandably never been made public. Authoritative estimates recently put it at from 7 to 12 million [2], and of these, 85% to 90% are men. If these figures are correct it would mean that approximately 16% of all adult males in Russia are forced labourers. Moreover, these figures do not include the millions deported for "forced colonization", *inter alia* from regions occupied during the war.

Labour camps are to be found throughout the country. The largest, however, are in the North and East. The camps are all administrated from a central body, the GULAG, which once formed part of the GPU (secret police), but which was later transferred to the People's Commissariat for Internal Affairs, the NKVD (or later, MVD). GULAG as such controls vast undertakings, in which the prisoners are put to work; but the more frequent procedure is for GULAG to conclude contracts with various State or other enterprises, whereby it guarantees to carry out some project or other with prison labour.

There is almost no kind of work for which prison labour is not used, forced labourers being employed extensively in agriculture, mining (gold, silver, platinum, hard coal, iron etc.), lumbering (in the North) and many other industries. During the war they were mainly used in war production, and since then the production of atomic weapons has occupied forced labourers exclusively. Forced labour has also been used for communication (canals, railways, roads, airfields, harbours, bridges) and housing projects (for example, in and about Moscow).

Many of the activities mentioned above depend to a considerable extent on forced labour. According to one estimate, since 1938 prison labour has accounted for 75% of the gold production [3]. Thus this system can be said to play a very important part in the national economy.

[1] See for recent situation also: Report of the Ad hoc Committee on Forced Labour, 1953, p. 82-98.

[2] Dallin, op. cit., p. 86-87. A. K. Herling, The Soviet Slave Empire, 1951, p. 11. Mora-Zwierniak op. cit., p. 127/9. C. Zamorski, Forced Labour in the Soviet Union. In: World Affairs, N.S., Vol. 4, 1950, p. 157.

[3] Herling, op. cit., p. 14.

As regards the people inhabiting the labour camps, these differ as much from each other as the work which is done. Only about 15% are criminals in the ordinary sense of the word, the rest being the so-called political offenders. Not that this means that these people necessarily hold any political convictions; on the contrary, most are as ignorant and primitive as the majority of ordinary criminals, and have ended up in the labour camps for a variety of different reasons. At the start of the first five year plan, many kulaks (more or less well-to-do farmers) were sent to the camps because they quite naturally did not take much to the idea of collective agriculture. Then too, there were vast numbers of the nomadic steppe inhabitants (Turkomen, Kirghiz etc.) and others who did not understand anything of these new ideas, and many of these would be arrested for "sabotage of the production programme" because they had in their ignorance, for example, allowed a piece of agricultural machinery to become rusty. "Sabotage" is in fact the primary cause putting most into camps since the smallest of misdemeanours fall under this category, even misdemeanours which in the West would be punished with some disciplinary action, a fine, or at the most a few days imprisonment. Also in the camps are disgraced communist functionaries, individuals prosecuted for their religious beliefs, and people with foreign connections. This last group is mainly made up of Jews, since practically every Jewish family in Russia has relatives in Poland or Rumania, and a number of foreign communists who had to flee their own countries because of their political convictions. Finally, many are sent to the camps on the merest suspicion of lack of sympathy for the regime; being related to a convicted man often being considered sufficient evidence against one.

Some prisoners are granted the privilege of a trial before being sent to the camps, but these trials are not what we are used to in the West [1]. In Russia, the principle of the independence of the judge is not adhered to. The Court is an instrument of the communist party and as such is used to combat any actions dangerous to the social order. The search for objective truth is thus not a primary objective [2]. However, only a small number of prisoners pass through a trial and by far and away the majority are simply sent to the camps on the decision of the NKVD (MVD). This body has the power to impose

[1] The statements in this paragraph were valid up to 1958.

[2] Mora-Zwierniak, op. cit., p. 20-22.

internment by an administrative process; that is to say, individuals may be simply rounded up and put into prison where they are then notified after awhile that they have been convicted to say 10 years forced labour, and deportation to the labour camps follows. Therefore, the corporation controlling labour forces, and hiring them out at considerable profit to other departments [1], is also responsible for the passing of sentences on prisoners without any form of trial. Understandably this contributes toward a state of affairs in which arrests are made only to fill the requirements for forced labourers.

The living conditions of prisoners vary in different camps, depending among other things on the nature of the work being performed. For example, the conditions are better in agricultural camps than in mining camps, and a few camps in the vicinity of Moscow are remarkably up to date. In most camps, however, the conditions are too shocking to be believed. By far the greater majority of those condemned to forced labour are deported to the arctic regions of Russia and Siberia, and have to work exceedingly hard in extreme cold and on very little food. Under these conditions it is hardly surprising that the death rate is high (although the official figures are not made known, one observer claims that the death figures vary from 5% in the (few) good camps to 40% in the very worst, especially in Kolyma where gold is mined [2]).

Because of their small chances of surviving their terms of forced labour, the victims are not particularly interested in whether their sentences are for 5, 8 or 10 years; and it is indeed very rarely that people return home after the termination of their official sentences. Usually they are informed that they have been sentenced anew, either to a further number of years in the same camp or to banishment to Siberia. Those banished to Siberia join settlements of "forced colonists", which will be discussed later.

It is very difficult to escape from the camps, and although many prisoners have succeeded, it should be remembered that they form a very small percentage of the total number of prison labourers.

Prison labour would appear to have given good results economically. Production in various branches of industry has been considerably increased with this labour [3], and the costs of pro-

[1] See page 182.

[2] C. Zamorski, Forced Labour in the Soviet Union. In: World Affairs. N.S., Vol. 4, p. 166.

[3] See figures in Dallin, op. cit., p. 210/11.

duction have been kept sufficiently low as to make competition on the foreign markets a favourable proposition, which in turn has made it possible to import articles vital to the economic development of the country. Besides this there is the fact that much virginal territory has been opened up, and prison labour can therefore be said to have fulfilled its purpose.

However, the (forced) colonization of Russian Asia has not been the work of prisoners alone. In about 1930, a start was made on the removal of undesirable population groups *en masse* to remote areas of Asia and Northern Russia. The first to fall victims to this scheme were the kulaks. As already stated, one of the main objectives of the first five-year plan was the forcible collectivization of agriculture, and to achieve this the kulak class—comprising 5,859,000 persons in 1928—had to be "liquidated", as made known later officially. What this amounts to is that many of the men were sent to labour camps and that the rest, thus women, children and the remaining men, were deported to Siberia and Central Asia. There was a further mass movement of "forced colonists" during the war years, and the eviction of undesirable persons continued in the post-war period. This time the victims were taken primarily from the occupied zones, where anyone in any way suspected of anti-communist sentiments would be deported together with his family. From the occupied zones of Poland alone almost a million people were resettled in this way in the years 1939-1941 [1]. Thus, as far as the Soviet rulers were concerned, large groups of population were being removed from places where they could only hinder Soviet progress to the uninhabited areas of Asia where they could be used to colonize vast tracts of country. Since the deportees are made to work as forced labourers, they fall under the control of a representative of the NKVD (later MVD), and the situation in the settlements is almost the same in many respects as in the labour camps. However, they have a few advantages over the prison labourers in that they are paid piece-work wages, from which food and other necessities can be bought in the stores run by the NKVD, and in that families are often allowed to remain together, which is not the case in the work camps; a man and his wife if both convicted to forced labour often being sent to different camps. Nevertheless, in the colonization settlements the work-day is long and the work heavy; absenteeism is

---

[1] Mora-Zwierniak, op. cit., p. 86.

punishable; and the food which can be bought is both scarce and of poor quality. Moreover, housing in most instances leaves much to be desired, and the climate in almost all cases is difficult to endure. All in all, it is not surprising therefore that the death-rate is frequently high.

However, in those countries that have come into the Russian sphere of influence [1], compulsory labour is not only the lot of those people who have been forcibly removed but also of the rest of the population, since in these countries the inhabitants are compelled to work in the same way as Russians are in Russia.

In the Baltic countries, the farmers were the first to feel this [2]. In the first place, anyone running a farm, man or woman, received specified tasks to be completed within a specified time. This included felling and transporting wood, road reparations, and haulage with their own vehicles of whatever was ordered by the authorities. In emergency cases, extra duties could be demanded; and, what is more, collective work could be demanded of the local communities, refusal to comply being severely punishable. If it so happened that there were no woods in the neighbourhood, or no roads in need of repair, this did not mean that compulsory labour was dropped. Far from it, for in such cases farmers were sent elsewhere, even if necessary to other districts. Altogether, this work constituted a very heavy burden, especially in the last case.

In Rumania, innumerable people were called up for so-called voluntary labour, which was in no sense recognizable as such, however [3]. Permanent brigades were formed, primarily composed of those who had till that time done little to no labour at all; and temporary brigades were made up of people on their summer vacations, while others were formed with people "willing" to work in their free time, after work. These brigades are utilized for all sorts of work—paving roads, laying railways, mining hard coal, etc., etc. and although newspapers report that all this is done with the greatest amount of enthusiasm, one cannot lose sight of the fact that the conditions of work are sometimes appalling, and that the mortality in these cases is shockingly high.

In Poland [4] a proclamation regulating compulsory labour appeared

---

[1] See besides the literature mentioned below also: Report of the Ad hoc Committee on Forced Labour, 1953.

[2] Herling, op. cit., p. 81-86.

[3] Id., p. 116-121.

[4] International Labour Office, Legislative series, 1946.

in January, 1946; and according to this proclamation, all men between the ages of 18 and 55, and all women between the ages of 18 and 45, with the exception of certain categories, were to register at the labour bureau. This bureau could then conscript them for a period of two years' labour at the most, without having to take into consideration where the persons concerned lived, except that persons called up to work away from their own villages or towns were given the right to choose between various possibilities. Anyone failing to appear at the place where the work was to be done when told, was liable for conviction to a maximum of 5 years imprisonment with forced labour and/or a fine.

A similar regulation is in force in Czechoslovakia [1]. All men between the ages of 16 and 55 and all women between the ages of 18 and 45, again with a few exceptions, can be conscripted for labour in or away from their places of abode. The managers of undertakings may send a request for labour to a labour bureau, which has the authority, possibly after investigating the urgency of the case, to send the requested number of workers for a maximum period of one year. Workers should be notified of conscription at least three days in advance of the commencement of work, and refusal to comply is of course severely punished.

People are also recruited for labour in East Germany [2]. Whenever workers are required on projects considered to be of importance, the labour bureau meets the demand usually by taking a certain percentage of the personnel in various undertakings and sending these. However, it has been known to occur in cases of emergency that people have been simply rounded up at random in the streets. The labour bureau pays no regard to the condition of health and the circumstances of the individual, even in regular recruitment. Workers in great numbers have often been required for the work involved in the dismantling of industries, but by far and away the majority of recruits are sent to the uranium mines. Here they have to work extremely hard under conditions which are dangerous from the point of view of health, and they are paid for 26 days work in a month although ordinarily having only one rest day. Guards are employed for the purpose of driving the people to work harder. In cases of absence or time wasted, food and pay are withheld, and on relapse a

---

[1] International Labour Office, Legislative series, 1945.
[2] Herling, op. cit., p. 184-196.

worker is removed to a "penal mine" where conditions are far worse and where smaller rations of food are given. The workers naturally frequently fall ill under such circumstances, but they are not given time off to recover except in cases of high fever. Doctors who declare workers sick when they have not got a high fever run the risk of being convicted for sabotage. 20% to 30% of the labour force in the uranium fields are women, who work above ground but are given equally arduous tasks as the men. Although the regulations stipulate that only persons between the ages of 18 and 45 may be recruited, it is known that there are children under 14 and men over 65 working on the mines; this is because the officers at the labour bureaus are expected, on penalty of discharge or worse, to supply the required number of recruitees at short notice and they are therefore not always too strict about applying the age limit. Finally, to prevent escape, the entire area of the mines and labour camps is heavily guarded and surrounded by barbed wire.

And this applied only to labour in the satellite countries themselves. But the people from these countries are sometimes also sent as labour-power to Russia. This took place in a peculiar form regarding youths for instance in Estonia. Boys between 14 and 17 years of age were recruited to be sent to Russian schools and formed into a labour reserve. Neither the boys nor their parents were consulted in the matter. It was intended to transfer 40,000 boys from Estonia to Russia in this way [1].

In addition to the fact that the people in the Russian satellite countries have no say whatever as regards the work which they are to perform, we also find severe stipulations here too concerning absenteeism, negligence, labour wastage etc. Sabotage of production programmes is countered with the same heavy penalties, even to the extent of the death sentence. And in Czechoslovakia, for example, it is laid down by law that any able-bodied person between the ages of 18 and 60 who refuses to work can be sent to a labour camp, and in fact all the satellite countries are as abundantly provided with labour camps as Russia herself.

Wherever we look we find compulsory labour, both in Russia and the countries that come within her sphere of influence, be it in the prison camps, the settlements of forced colonists or in the so-called free society. Resistance from within would appear an impossibility.

---

[1] Herling, op. cit., p. 75/6.

From the outside world, one counter-action has been endeavoured. That was in 1930, when the conditions in the camps in the arctic regions became known through the stories told by escaped prisoners and seamen, especially Scandinavians, whose ships had called in at northern ports to load timber. Public opinion in Europe and America was deeply shocked, and in the United States an embargo was declared against the importation of Russian timber on the basis of an article of law decreeing that goods produced with prison or forced labour might not enter the country. However, since material interests were involved, the whole issue became confused. Both in England and the United States, industries adversely affected by competition from Russian products demanded a complete importation embargo, but others again, such as the paper industry that could well do with Russian timber, strongly opposed any such action. This gave the Soviet regime an opportunity to describe the whole action as a capitalistic manipulation, and the English Labour Government was unable to come to a decision. Nor was it long before the American importation embargo was lifted, and in Russia everything went on just as it had before, the system of forced labour even increasing in extent and elaboration as time went on. Today it has reached a point at which economic life in Russia would appear to be impossible but for this form of labour, its role having become so essential.

We can only conclude therefore that compulsory labour has been realized in Soviet Russia on a scale such as would have been impossible even to conceive of in any European country up to not so very long ago.

LITERATURE

Beausobre, Julia de, The Woman Who Could Not Die, New York, 1938.
Dallin, David J., and Boris I. Nicolaevsky, Forced Labor in Soviet Russia, London, 1948.
The Dark Side of the Moon, With a pref. by T. S. Eliot, London, 1946.
Eccard, Frédéric, Le travail forcé en Russie Soviétique. In: La revue hebdomadaire, 40me année, 1931, p. 457-472.
Herling, Albert Konrad, The Soviet Slave Empire, London, 1951.
Herling, Gustav, A World Apart, Transl. from the Polish, London, 1952.
Hubbard, Leonard E., Soviet Labour and Industry, London, 1942.
Industrial life in Soviet Russia 1917-1923, Geneva, 1924 (International Labour Office).
International Labour Office, Legislative series, 1945, 1946.
Kolarz, Walter, Russia and Her Colonies, London, 1952.
The Labor Laws of Soviet Russia, 3rd ed., 1920 (The Russian Soviet Government Bureau, New York).

Littlepage, John D., and Demaree Bess, In Search of Soviet Gold, London etc., 1939.

La "main-d'oeuvre" soviétique, le régime des détenus à Solovski, Par D.H.B. In: La nouvelle revue des jeunes, 3me année, 1931, p. 305-320.

Malsagoff, S. A., An Island Hell: a Soviet prison in the Far North, Transl. from the Russian, London, 1926.

Mora, Silvester, (ps. of C. Zamorski), Kolyma, Gold and Forced Labor in the USSR, Washington, 1949 (Foundation for Foreign Affairs).

Mora, Sylvestre, (ps. of C. Zamorski) — Pierre Zwierniak, La justice soviétique, Rome, 1945.

Petrov, Vladimir, It Happens in Russia, seven years forced labour in the Siberian goldfields, Transl. from the Russian, London, 1951.

Report of the Second Session of the "Ad hoc Committee on Forced Labour" of the United Nations. In: Bulletin de l'Organisation Internationale du Travail, E/AC. 36/4, Add. 1, 27 juin 1952.

Report of the Ad hoc Committee on Forced Labour, Geneva, 1953, (United Nations — International Labour Office).

Schwarz, Solomon M., Labor in the Soviet Union, New York, 1952.

A selection of documents relative to the labour legislation in force in the Union of Soviet Socialist Republics, London, 1931, Cmd. 3775.

Solonevich, Ivan, Russia in Chains, Transl. from the Russian, 1938.

Le travail forcé en Russie Soviétique (Centre Belge de l'Entente Internationale Anti-Communiste).

The White Sea Canal, being an account of the construction of the new canal between the White Sea and the Baltic Sea, Transl. from the Russian, London, 1935.

Zamorski, C., Forced Labour in the Soviet Union. In: World affairs, N.S., vol. 4, 1950, p. 154-167.

CHAPTER FOURTEEN

CONCLUSIONS

We have established in the foregoing chapters that the abolition of slavery did not necessarily mean the end to compulsory labour, other forms having been evolved wherever this seemed necessary or advantageous from an economic point of view.

In Spanish America, enslavement of the Indians was forbidden (except in certain specific cases) from the very outset of colonization. Nevertheless, other forms of compulsory labour were instituted. To start with, the Indians were divided among the Spaniards who could then dispose of their labour, for comparatively short periods at first, but longer periods for later generations (the *encomienda* system). When this system became inadequate after some time—newcomers finding that there were no Indians available for them—it was abolished, to be immediately replaced by another form of compulsory labour. Now every Indian village had to deliver a stipulated number of labourers to an entrepreneur—the labourers being chosen in rotation from among the inhabitants. When this system (called *repartimiento* or *mita*) became in its turn no longer economical—the system of a rotating and primitive labour force no longer being satisfactory in view of the increasing demands for skilled labour—it also disappeared from the scene. But there was something to fill the gap, for by that time debt bondage had become prevalent—and this form of labour compulsion remained to stay.

Something very similar to this can be seen to have happened after the abolition of Negro slavery in the course of the 19th century. Where slavery had been widespread, emancipation was followed by the imposition of drastic measures to retain a labour force. Apart from other stipulations there was almost in all cases a decree against "vagrancy" (Jamaica, Mauritius, South Africa, the United States, the Portuguese colonies, etc.) which in effect always amounted to compulsory labour when strictly applied. In a few of the Southern states in the U.S.A., for example, anyone without regular work was declared to be a "vagrant" and as such liable (in the likely event of his not being able to pay the very high fine imposed) to forced labour on a plantation. In other instances the general obligation to work was even emphatically established by law (Mauritius); and in the Portuguese colonies the prohibition of vagrancy went coupled to another regulation covering contract labour, whereby officials presiding over the conclusion of contracts were to receive a fee for every contract concluded in their presence.

In the Cape Colony (South Africa), the settlers can be said to have been more strongly opposed to the abolition of the slave trade by England in 1807 than to the abolition of slavery as such in 1833. This was mainly because the settlers had until then relied on imported slaves, and the native Hottentots were left in comparative peace. After 1807, however, these were subjected to what amounted to compulsory labour even if expressed in other words in the relevant legislation; and when England decided to abolish slavery as well as the slave trade, a law was immediately passed by the Legislative Council in the Cape which could only mean compulsory labour for both the Hottentots and the liberated slaves. When the mother country rejected this law, the settlers decided that they had had enough of British interference, and this was one of the main causes leading to the Great Trek, and the consequent colonization of vast new territories. The Boers in this new land were their own masters and they made free use of forced Bantu labour in meeting their limited requirements as cattle farmers.

The harshness of the measures taken in many countries directly after abolition is not surprising since there where the use of Negro slaves was widespread and almost essential for the economy, the direct result of abolition was chaos. The Negroes wanted to get away from their old work on the plantations, for to their minds it was slavery under any name; and the climate in most areas concerned was such as to make it possible for them, at least for a while, to live without having to work at all. That was the situation in the West Indies and Mauritius after 1834; and it was the same in the United States when slavery came to an end there thirty years later: the Negroes would not hear of labour contracts, especially after the rumour spread that every emancipated slave was to receive forty acres of land and a mule. In the thinly-populated South, with its mild climate, it was not difficult to live for a while without doing any special work. And in the vast, thinly populated Portuguese colonies the Negroes were certainly not dependent on the employment opportunities of the white settlers.

In Java, however, the set up was different. After the abolition of forced labour under the culture system (more or less synonymous with the abolition of slavery elsewhere) the private planters then appearing in greater numbers had no real difficulty in procuring labourers because of the over-population. But here the difficulty lay in the fact that this labour, once procured, could not be depended upon since the Javanese labourer only worked for as long as he desperately needed the earnings, and as soon as he had a little laid aside he left his employment. It was for this reason that labour compulsion was resorted to, although it was not carried to the same lengths as in other countries where the labour problems were more pressing. Penal sanction, and, after the mother country had repealed that, the creation of debt relationships, and the exercising of pressure through the *desa* chiefs or European officials were, among others, the means used to improve the situation.

In some countries, the extreme measures adopted immediately after abolition were dispensed with fairly soon. Such was the case, as we have seen, in the United States where the "vagrancy" laws, if not entirely abrogated, were at least applied much more leniently. But then, neither did the need for severity last long here. The Negroes did not succeed (except in a few cases) in acquiring small farms of their own, and, since there were no other ways open to them of becoming independent, they had no other choice but to work for Europeans. Under such circumstances, matters could be left to run their own course. In a few such cases, compulsory labour was indeed resorted to again later, but then only incidentally, when there was an unusual emergency, or when labour was not to be obtained by normal methods.

The situation in the United States, as described above, was comparable to that which had been found earlier in the British West Indies on a few small islands. On Antigua, St. Kitts and Barbados, the rising density of population entailed that there was no more free land available—a factor which very soon put an end to any difficulties the planters might have encountered earlier in procuring labour [1]. On the larger islands, however, and in British Guiana, the situation was quite different and more closely corresponded to that found in Mauritius. Large numbers of emancipated slaves found ways and means of supporting themselves, and the colonists expe-

---

[1] See: William Law Mathieson, British Slave Emancipation 1838-1849, 1932, Chapter 1: Developed Colonies.

rienced acute labour shortages. This was coped with through the importation of vast numbers of coolies by means of an indenture system subject to penal sanction; a labour system which, if not in principle, at least in practice (methods of recruitment, treatment, and, in some cases, failure to release labourers when their contracts expired) bore a strong resemblance to compulsory labour.

In the sparsely populated Portuguese colonies there was also, generally speaking, little need for the Africans to work for the Europeans, and here too, compulsory labour persisted, the early legislative measures remaining in force and being made even harsher from time to time.

However, in many territories a great advance in the economic life, bringing with it a great need for a labour force, occurred a long time after the abolition of slavery. This was, for example, the case in South Africa (where the really great demand for labour first arose with the exploitation of diamonds and gold after 1870), in the Outer Provinces of the Dutch East Indies (where large-scale colonization began at about the same time), and in Kenya (where the Europeans only began to come in large numbers at the beginning of this century). Similarly, at the turn of the century, there was also a switch to large-scale economic activity in the Congo Free State, and in those regions of Latin America where rubber was obtainable, the rapidly rising demand for this product creating an urgent need for labour in distant, sparsely populated country. And the French were faced with the same difficulty when they took over the administration of Madagascar in 1896 (i.e., almost 50 years after they had abolished slavery), and wished to develop it.

We have seen how compulsory labour was resorted to in all these cases, sometimes ruthlessly—if the difficulties were great and there seemed no other solution (e.g., the rubber regions in Latin America, and, to a lesser extent, Kenya and Madagascar)—sometimes more subtly—as for example in the Outer Provinces of the Dutch East Indies, where labourers could be drawn from nearby, overpopulated areas—or sometimes even altogether indirectly, as in South Africa where the country itself is heavily populated.

We have also established that compulsory labour is not only found in countries where two races of unequal economic power confront each other, such as in the colonial territories, but that it has also been applied in some Western countries to the people of the country itself; our prime example being Soviet Russia. To achieve the tremendous economic expansion here, labour compulsion was resorted to; and then not only in the well populated areas—by means of a ban on non-working, the forcible removal of labour forces, etc.—but also in the more inaccessible areas of the North and East which were to be colonized. But Soviet Russia is not the only example, since compulsory labour has also been imposed on whites in the United States, although only in sporadic cases. Here it concerned the development of industries in areas far removed from a source of labour supply (e.g., the Maine lumber companies).

An important factor in these differences in the use of compulsory labour in the United States and Soviet Russia is undeniably the difference of approach to social-economic questions. In a system in which the economy is planned by the state, a severe regulation of labour such as is found in Russia is normal. A general lack of respect for the individual which may occur in such a system can, in special circumstances—when normal methods of providing labour are inadequate for work in distant places with forbidding climate—lead to the worst sort of forced labour. Where *laisser faire* is the social ideal, as in the United States, such a situation (for its own people) is only possible in cases of national emergency, such as war. However, it should not be forgotten that there are other factors besides the social-economic ideals which influence the issue of compulsory labour. In the United States there was a great tide of immigration during the period of industrialization, which to a great extent filled the demand for labour, whereas Russia, when later on industrialization began there, had to draw on its own population resources. Moreover, when we compare the situation in Soviet Russia with that in the Western European countries in their period of developing industry, it is clear that where these countries colonized they needed to provide relatively few people—the native populations (not, as a rule, willingly!) supplying the labour requirements—while Soviet Russia used, at a time when she was in the throes of an industrial revolution, its own people (plus those from neighbouring countries) to open up the vast, uninhabited expanses of Asia and Northern Russia. And it is this simultaneous industrialization at a previously unheard of rate on the one hand, and colonization of vast, uninhabited territories without much help by the native population on the other, which makes the Soviet-Russian situation unique.

As yet we have only spoken of cases where compulsory labour was imposed by whites. However, the whites have not been the only people to resort to the use of this form of labour. In Liberia, for instance, which was founded as a settlement for emancipated slaves from America, these emancipated slaves used the natives of the country in exactly the same way as the Europeans set about using the native populations of their colonies; and in the Negro State of Haiti the rulers, when their subjects showed signs of reverting to a life of idleness, even instituted an official system of forced labour, whereby non-working was not permitted, and strict supervision made hard work unavoidable.

We also learn something else from the history of Haiti. When later Governors dispensed with the use of force the country deteriorated. Under certain circumstances therefore compulsion would appear to be indispensable, at any rate, if the object is to develop a country. In Haiti, it soon became clear that there were no native leaders able to make people work, whereas the whites have never hesitated to make the native populations labour for them wherever they colonized, and their appearance in a new country has led to the introduction of compulsory labour whenever it was profitable—compulsory labour for the authorities *and* for private individuals.

In general, there is less to be said against the former than against the latter. In many cases, its institution can be compared to taxation in our society. And if it is not too heavily imposed, and is used for purposes which also serve the interests of the native population it is in most cases carried out without resentment.

However, so much misuse is often made of this system of labour that it can frequently become an almost unbearable burden for the labourers who are in most cases put to work on projects which can make no direct contribution to the welfare of their community; the construction of great highways and railways, for example. Moreover, in most cases, the labourers have to work far too long on these projects, sometimes far from their homes (which factor can only serve to disrupt their lives). And sometimes even the women are made to do such work.

However, when we come to examine compulsory labour for private individuals we find that what it really amounts to is complete exploitation of the weak by the strong. This compulsory labour has taken many forms, although these various forms again are repeated in many places. And an added factor to such labour is almost always that the authorities in charge prove themselves to be the willing servants of the employers.

The measures adopted by the authorities to compel a population to work range from the levying of taxes and other indirect measures to mediation, persuasion, pressure by officials (often with the assistance of the native chiefs) to a ban on "vagrancy" and the passing of laws decreeing work to be obligatory for all; while prison labour is sometimes also put at the disposal of the employers. Those whose interests were directly involved (i.e. the planters etc.) went in for recruitment, in most cases resorting to deceit and sometimes even to force, which lent to the work of the recruitees an element of compulsion, even though this work might have been free in theory. Keeping people at work once they had "accepted" to work was almost everywhere done by means of penal sanctions on breach of contract. The employers themselves often found it a better system to incur their labourers in debt, since in most countries there were laws binding the labourers to work on their employer's estates etc. in such cases. The worst cases of compulsory labour for private individuals were those in which a reign of terror kept people working.

As we have seen, there have been instances where measures such as described above were unnecessary and superfluous, and in the main in such instances there was an acute shortage of land; the natives, not being able to acquire their own land, being compelled without pressure to work for Europeans. In a few cases this native land shortage was not the result of natural circumstances but of a deliberate policy put into practice by the ruling class. This policy therefore by and large served in place of legal measures.

Primarily indirect methods to force the people to work were used in South Africa. But there have been many other countries in which for example taxes have been levied to make it essential for the natives to earn wages (e.g., Belgian Congo, Kenya, Madagascar).

During this study we have frequently found cases of direct or indirect intervention by officials. The systematic use of pressure by government officials was the principal means of getting people to work in Kenya; and in the Portuguese colonies it was the essential basis on which the whole system of compulsory labour was built up. Immediately after the abolition of slavery, officials were encouraged to assist as much as they could in the provision of labour by the prospect of a reward for their efforts, and until well into the 20th century they were repeatedly given express orders to facilitate the recruiting of natives for work as much as lay within their power. In the Belgian Congo, government officials would accompany recruiting agents on their trips to "track down" the natives; while in Madagascar, labour bureaus were set up to assist the recruitment of labour —although their task was not precisely defined as such. In South Africa too, we find that officials took upon themselves the responsibility of providing labour; as was the case to a certain extent in Indonesia, where the officials were not a disinterested party in recruitment. Pressure on the people through native chiefs and headmen was frequently made use of (South Africa, Kenya, Indonesia etc.).

The regulations against "vagrancy", as we have seen, were a common feature in most colonies etc. in the immediate post-abolition period (e.g., Jamaica, the United States, the Portuguese colonies), but we also find them being used in later periods (e.g., South Africa). When strictly applied such regulations amounted to nothing less than the imposition of widespread compulsory labour; and in some countries the obligation (or duty) of all able-bodied members of a community to work was a clearly expressed principle. This was the case in Mauritius straight after abolition and also later when it was found that Indians were not willing to hire themselves out again on the completion of their contract periods. More or less the same happened in Madagascar when the French took over the administration of the island: all men of good health had to be able to show that they had work; if they were not able to do this, penal servitude followed, in turn followed by a period of forced labour. Portugal went furthest in formulating labour compulsion: according to a law of 1914, every able native in the colonies stood under a legal and moral obligation to support himself by work. For the rest, the regulation more or less approximated the cases mentioned above.

In these countries, the necessity to labour, as imposed by law, sufficed and the choice of employer was left to the labourer (at least in theory), but elsewhere matters took a slightly different course. In the Negro State of Haiti, for example, there was not only a ban on non-working in the first period—all citizens having to be either workers or soldiers—but also no freedom of choice in employment, all the labourers being allocated to specified plantations. Also, the work fell under the direct supervision of the administration.

Here a comparison can be drawn to the situation in Soviet Russia, for here too, non-working is not permitted, nor an independent change of employer. It should, however, be noted that the compulsion used was meant to promote the progress of the people on whom it was applied in both Haiti and Soviet Russia. This of course is very different from the situation in the colonial territories where the first and foremost criterion of labour compulsion on the natives was the enrichment of another people; if it happened at the same time to be to the advantage of the natives, good and well, but this was merely secondary.

That the recruitment of labourers for the enterprises requiring labour frequently went hand in hand with abuses of fundamental human rights—and often the worst possible abuses—is shown in many examples in the preceding chapters. The worst examples of all came up in the recruitment of Indians and Chinese for Mauritius and the English West Indian colonies in the early days, and that of the Africans in Angola for St. Thomas and Principe.

Penal sanction on breach of contract was another practically universal phenomenon, and the regulations covering it did not differ much in content in all the countries in which it was applied. A listing of instances is unnecessary.

Debt bondage was a frequent occurrence there where there were native tenement farmers. We have seen, for example, how these tenant farmers would become bound to their landlords through a debt relationship in such places as Latin America, the United States and Madagascar. But the system of debt relationship was not only used in such cases. With labourers, the granting of an advance payment at the time of recruitment served the same purpose (e.g., Java, the United States, South Africa, Surinam, and the recruitment of coolies for the West Indies and elsewhere). The individual would then be bound to his work for as long as the debt existed, either because of legal provisions, or, in a few cases, tradition. Also, it was customary to keep contract labourers on after the expiration of their contracts by endeavouring to incur them in debt toward the end of the period; examples of this being found in the Outer Provinces of the Netherlands East Indies, and the Portuguese colonies.

The worst conditions of compulsory labour are of course those where it is nothing but terror which keeps the people at work. The labour of the rubber tappers in South America and the Congo Free State are examples of this; and there was also a strong element of terror in the employment of Angolese Negroes on the islands off the West Coast of Africa.

In conclusion, the question of land shortage. In Java, there was such a large native population that many were unable to acquire land and thereby became available to the Europeans as labourers.

More often, the natives would have to go to work because of a land shortage after the whites had taken over all the good land for themselves. We saw this happen in Mexico, for example. But not infrequently the limited amount of land available to the natives and Negroes was more or less the result of a deliberate policy on the part of the whites, aimed at increasing the labour supply; examples of this having been found in the United States, South Africa and Kenya.

Where we have witnessed the occurrence of compulsory labour in colonial territories, we have seen that the representatives of the ruling class would, as a rule, form a united front against the natives. As we know, government officials often lent their assistance to the provision of labour, but this is not the only aspect of the question; for the courts too have shown a tendency to stand in support of the ruling class, treating the native with extreme arbitrariness where this might be to the advantage of their own group. Examples would be superfluous since they can be found in every chapter. Because of this attitude on the part of officialdom, the native population in almost all cases lost their last chance of a certain degree of protection. The few officials who stood up for the native's rights were usually powerless to change the general situation.

The justification given for compulsory labour, by government representatives as well as by those whose interests were directly involved, was often remarkable. Repeatedly it was stated that the imposition of compulsory labour would be for the benefit of the native population, incredible as this might sound. During the Spanish colonization of America [1], it was justified on the grounds that working for the whites would bring the Indians into contact with Christianity. So that they might feel the blessing of Christendom even more profoundly, the Indians were moved from their own spread out settlements and made to live in special towns—close to the mines. And when Indians were brought from the "useless" islands—where there was no gold—to the islands where labourers were needed in vast numbers, the argument was once again that they would thereby get the chance to live among Christians and be converted. According to a later variation of the theme, the well-being of the native in general would be promoted if they worked for the whites.

---

[1] See Lesley Byrd Simpson, The Encomienda in New Spain, 1929, pp. 28, 31, 36, 50, 108.

We have already quoted the words of a former Prime Minister of England concerning the "labour tax" in South Africa: the new regulations would help the Bantu to overcome his laziness, teach him the value of work, and give him the chance to do something in return for the wise rule of the Europeans [1]. At the beginning of this century, it was especially Joseph Chamberlain in England who was zealous in this direction: The African would not advance in civilization until he had been convinced of the necessity and dignity of labour, he said [2]. It would be a good thing for the Africans to be industrious, and by every possible means they must be taught to work. A similar argument was used in the Portuguese colonies to justify the conditions there, in reality amounting to little less than slavery. It was claimed that anyone working for the whites was in a position to come into contact with the higher culture of the Europeans, and was therefore in every sense better off [3]. The Africans were in effect not able to take care of themselves; it would be best for them to come to work on a cacao plantation under the protection of the Europeans [4]. In the chapter on the United States we realized what the Governor of Mississippi meant by "to work is the law of God" [5]; and the Black Codes had their origin in such an attitude. In the Mexico of the turn of the century, it was the general belief that the lower classes did not have the slightest idea of what freedom entailed, thus they were very well off, although their position was as good as slavery. They had to be compelled to work for the sake of progress; they would neither benefit themselves nor the world if they were not driven to work with a whip [6]. That this attitude has prevailed a long time in some quarters is illustrated in a speech given by the Governor-General of Madagascar in 1930 [7]. Among other things, he said that the interests of the Europeans and natives are reconcilable at all times. The colonists need the natives as a labour force, at the same time, through contact with the Europeans, the natives are able to

---

[1] Page 24.
[2] J. S. Furnivall, Colonial Policy and Practice, 1948, p. 342.
[3] Henry W. Nevinson, A Modern Slavery, 1906, p. 54.
[4] William A. Cadbury, Labour in Portuguese West Africa, 2nd ed., 1910, p. 15/16.
[5] Page 57.
[6] John Kenneth Turner, Barbarous Mexico, 1911, p. 203, 276.
[7] Madagascar en 1930, Texte du discours prononcé par M. Léon Cayla, gouverneur général de Madagascar et dépendances . . . 13 octobre 1930. In: L'Europe nouvelle, Année 14, 1931, p. 24-26.

attain a higher level of culture The Government therefore has a moral duty to gradually train them to a life of industry.

These are but a few of the many examples that could be taken from any period in the history of any country in which there was insufficient free labour available; but since they all amount to the same thing, we will leave it at that.

THE ABOLITION OF COMPULSORY LABOUR IN VARIOUS COUNTRIES

In the previous chapters we have seen compulsory labour come to an end in various ways. Certain systems of compulsory labour disappeared when they no longer fulfilled their purpose (e.g., in colonial Spanish America)—only to be replaced by another system. Compulsory labour really came to an end in the first place where it was no longer necessary. This was the case in the United States, as regards the worst practices at any rate immediately after slave emancipation. For the same reason the immigration of Indian contract workers to Mauritius ceased in 1911; the Indian population of the island being so great by that time as to make further immigration unnecessary. And something similar happened in Surinam and the Dutch East Indies (Outer Provinces); after some time there was a sufficient offer of free labour in these territories, mainly because with improved labour conditions many coolies stayed on after their contract periods, thereby forming a labour reserve. Under these circumstances, contract labour under penal sanction became superfluous and was gradually abolished in 1931/1941.

In some cases, compulsory labour came to an end because of opposition from the labourers themselves, or from governments representing them; as for example the Indian Government, which in 1917 prohibited all emigration of Indians for contract labour subject to penal sanctions. For an example of the impetus toward the abolition of compulsory labour coming from the labourers themselves, we can cite what happened in the Mexico of this century. In the revolution of 1910/11, during which a start was made on the division of the large estates, an important role was played by the Indians who had till then lived to a great extent in debt bondage or a kind of serfdom. But all the same, these cases of compulsory labour coming to an end because of opposition form the exception rather than the rule, particularly when such opposition comes from the labourers themselves.

It is not easy to define the role played by ethical influences in the abolition of compulsory labour or of some of its forms. Naturally, ethics have played an important part in many decisions in this field; indeed the abolition of slavery itself was largely fought for on ethical grounds. The question, however, remains whether a ban on compulsory labour based on such grounds has much effect in actual practice. Almost always the people in the mother countries concerned have been much more open to a consideration of colonial questions from an ethical point of view than the people in the colonies as such. We have repeatedly seen how laws passed in the colonies were repealed in the mother country if they were too severe, and how the impetus toward forbidding practices which were too inhumane always seemed to come from the same source. However, all too often such a ban would be unwelcome in the colonies, and would be simply ignored; or, if necessary, the colonists would continue in their former practices a little less obviously, and, if that did not work, would resort to other methods which had the same effect in practice. In Spain, laws were continuously being passed to improve the lot of the Indian labourers, and, on paper, the encomienda system was repealed more than once. Nevertheless, this system only really came to an end when it no longer served any purpose, and even then, the subsequent position of the Indians was certainly not an improvement. More useful forms of compulsory labour would replace the repealed system. The Portuguese ruling of 1878 (when slave emancipation became a reality in the colonies) contained measures covering the protection of native rights as well—but in Africa these were simply ignored. The Dutch Government repealed penal sanction for Java after it had been in force for several years; but the planters took to other ways of enforcing compulsory labour: clauses were introduced in the labour contracts, and if the labourers did not adhere to these, they did so at their peril; debt bondage was resorted to; and unofficial assistance by the authorities did the rest. In France, public opinion was disturbed at the high death rate among those employed on the public works in Madagascar. As a result, compulsory labour for the Government was abolished—but here again, other ways were immediately provided for putting the natives to work. Public opinion in England has very often—perhaps more often than anywhere else—strongly opposed the imposition of compulsory labour; and as a result the British Government has on many occasions repealed laws drafted in the colonies. We have seen how the most rigorous laws which were passed just after the abolition of slavery in the West Indies, in Mauritius and in the Cape Colony, were promptly rejected in London. And when in Kenya, at a much later date, all the Government officials became involved in the recruitment of labour there was such a storm of protest in England that the Government had to take action. But was there much result in the colonies? In the West Indies and in Mauritius, the Negroes could not be persuaded to work in sufficient numbers or sufficiently, and the colonists set about bringing in coolies under an indentured system which was anything but free. And in Mauritius a system of compulsory labour closely resembling that which had been banned in England came into effect later again (this time for the Indians). In Kenya, the pressure exerted by the officials on the native population to get them to work was just as great after the intervention from London—now differing only in terms of subtlety—and there were many other measures to support this pressure. In the United States, the influence of the Northern States on the Southern, accustomed to enormous resources of Negro labour, is comparable to that of a mother country on its colonial territories. The laws passed in the South shortly after the liberation of the Negroes, and aiming to keep them on the plantations, were declared unconstitutional under the influence of the North. But in reality, nothing very much changed till years later—when the situation was so far developed that the laws were no longer necessary.

Criticism from outside countries also played a role in the abolition of compulsory labour, or a particular form of it. In the Dutch East Indies an import embargo by the United States hastened the process of abolishing contract labour under penal sanction—a process which was, however, already in full swing because of the economic development of the territories. Moreover, the interference by the United States was not so much due to moral disquiet as to a fear of competition: the embargo did not apply to the import of Indian rubber, for which there was a heavy demand, but only to tobacco, which was being grown extensively in the United States itself. World-wide criticism of the state of affairs in the Portuguese colonies was probably unprejudiced by economic motives, and continued throughout the first two decades of this century, and it was more than likely under the influence of this criticism that the principle of moral and legal obligation to work was relinquished in 1928. But that which was given with one hand would seem to have been taken with the other: the "moral and legal" obligation disappeared, but there remained the moral obligation to ensure one's livelihood by means of work; officials were forbidden to recruit natives for private employers, but it remained their duty to facilitate the work of recruiting agents as much as possible; etc. Thus in effect, these changes in the Portuguese colonial laws seem to have made as little difference in practice as the reformations in the legislation of many other countries.

With the rise of the League of Nations and the institution of the United Nations Organization, action against the occurrence of compulsory labour has been taken on an international level. In the course of years various conventions were accepted prohibiting compulsory labour or, at any rate, drasticly restricting it. The International Slavery Convention of 1926 drafted a resolution declaring that compulsory labour for private ends should be abolished as soon as possible, and that compulsory labour on projects of public importance should only be resorted to in the event of there being absolutely no possibility of obtaining voluntary labour. The Convention pertaining to forced labour ratified by the International Labour Conference in 1930 demanded the immediate abolition of compulsory labour for private individuals; concerning the labour imposed by an administrative body, their statement paralleled that of the previous Convention. In 1936, there was a further Convention pertaining to the recruitment of labourers; the aim being to forbid the malpractices which made labour obtained by recruitment tantamount to compulsory labour. Later there followed another Convention that declared itself to be against the use of forcible persuasion in the conclusion of labour contracts, and a convention demanding the speediest possible abolition of all penal sanctions. Nevertheless, many countries with colonies in which compulsory labour was being imposed in one form or another were very reluctant to ratify these conventions [1]. The first-named Convention (primarily directed against slavery) was indeed ratified by 41 countries; the second by 25 countries—but of the four countries with colonies (England, the Netherlands, France and Belgium) three (the Netherlands, France and

[1] See: Report of the Ad hoc Committee on Forced Labour, 1953, p. 146/147.

Belgium) indicated that the Convention would be applied with certain modifications. The Convention of 1936, pertaining to recruitment, has as yet only been ratified by Norway, Japan, England (1939), New Zealand, Belgium (1948) and Argentina; and the two last-mentioned conventions have only been ratified by England, New Zealand and Belgium, and by England and New Zealand respectively. We see therefore that even international conventions have not been put into practice too speedily by the governments concerned. In spite of this, the value of international action must not be underestimated. Through it certain norms at least become acknowledged by degrees, and when the economic situation is not unfavourable for the elimination of compulsory labour, measures in that direction are perhaps taken sooner than would otherwise have been the case. That the economic situation remains the determining factor even today, however, is indicated by the fact that during the slump of the thirties when far fewer labourers were required steps were often taken to abolish compulsory labour, while compulsory labour sprang into life again in many places during the war years when there was an increasing demand for man power [1].

COMPULSORY LABOUR IN THE LIGHT OF NIEBOER'S THEORY

In conclusion, we will examine the phenomenon of compulsory labour (since the abolition of slavery) in the light of Nieboer's theory, as presented in his "Slavery as an Industrial System" [2]. The main argument of his theory can be expressed as follows: Slavery will generally occur where there is still free land available (through which a livelihood can be found without the help of capital), where there are, in other words, still "open resources". In areas where there is no longer any free land available (or where capital, not available to all, is necessary to provide subsistence), thus where there are "closed resources", there will on the contrary generally be no slavery, since in the latter case there will generally be people prepared to work for wages (not being able to support themselves independently) and slavery thus becomes superfluous. Where there are "open resources", however, no one is dependent on another for his earnings, and it is therefore necessary to use force if others are to be made to work for an individual. The author discusses slavery in his book,

[1] Report of the Ad hoc committee on forced labour, 1953, p. 147.
[2] H. J. Nieboer, Slavery as an industrial system, 2nd, rev. ed., The Hague, 1910.

but not other forms of compulsory labour, although he does occasionally refer to these as disguised slavery to which his theory is also applicable [1]. Indeed one cannot see why, under the circumstances mentioned by Nieboer, it should be precisely slavery that exists if there is not a sufficient offer of voluntary labour, and not another form of compulsory labour—as pointed out by J. J. Fahrenfort in his article "Over vrije en onvrije arbeid" (On voluntary and involuntary labour) [2]. If Nieboer's thesis is valid, then the realities of compulsory labour other than slavery will be in agreement with it; and therefore we should check the theory against the data in the preceding chapters.

As far as Spanish America is concerned [3], the thesis fits the circumstances of the first period well. Here there were originally "open resources": The Indians were allowed to retain possession of their land for a long time, and there was actually still a lot of land not yet in use. In these circumstances, compulsory labour came into being, first under the encomienda system, and then under the repartimiento and mita systems. And then we find compulsory labour prohibited officially at about the time when all the good land was in use, with a resultant "closed resources" situation. Thus far the theory is substantiated therefore. But, after this period, compulsory labour again occurred—if not officially—in the form of debt bondage; and it persisted for a long time. Here therefore the facts of the matter seem to contradict Nieboer's theory. However, there might have been one condition which, if valid, would make the theory fit better than it seems to at first glance. For although there was no longer any directly usable free land available [4] there were still fairly large areas of so-called no-man's-land with only a very scanty Indian population in the infertile regions of the country [5]. This land as such was certainly not suited for agriculture. All the same, it is not impossible that these unattractive regions offered to the Indians working on the haciendas a way, however primitive it may have been, of living independently. And if these regions did indeed tempt the hacienda Indians, the existence of debt bondage would then be entirely consistent with Nieboer's theory.

---

[1] E.g., p. 420.

[2] This article appeared in the Dutch periodical Mensch en Maatschappij, Vol. 19, 1943, p. 29-51.

[3] We are primarily concerned here with Mexico, for which country we gave a short description of the land situation in the chapter on Latin America.

[4] George McCutchen McBride, The Land Systems of Mexico, 1923, p. 31.

[5] Id., p. 72/73.

It seems to us, however, that the actual state of affairs was somewhat different. In the first place it is conceivable that there will not always be an *immediate* labour surplus as soon as all the arable land is taken up. If the population increase is not rapid, there might be a fairly long transitional period in which the farmers prefer to lead a poverty-stricken existence rather than work for wages. (One is reminded here of the destitute farmers in Erskine Caldwell's *Tobacco Road* who preferred to go hungry on their delapidated farms to going to work for others). In such circumstances compulsory labour can fulfil a purpose under a situation of "closed resources".

But even if the circumstances of the land situation compelled the majority to work for a minority group, the landowners might still find a reason to bind labour as strongly as possible; to wit, in the case of landowners competing for labour; a possibility if there remained an acute labour shortage even after all the Indians (in the case of Mexico) had been put to work. Thus here we have another case of compulsory labour still having sense even under a system of "closed resources". And at the same time we see here the particular character which debt bondage has as a form of compulsory labour. Measures designed to drive the population to work have no point if the population have to go to work anyway under stress of circumstances; but debt bondage might very well have point under such circumstances, since every employer attempts to get as many employees for himself at the expense of other employers.

A case comparable with the above-mentioned one is met with in the United States. After the abolition of slavery most of the Negroes were unable to acquire land of their own and were therefore compelled to work for the whites; thus, "closed resources"; and we see also how, in agreement with the theory, the strict application of the "vagrancy" laws, amounting in effect to compulsory labour for all, was soon dispensed with. But even though an end was made to the systematic compulsion of all Negroes to work, this did not mean that compulsory labour was altogether done away with. For a long time afterward, debt bondage remained a comparatively common phenomenon, even though not widespread. In our opinion the primary cause for this again lay in the relation between the demand for and supply of labour. The South, after a period of extreme depression—a result of the Civil War and the sudden liberation of the slaves—began to recuperate economically toward the end of the seventies. Agricultural output was normalized and there was a start made in industrialization. The resulting demand for labour, especially heavy at times of unusual activity, caused the employers themselves to try to bind their labourers to work for them. A very important corollary factor was the generally prevalent attitude of low evaluation of the Negroes—until so recently still slaves. For this reason the whites did not have many scruples about rounding up Negroes—usually by dubious means—and holding control over them through a debt relationship when there was need of labour, and specially of cheap labour. Once again thus we find labour compulsion imposed by the authorities on the whole labouring population (by the rigorous application of "vagrancy" laws) disappearing as soon as the labourers themselves found it essential to work; but in the face of a comparative shortage of labour each employer trying to provide for his own needs. In this they were assisted by laws permitting a creditor to compel his debtor to work for him. But that remains quite a different thing from labour compulsion imposed from above and applicable to all, which only has sense in cases of "open resources" [1]. Debt bondage—whether supported by legal provisions or not—can in certain circumstances still serve a purpose in a situation of "closed resources".

Nieboer's theory is applicable to the situation as found in the British colonies in the West Indies, and Mauritius. In by far and away the majority of West Indian colonies "open resources" existed. As has already been pointed out, all the land was in use in only a small number of West Indian islands, whereas on most of the islands (including Jamaica where half of the English West Indian Negroes were situated) and in British Guiana, there was still a lot free land available, and the Negroes could easily support themselves. In Mauritius too, they could make ends meet without being dependent on the whites. In agreement with the situation of "open resources" we see the appearance of compulsory labour. To start with, various methods of obtaining compulsory labour were imposed on the recently freed slaves; when these methods were dropped, in part due to the opposition in London, in part to the difficulty of enforcing them effectively (it being found too easy to escape in some places!) another system of compulsory labour was substituted: contract labour under penal sanction, together with all sorts of practices which greatly intensified compulsion.

---

[1] And sometimes, as stated, in the period of transition to "closed resources".

The theory is also applicable to the Boer Republics in South Africa, which were formed after the English Government abolished slavery. The harsh measures adopted by the Boers in the beginning—official distribution of natives to employers, and an apprenticeship system that amounted to something appalling in practice—only lasted until such time as the whites had taken up all the land; until such time as the "open resources" had become "closed resources" therefore.

In examining the situation in the African colonies belonging to Portugal (Angola and Mozambique) we find a case of "open resources"—vast, thinly-populated territories—and the institution of compulsory labour following immediately upon the emancipation of the slaves, and continuing far into the 20th century. Thus, here too the facts substantiate Nieboer's hypothesis.

As we have seen, at the time of the abolition of the culture system in Java the population density was very great and many Javanese natives were unable to acquire land. In other words, a situation of "closed resources". Nevertheless, all sorts of practices were rife which definitely lent an element of compulsion to the labour situation. So we have here an example of compulsory labour in a case of "closed resources". But this compulsion was of a special kind; it served not so much to make people work as to provide that they did so with more regularity. This was because the needs of the natives were modest, and it was unknown to desire more than was strictly essential, so that, although it was essential for them to work for the Europeans because of the land situation, they only did so from time to time, when it was most needed. "Closed resources" therefore do not always supply *sufficient* labour. In Java, the circumstances required that there should be some measure of compulsion if adequate labour was to be had.

On Haiti too, the situation closely resembled one of "closed resources". In time when it was administrated by France, and passed for the richest colony of France, all the land suitable for agriculture, or made so by irrigation, was devoted to sugar cane. Just after the declaration of independence in 1804, all the land which had belonged to the French (by far the greatest part) was proclaimed to be State property [1]. Of the land which had been in the possession of mulatto planters, part also went to the State, while the other part remained

[1] James G. Leyburn, The Haitian People, 2nd printing, 1945, p. 38.

in the possession of the previous owners [1]. There was thus no opportunity for the freed slaves to settle outside the former plantations unless it was to be in the mountains where conditions were most unfavourable; therefore the great bulk of the population had to resign themselves to making their livelihood on the old plantations. In this way the situation closely resembled that which developed on the thickly populated islands of the British West Indies and in the South of the United States immediately after the abolition of slavery in 1833 and 1865 respectively. Under these circumstances one might have expected that the freed slaves would go to work sooner or later, probably, as was usual in such cases, on a share-cropping basis. And share-cropping did indeed appear later in the history of Haiti, as described in the chapter on this territory. But the immediate result was that the small farmers abandoned the cultivation of sugar—an important export crop—and only grew that which was needed to support the family from day to day, any desire for economic prosperity being unknown among the Negroes and most mulattos. Nevertheless, those who first ruled Haiti after it became free had other ideals for their country. They wished to recreate the prosperity of colonial times and develop the country economically as far as was possible. They knew too that force would be absolutely indispensable when dealing with a people who had only just left slavery behind them and were living in a climate where it takes little work to provide necessities. So we find here another case in which compulsory labour in a situation of "closed resources" can serve a purpose, namely to get people to work more than demanded by the circumstances. Actually this was more or less the case as we have seen it in Java, except that compulsion there was from individuals whereas in Haiti it was the State itself which exercised severe compulsion on the population. Such a situation is understandable in view of a) the chaotic state of the country because of the years of war, b) democratic ideals were not yet formed, and c) the personalities of the first leaders.

Having tested Nieboer's theory on countries faced with labour problems directly after the liberation of the slaves, we will now go on to test it on the cases in which the labour demand first arose only long after emancipation.

We will direct our attention first to the situation in territories where the native population was very small so that even under

---

[1] Id., p. 37/38.

the most favourable conditions they could in no way satisfy the labour demand. Always, in such cases, labour would be brought in from elsewhere—e.g., the Outer Provinces of the Netherlands Indies (importation of contract labourers), a few thinly populated sections of Mexico (labourers obtained by methods amounting to kidnapping), the Siberian territories colonized by Russia (transfer of "undesirables"), and the operation of exploitation companies in the remoter parts of the United States where there was a sudden demand for labour (such as the Maine lumber companies at the turn of this century). We have here to examine the situation with regard to "closed" and "open resources" a) in the country of origin of the workers, and b) in the country to which they were taken.

It seems clear that if there was a situation of "open resources" in the country of origin force would have to be used to obtain labour, whereas with a situation of "closed resources" this would not be necessary. However, we see that, with regard to the recruitment of Javanese labour for the Outer Provinces and the recruitment of coolies from overpopulated China and India for the British West Indies and elsewhere, deceipt and even force were used just as in the recruitment of labour in the North American cities (where there was plenty of opportunity for work) for the Maine lumber companies. Not many people were apparently prepared in those days to recruit of their own free will, even in grossly overpopulated countries: Nothing was usually known of the circumstances in the new countries; distances were, relatively speaking, far greater, and the supervision of emigration on the part of the authorities was not a fraction then of what it is today.

As far as the "open" or "closed" resources in the countries to which the emigrants went is concerned, the penal sanction in force in many cases may in part have depended on circumstances of "open resources" present in a lot of the cases, but to a far greater extent it was no doubt a result of the unattractiveness of the life in distant places where labourers escaped whenever possible. In Soviet Asia too this was certainly the principal reason for the compulsion, since no one relished the prospect of having to do the heavy work involved in clearing the land in such an unfavourable climate. Thus, in the opening up of almost inaccessible territories compulsory labour is quite conceivable, even though there might be a situation of "closed resources" nearby and in the same country.

In these instances, therefore, Nieboer's theory has a very limited application.

In other countries the density of the native population was such that there was at least potentially sufficient labour available for the needs of the whites. This was the case in Kenya, South Africa, the Congo Free State and in those regions in South America where a start was made to the development of the rubber industry at the turn of this century. In the two latter instances there was certainly a situation of "open resources", and the severely rigorous systems of compulsory labour occurring there fit the picture. In Kenya, the situation was almost one of "closed resources": because of the limited extent of the native reserves there, there were already people dependent on the opportunities to work for the Europeans, even though the greater majority of the natives were still able to support themselves independently up to a degree. In South Africa, it went far further in this direction. Here the population was such that the small areas set aside for them as reserves were totally inadequate; thus, clearly a case of "closed resources". However, in both Kenya and South Africa measures were taken with a view to compelling the natives to work. It would appear that the situation of "closed resources" was not enough to guarantee an *adequate* labour supply. In Kenya, where only a comparatively small proportion of the natives were as yet dependent on European employment, both direct and indirect measures were taken to improve the labour supply; in South Africa, where a much greater proportion of the population had to seek employment by Europeans, measures were primarily indirect.

In the territories here mentioned there seems to have been a direct relation between the degree of compulsory labour and the extent of the "open" or "closed" resources; in South America and the Congo Free State, with "open resources", a reign of terror to get the people to work; in Kenya, on the borderline between "open" and "closed" resources, pressure from government officials and indirect measures; in South Africa, with its "closed resources", intervention of an indirect nature only. But we must be careful not to draw conclusions too hastily. There are naturally other factors that play a role in this matter. In the rubber regions of South America, for example, employers were far freer to do as they pleased because they were far from all inspection and partly because it was not quite clear to which country the rubber regions really belonged. In Kenya and South Africa, however, employers had to show more discretion seeing that these countries were more or less under England's direct influence. Furthermore, here we see once again that "closed resources" do not always yield sufficient labour; additional measures being in many cases necessary if the ruling class are to satisfy their desire for profits.

The situation in Kenya and South Africa gives occasion to commentary of another sort. In so far as there is a case of "closed resources" here, this was by and large the result of a deliberate policy on the part of the Europeans to compel the natives to seek work. Artificially created "closed resources" can (to a great extent) take the place of compulsory labour. The situation in the southern United States after the abolition of slavery is in a sense comparable to this, for although there was actually a lot of free land available at the time, the Negroes were not able to acquire much of this, since they did not have the money to buy—even though the prices were often low—and there was never any question of giving it away to them for nothing. In all these cases we are concerned with another type of "closed resources" situation than that meant by Nieboer, since his examples are of countries in which the "closed resources" situation had a natural origin, whereas in the cases here cited it was largely the result of a deliberate land policy on the part of the governing group. In the dualistic societies with which we are concerned here, the ruling clases have as it were consciously imitated what sometimes is the natural development with primitive peoples.

We will summarize the applicability of Nieboer's theory in the more complicated relationships which as a rule existed after the abolition of slavery.

In many cases the theory fits well. In colonial Mexico, for example, the authorities used compulsory labour just as long as there were "open resources"; when this situation no longer existed compulsory labour was abolished. In the Boer Republics of South Africa compulsory labour also existed just as long as there were "open resources". And in many other cases there was a correlation: compulsory labour in the British West Indian colonies, the Portuguese African colonies and the rubber regions of South America—all areas with "open resources"; and in the United States where the Negroes were faced with a situation of "closed resources" compulsory labour was resorted to on a limited scale only.

In some cases, however, the facts of the matter differ from those which we would expect to find by applying the theory. In the first place, we met with quite a few examples of forced labour in situations of "closed resources". Although this may have been due to a transitional period in which the small farmers were inclined to prefer to starve, when there was no longer any available land, rather than become wage labourers, it was more often due to the fact that a labour shortage was not eliminated by the labour supply made available in a situation of "closed resources". Such an absolute labour shortage is more likely to arise in countries here described—colonial societies with their frequently excessive labour requirements in relation to the number of native inhabitants; and in countries with a rapidly developing economy—than in the primitive societies discussed by Nieboer.

In Western societies circumstances also arise which make compulsory labour purposeful for reasons other than "open resources"; and here we mean the exploitation of distant, practically inaccessible regions—a phenomenon unknown to the societies discussed by Nieboer. The compulsory labour occurring in these cases is not dependent on any existing situation of "open resources" so much as on the hardships of life in such places.

Further, it can also occur in Western countries that there is no compulsory labour even in a situation of "open resources". In contrast with what is found for primitive peoples, as described by Nieboer, in modern society preference is more likely to be given to a dependent, but comfortable existence above an independent, though more primitive life; which naturally leads to an offer of labour in a situation of "open resources".

All in all, Nieboer's theory is on the whole valid also to the societies represented in this work; nevertheless it clearly has more application to the largely balanced societies which he discusses than to the more complicated relationships in Western or Western-influenced countries.

SUMMARY OF CONCLUSIONS

After the abolition of slavery other forms of compulsory labour were resorted to, and enforced until such time as they were no longer necessary from an economic point of view, or—in a few isolated cases—until such time as action by or on behalf of the compulsory labourers successfully brought them to an end.

Although ethical considerations can be seen to have played a role in the abolition of compulsory labour, this influence has only been secondary. The most important motives have always been of an economico-commercial nature.

Nieboer's theory can be shown to be generally applicable to Western or Western-influenced post-abolition societies. It does, however, require some modification then.

LITERATURE ON COMPULSORY LABOUR IN GENERAL

For literature concerning particular countries, see list at the end of each chapter

Bouillier, Louis, De l'obligation au travail pour les indigènes des colonies d'exploitation (spécialement dans les territoires français de l'Afrique centrale), Paris, 1923.

Buell, Raymond Leslie, Forced Labour: its international regulation. In: Foreign Policy Association, Information service, vol. 5, 1929/30, p. 411-428.

—— Slavery and forced labour. In: The Nation, vol. 131, 1930, p. 699-701.

Bülck, Hartwig, Die Zwangsarbeit im Friedensvölkerrecht, Göttingen, 1953 (Veröffentlichungen des Instituts für Internationales Recht an der Universität Kiel, 36).

The Colonial problem, a report by a study-group of members of the Royal Institute of International Affairs, London etc., 1937, Chap. 10.

Crétois, Pierre-Jean, Le travail obligatoire dans quelques législations, Alger, 1927.

Fahrenfort, J. J., Over vrije en onvrije arbeid. In: Mensch en Maatschappij, vol. 19, 1943, p. 29-51.

Fayet, Charles-J., Esclavage et travail obligatoire, la main-d'oeuvre non volontaire en Afrique, Paris, 1931.

Forced labour, report and draft questionnaire, Geneva, 1929 (International Labour Conference, 12th session, 1929).

—— Supplementary report, Geneva, 1929 (International Labour Conference, 12th session, 1929).

Forced labour, Geneva, 1930 (International Labour Conference, 14th session, 1930), 1 vol. and 2 supplements.

Forced labour, Geneva, 1956 (International Labour Conference, 39th session).

Furtwängler, F. J., Koloniale Zwangsarbeit. In: Arbeit, 6, 1929, p. 789-796.

Goudal, Jean, The question of forced labour before the International Labour Conference. In: International labour review, vol. 19, 1929, p. 621-638.

Harris, John H., Slavery or "sacred trust"?, London, 1926.

Heusch, Michel Halewyck de, L'esclavage et le travail forcé dans les colonies. In: Revue de l'Université de Bruxelles, année 38, 1932/33, p. 145-160.

Mercier, René, Le travail obligatoire dans les colonies françaises, Vesoul, 1933.

Morel, E. D., The black man's burden, Manchester etc., 1920.

Neytzell de Wilde, A., Genève en de arbeid onder dwang in overzeesche gewesten. In: Koloniaal Tijdschrift, 21, 1932, p. 143-161.

Olivier, Sydney, White capital and coloured labour, London, 1906.

Padmore, G., Forced labour in Africa. In: Labour monthly, vol. 13, 1931, p. 237-247.

Rapport de la Commission Temporaire de l'Esclavage. In: Journal officiel de la Société des Nations, année 6, 1925, p. 1413-1426.

Rémond, Marcel, La main-d'oeuvre dans les colonies françaises, Paris, 1903.

Report of the Ad hoc committee on forced labour, Geneva, 1953 (United Nations - International Labour Office).

Warnshuis, A. L., Joseph P. Chamberlain and Quincy Wright, The Slavery Convention of Geneva, Sept. 25, 1926 (International Conciliation, no. 236, 1928).